AS Fast-Track

Business Studies

Barry Brindley

Martin Buckley

Series consultants **Geoff Black and Stuart Wall**

Page designer **Michelle Cannatella**

Cover designer **Kube Ltd**

Pearson Education Limited
Edinburgh Gate
Harlow
Essex CM20 2JE, England
and Associated Companies throughout the world

ISBN 0 582 43234-0

British Library Cataloguing-in-Publication Data

A catalogue record for this book is available from the British Library.

Set by 3 in Optima and Tekton
Printed by Ashford Colour Press, Gosport, Hants

Contents

Read this first!

TWO WAYS TO USE THIS BOOK...

This book is designed to be used:

Either

- On its own – work through all the exercises for a quick run-through of your subject. This will take you about 24 hours altogether.

or

- As part of the *Revision Express* system:

1 Read through the topic in the *Revision Express A-level Study Guide* (or similar book).

2 Work through the exercises in this book.

3 Go to www.revision-express.com for extra exam questions and model answers.

4 For even more depth and detail, refer back to your textbook or class notes, and visit the web links from www.revision-express.com.

HOW THE BOOK WORKS

The book is divided into two-page revision sessions. To make your revision really effective, study one session at a time.

Have a short break between sessions – that way you'll learn more!

Each session has two parts:

1st page: the first page on each topic contains interactive exercises to nail down the basics. Follow the instructions in the margin and write your answers in the spaces provided.

2nd page: the second page contains exam questions. Sometimes you'll answer the exam question directly, but more often you'll use it as a starting point for in-depth revision exercises. In each case, follow the extra instructions in the margin.

REMEMBER: the answers in the back are for the revision exercises – they are not necessarily model answers to the exam questions themselves. For model answers to a selection of exam questions go to www.revision-express.com.

All the pages are hole-punched, so you can remove them and put them in your folder.

TRACK YOUR PROGRESS

The circles beside each topic heading let you track your progress.

If a topic is hard, fill in one circle. If it's easy, fill in all three. If you've only filled in one or two circles go back to the topic later.

TOPIC HEADING ● ● ○

EXAM BOARDS

You might not need to work through every session in this book. Check that your exam board is listed above the topic heading before you start a session.

(AS) AQA EDEXCEL OCR WJEC

This book covers the most popular topics. For full information about your syllabus, contact the relevant exam board or go to their website.

AQA
(Assessment and Qualifications Alliance)
Publications department, Stag Hill House, Guildford, Surrey GU2 5XJ – www.aqa.org.uk

EDEXCEL
Stuart House, 32 Russell Square, London WC1B 5DN – www.edexcel.org.uk

OCR
(Oxford, Cambridge and Royal Society of Arts)
1 Hills Road, Cambridge CB2 1GG – www.ocr.org.uk

DON'T FORGET

Exam questions have been specially written for this book. Ask your teacher or the exam board for the official sample papers to add to the questions given here.

COMMENTS PLEASE!

However you use this book, we'd welcome your comments. Just go to www.revision-express.com and tell us what you think!

GOOD LUCK!

The market

When buyers and sellers of a product meet, a market is created. The idea of the market is important because it is through the interaction of buyers and sellers that prices are determined.

DEMAND ○○○

THE JARGON
Aggregate demand refers to the total quantity of a product demanded by consumers within a country.

Demand refers to the quantity of a product that consumers will buy at a given price. The demand curve normally slopes down from left to right. This is because:

Why does the demand curve slope down from left to right?

> *as price falls – it becomes more attractive to consumers.*

SUPPLY ○○○

The supply curve slopes upwards from left to right. This is because:

Why does the supply curve slope upwards from left to right?

THE DETERMINANTS OF SUPPLY AND DEMAND ○○○

THE JARGON
Supply refers to the quantity of a product that producers are capable of supplying at a given price.

Where there is a shift in the position of either a supply or a demand curve it means that a factor other than price has changed – this factor is the determinant.

Here are some of the factors that may cause a shift in a supply or a demand curve. Which curve do they affect – or is it both? (Tick the relevant columns.)

WATCH OUT
Some of these factors may affect both supply and demand.

Factor changed	Shift in demand curve	Shift in supply curve
Consumer income		
Prices of other goods		
Consumer tastes		
Cost of production inputs		
Technological advances		
Social or cultural attitudes		
Tax changes		
Substitute prices		

PRICE DETERMINATION ○○○

Identify and label the vertical axis 'Price'.
Identify and label the Quantity axis.
Draw a horizontal line to identify the equilibrium price. Label this P.
Draw a vertical line to identify the equilibrium quantity. Label this Q.

The diagram below shows how the interaction of supply (S) and demand (D) determine price.

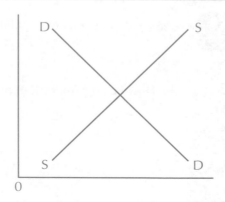

Turn the page for some exam questions on this topic ➤

EXAM QUESTION 1

●●●

House prices have sometimes risen sharply in the south-east of England.
(a) What factors might have contributed to this situation?

> Some of the factors listed helped cause the rise in prices. In each case you are given a choice. Highlight the correct word.

Fall/increase in price of rented accommodation

Difficulties in obtaining building land in south/north

Rise/fall in numbers of jobs available in south

Rise/fall in mortgage interest rates

Fall/rise in building society lending

Lower/higher paid jobs in the south

Availability/non-availability of council houses for purchase

Increases/decreases in prices of building materials

(b) Give one way the government might be affected by the rise in house prices.

> Now have a go at parts (b) and (c).

(c) Give one way that rising house prices might affect businesses based in the south-east.

EXAM QUESTION 2

●●●

From time to time governments intervene in the market to control prices. The diagram below illustrates a situation where minimum wage legislation has been imposed.

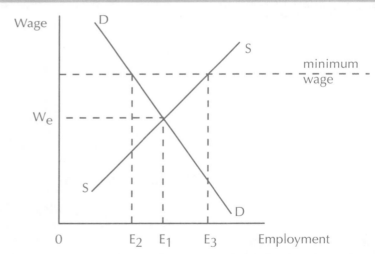

EXAMINER'S SECRETS
Examiners are impressed if you can use supply and demand analysis to explain why prices have changed.

> Answer these two questions with reference to the graph.

(a) What is the market equilibrium wage and employment level?

(b) How has the imposition of a minimum wage affected employment?

EXAMINER'S SECRETS
Some firms, in the longer term, may seek to replace the more expensive labour with labour-saving capital machinery.

Markets and competition

Competition refers to the degree of rivalry between firms in a market to sell you their products and services. Where a firm is in a competitive situation the consumer is likely to get a better deal in terms of price and quality.

THE SPECTRUM OF COMPETITION ○○○

The degree of competition in a market varies. At one end there is the perfectly competitive market and at the other end monopoly where there is no competition. In between these extremes are monopolistic competition and oligopoly. These are the forms of competition that exist in most markets.

The characteristics of monopolistic competition are:

> Here are some characteristics of different market structures. List those that relate to monopolistic competition in the space provided:
>
> - many sellers
> - single seller
> - free entry
> - low profits
> - price makers
> - price takers
> - undifferentiated product

An oligopoly has different characteristics from those listed above. Its characteristics are:

> List three characteristics of an oligopoly that makes it different.

THE IMPACT OF COMPETITION: CASE STUDY ○○○

The holiday package industry is very competitive, and this is reflected in what firms offer the consumer. For example, one might offer free child places, another discounts for booking two holidays in a year. Other enticements include:

> List other ways holiday companies seek to attract customers. Try to think of at least three.

EXAMINER'S SECRETS
Governments encourage competition because it means the consumer gets a better quality product at a lower price. You will often find that it also means the business will provide a product or service closer to what the consumer wants.

FIXING THE MARKET ○○○

There are various forms of unfair competition:

> List at least three forms of unfair competition.

THE JARGON
Sometimes firms try to manipulate the market to their own advantage. This is termed fixing the market. They try to do this to protect their prices and profits.

Turn the page for some exam questions on this topic ➤

THE JARGON

OPEC is shorthand for Organization of Petroleum Exporting Countries. A cartel is a group of businesses that come together to agree selling area, exchange information or agree prices.

EXAM QUESTION 1

● ● ●

In some exam papers you may be given a press cutting to read. You are then required to answer some questions based on that material. The questions below are typical and would be based on a press cutting about OPEC. The press cutting might start 'OPEC is a cartel created by some of the oil exporting countries. . .'

(a) Give one reason why OPEC wants to regulate the supply of oil.

> Answer the questions in the spaces here.

(b) OPEC is able to do this because oil has an inelastic demand curve. Explain this statement.

THE JARGON

A necessity is a product that many consumers are unable to do without

IF YOU HAVE TIME

Draw an inelastic demand curve!

(c) What impact does this have on consumers?

> Give two points in response to this question.

EXAM QUESTION 2

● ● ●

Both the UK government and the EU are keen to ensure competition exists in all markets. Think of three things that have been used to achieve this aim and write a short paragraph about each.

> An answer to this question might mention Article 86 of the Treaty of Rome. Write one or two sentences about this here.

> You could also write about the Fair Trading Act, and Competition Act. Remember to give the dates of the Acts when you mention them.

WATCH OUT

Legislation passed by the UK government applies to situations that occur within the UK. EU legislation applies to situations where more than one member state is involved.

> Finally, you could write about Articles 92–94 of the Treaty of Rome.

8

BUSINESS STUDIES

Macro-economic factors

The macro-economic environment refers to the part of the economic environment over which the firm has no control. Firms must try to understand these economic processes to best guess future developments and thus protect their interests and exploit opportunities.

INFLATION ○○○

Inflation may be caused by cost push or demand pull influences. It may also be imported.

> **Draw a line to match each statement to the correct cause of inflation.**

THE JARGON
Hyperinflation refers to a situation where prices rise so fast that money may cease to be used and people return to bartering.

1 Cost push	Increases in the prices of raw materials or components from abroad force British manufacturers to raise the prices of their products.
2 Demand pull	Rising business costs, such as wages or interest payments, force firms to increase prices so as to protect profit margins.
3 Imported	A situation where demand is growing more quickly than the ability of firms to meet that demand. It often arises in 'boom' conditions.

THE JARGON
Structural unemployment occurs where a region is heavily dependent upon a declining industry, e.g. mining.

UNEMPLOYMENT ○○○

There are various forms of unemployment including frictional, cyclical and structural. The government might use a range of strategies to reduce structural unemployment.

> **Suggest three ways the government might reduce structural unemployment.**

THE JARGON
The exchange rate is the value of one currency in terms of another. For example, the sterling: peseta exchange rate might be £1 = 250 pesetas.

EXCHANGE RATES ○○○

Exchange rates often fluctuate and this may cause problems for businesses trading internationally. Exchange rate appreciation occurs where one currency increases in value against another (e.g. £1 might now buy 275 pesetas). Thus exchange rate appreciation might affect a British firm importing from, or exporting to, Spain as follows.

> **Explain the effect of exchange rate appreciation on a British firm importing from Spain. Then explain the effect if the firm is exporting to Spain.**

Exchange rate depreciation might affect a British firm importing from Spain, as follows.

> **Now explain the effect of exchange rate depreciation on a British firm importing from Spain.**

Turn the page for some exam questions on this topic ➤

EXAM QUESTION 1

● ● ●

What benefits and problems might a firm face from a period of rising inflation?

The table lists some benefits and problems that are associated with rising inflation. Tick a column to indicate whether each statement is a problem or a benefit .

	Benefit	Problem
Rising prices lead to higher profits		
Exchange rates may depreciate		
Inflation may damage business confidence		
Interest rates may be forced up		
Real value of loans less when repaid		
Financial planning may be more difficult		
General increasing demand for goods		
Exports may become uncompetitive		

Now write two or three sentences to explain why financial planning might be more difficult in a time of rising inflation.

EXAM QUESTION 2

● ● ●

EXAMINER'S SECRETS
The key to this question is to realize that it implies that a recession is imminent.

How might a firm alter its plans if a prolonged period of heavy unemployment is predicted?

Use the instructions on the left to help you plan your answer.

What might the production department do? Give four ideas.

THE JARGON
Outsourcing arises when a firm buys in services that it previously did itself, for example, market research.

What might the marketing department do? Give four ideas.

What might the finance department do?

THE JARGON
Sale and leaseback is a method of raising money by selling land and buildings. At the same time another agreement is entered into, leasing the property back from the new owner.

What might the human resources (or personnel) department do?

Social and demographic influences

People have always had an important influence on business. Changes in social attitudes have provided businesses with many opportunities and threats. The same may also be said for changes in population size and age structure.

BUSINESS STUDIES

PEOPLE AND BUSINESS

○○○

EXAMINER'S SECRETS
Make sure you can quote some examples of the different ways people influence businesses.

Businesses rely on people in many ways. Their attitudes and actions can influence a business, both favourably and unfavourably. There are numerous examples of businesses that have changed (or been forced to change) direction because of the influence of people. Here are some examples of the relationship people may have with business:

- as customers
- as shareholders
- as suppliers
- as pressure groups
- as employees
- as government.

The relationship between a business and its employees is important. Give at least two problems that might occur if the relationship is poor.

DEMOGRAPHIC CHANGES

○○○

The UK is facing demographic changes including a reduction in the birth rate, an increase in the size of the retired population and more young people going into higher education. Various groups might be worried by these demographic changes.

Explain how the two groups mentioned here might be affected.

The government

Businesses

There are various ways firms might avoid these problems.

Give two ways firms could avoid problems associated with demographic change.

These trends provide both opportunities and threats to a firm or industry. For instance, there might be more demand for academic textbooks and pensioner holidays (often out of season), but there will be less demand for products such as baby goods and toys.

Turn the page for some exam questions on this topic ➤

EXAM QUESTION 1 ●●●

One major trend during the twentieth century has been the increasing use of cars by people in their everyday lives. Assess the possible implications of this for business and society.

Here are some of the points you could make:

> Indicate whether you think each point is a benefit or a problem (with some of these points you might be able to argue that it is both a benefit and a problem).

	Benefit	Problem
1. Car fumes a major pollutant		
2. Cuts journey times		
3. The car industry provides much employment		
4. Increased road congestion		
5. Car taxes are source of government revenue		
6. Major cause of accident and injury		
7. Improved social and work mobility		
8. Health problems caused by lack of exercise		
9. Forces government to invest heavily in roads		

> **EXAMINER'S SECRETS**
> In an exam you would not be expected to use all these points. You would be required to select what you consider to be the most important and develop a short paragraph round each of those points.

Develop the statement in point 3.

> List some jobs that are created by the car industry.

Explain point 9.

> Write a short paragraph giving the reasons why the government has had to invest in road building schemes. You could mention what effect this investment has had.

EXAM QUESTION 2 ●●●

Female employment rates have grown throughout the twentieth century. Women now form nearly 50% of the workforce. However, their weekly earnings are only 75% of their male counterparts'.

Explain these trends.

> Here are some points you could use to explain the rise in female employment rates.
> • Women can control family size.
> • Growth of tertiary sector jobs.
> • Social attitudes have changed.
> • More highly educated women.
> • Gender discrimination unlawful.
> Write a paragraph explaining how social attitudes have changed.

> Now explain why women's earnings are so much lower than men's. Try to think of up to four points.

BUSINESS STUDIES

Technological influences

When we use the term 'technology' we are referring to the application of existing knowledge and skills to create and use materials, processes and products. Technology is often seen as determining the products made, the processes by which they are made and the organizational structure. Technology may also affect an individual's motivation and attitude to work.

TECHNOLOGY – SOME IMPORTANT TERMS ○○○

> **Draw lines matching each term or phrase with the correct definition.**

> **REVISION EXPRESS**
> For more on CAD/CAM see pages 132–133 of the *Revision Express A-level Study Guide*

1 Information technology	The process by which an interesting job is replaced by a more monotonous one through the use of machinery.
2 Management information system	A computer based system used to produce a detailed product design. Designs can be modified or refined using a computer based system.
3 Computer aided design	The use of robots in the production process, particularly where work is hazardous or monotonous.
4 Deskilling	The acquisition, processing, storage and dissemination of information using computers.
5 Robotics	Any system of production where manufacturing equipment is controlled by a computer.
6 Computer aided manufacturing	A computerized system which provides management with the information with which to plan, organize, coordinate and control.

INFORMATION TECHNOLOGY (IT) ○○○

Strategies for managing IT involve the whole organization. Here are some of the issues to be considered:

- selecting staff to set up and run IT-based management systems
- identifying changes to products, processes and administrative systems to take advantage of IT
- ensuring all departments recognize the importance of IT
- deciding whether to develop a customized system or purchase a standard commercial package.

In addition, IT can change the <u>organizational structure</u>.

> **How might the organizational structure be changed by the introduction of new information technology?**

not so much delegation – manages are free to take on more hand jobs – Manages have a wider span of control.

> **EXAMINER'S SECRETS**
> The implications of adopting 'new technology' are an important exam topic.

Turn the page for some exam questions on this topic ➤

EXAM QUESTION 1   ● ● ●

The benefits arising from the introduction of new technology far outweigh the problems. How far do you agree with this statement?

Write an introductory paragraph, setting the scene for an answer to this question. You might want to begin by saying something about the term 'new technology'. What exactly does it mean?

Here are some of the points that could be made. Highlight those points that you consider to be problems.

- The cost is often high and the firm may have to compromise in order to stay within budget.
- There is an opportunity to reduce staffing levels.
- Improved communication may result within the organization.
- There is the likelihood of employee resistance to change.
- Better management control as a result of more accurate information.
- Change is often rapid and some staff find it difficult to adjust.
- In the short term costs are going to outweigh benefits.
- Embracing new technology prevents other firms using this as a means of gaining competitive advantage over you.

Now write a concluding paragraph, summing up the arguments. You might want to distinguish between the short-term impact and the long-term impact.

EXAM QUESTION 2   ● ● ●

Mountbatten Estates is a property company that has just introduced a new Management Information System into its office. As a result some employees have left, absenteeism is higher and morale is lower. To what extent could these problems have been avoided?

Briefly state why employees might react unfavourably to change.

Now write at least two sentences to summarize the points you would make in the main part of your answer.

Business, law and society

Increasingly, businesses are being expected to act in a socially responsible manner, particularly in relation to the environment, employees and consumers. You will also find that the law often intervenes to protect these groups' interests.

SOCIAL RESPONSIBILITY AND ETHICS ○○○

A firm's profit might increase as a result of being socially responsible.

Give one reason to explain a rise in profits. Then give a reason for a fall in profits.

However, it is equally likely that a firm's profits will fall, since...

THE JARGON
Business ethics are the moral principles that guide a manager's behaviour. Business ethics are greatly influenced by the corporate culture of the firm.

Firms often face ethical dilemmas.

Think of an ethical dilemma for firms working with suppliers in developing countries.

It is important to distinguish between a firm behaving legally and behaving ethically.

Explain the difference.

The most ethical behaviour can be difficult to identify. For instance:

Explain why the management of a polluting factory might face a dilemma due to the conflicting interests of stakeholders.

THE JARGON
The shareholder approach to social responsibility argues that a firm is responsible only to its shareholders. The stakeholder approach acknowledges a responsibility to many other groups as well as shareholders.

Draw a line linking these statements to the correct Act.

EXAMINER'S SECRETS
You will not be required to know these Acts in great detail. You will be expected to know about the impact on the firm and the consumer.

CONSUMER PROTECTION LAW ○○○

The rights of the consumer are protected by a number of Acts. These include:

1 Trade Descriptions Act 1968/72	This act requires that goods should be of merchantable quality, fit for their purpose and as described.
2 Sale of Goods Act 1979	This act requires retailers and manufacturers to provide safety advice and instructions for all dangerous goods.
3 Consumer Credit Act 1974	This act makes it illegal for a trader to give false or misleading descriptions of goods on offer.
4 Consumer Protection Act 1989	This act ensures that the customer gets the quantity of a product asked for or stated on a label.
5 Weights and Measures Act 1985	This act requires the true cost of borrowing to be disclosed.

Turn the page for some exam questions on this topic ➤

EXAM QUESTION 1

● ● ●

In the twenty-first century we have a right to expect firms to act in a socially responsible manner.
To what extent do you agree with this statement?

Here are some arguments for and against the statement.

Tick to indicate which statements are for and which are against.

EXAMINER'S SECRETS
In an exam you would not have time to develop all these points, so highlight those you consider to be the most important and concentrate on these. Also make sure that you choose arguments both for and against.

Now write a short paragraph developing point 5 above.

	For	Against
1. Acting responsibly may reduce a firm's competitiveness.		
2. Acting responsibly creates a favourable image.		
3. Directors have a legal duty to shareholders.		
4. The prime task of business is to maximize profits.		
5. The interests of stakeholders may conflict with each other.		
6. Acting responsibly may attract good employees.		

EXAM QUESTION 2

● ● ●

Identify and illustrate the different kinds of law that affect management. What problems can these cause for management?

Write at least two sentences explaining how the law affects the marketing function within a firm.

Now write a short paragraph about the effects of the Companies Acts on information that must be given to investors. Also mention the responsibilities of directors if a business becomes insolvent.

Think about problems that legal controls give management. What is the impact on costs, time and freedom of action?

EXAMINER'S SECRETS
To get a good mark you would have to identify legislation that also affects the human resources and production function. You could talk about 'equality' legislation as well as health and safety legislation.

Nature of business

Business involves the transformation of inputs into an output that is designed to satisfy a customer's needs. For a business to be profitable it must 'add value' during the transformation stage so that a price can be charged that is higher than the cost of the inputs.

THE JARGON

'Value added' is the difference between the cost of materials and the price customers are prepared to pay for the finished product.

Define each of the types of output and give at least two examples of each.

IF YOU HAVE TIME

Make a list of the goods and services that you consume in a typical week classifying them into the different kinds.

INPUTS AND OUTPUTS ○○○

Inputs are the resources needed to produce goods or a service. They will include a combination of the four factors of production: land, labour, capital and enterprise. These resources are transformed into the following outputs:

Consumer durable goods:

Consumer non-durable goods (consumables):

Capital goods:

Services:

PRIVATE AND PUBLIC SECTOR ○○○

Goods and services are provided for consumers and firms by either the private sector or the public sector.

Private sector: the section of the economy consisting of privately owned firms ranging from sole traders to multinational companies.

Public sector: the part of the economy consisting of organizations owned and/or financed by local and central government.

Put the following organizations, services or products in the correct part of the table: local authority leisure centre, Post Office, British Telecom, libraries, McDonalds, BBC, local hairdresser, Asda, NHS, Virgin rail services.

Private sector	Public sector

THE CHAIN OF PRODUCTION ○○○

The production chain is the entire sequence of activities required to turn raw materials into a consumer product. These activities can be classed by the type of production that takes place.

In each case, after the words 'Activities include', write the relevant examples from this list: transport, mining, insurance, refining, communications, oil exploration, construction, farming, manufacturing.

Primary sector: the extraction or harvesting of basic raw materials.
Activities include

Secondary sector: the conversion of raw materials into finished goods.
Activities include

Tertiary sector: the provision of services for firms and individuals.
Activities include

Turn the page for some exam questions on this topic ➤

EXAM EXERCISE ● ● ●

For each of the activities listed, indicate the relevant economic sector.

In each case, tick the relevant column.

	Primary	Secondary	Tertiary
Retailing			
Nursing			
Mining and quarrying			
Construction			
Energy and water supplies			
Engineering			
Banking			
Teaching			
Farming			
Steel fabrication			
Forestry			
Motor assembly			
Dentistry			

DON'T FORGET

The sectors are interdependent. For example, the produce from farming in the primary sector is processed by the secondary sector and distributed and sold by the tertiary sector.

EXAM QUESTION 1 ● ● ●

Economies are dynamic in that they are constantly changing and adapting to new technologies, new material and new consumer demands. Organizations and workers must adapt to these changes if they are to remain in business or employment.

(a) Using the following data, calculate the percentage share of total employment for the manufacturing and service sectors for each year.

Employment in UK industries (000s)		
	1990	**1998**
All employment	22 920	23 237
Manufacturing	4 708	4 056
Service industries	16 350	17 664

Write your calculations in the spaces provided.

Manufacturing % share 1990 =

Manufacturing % share 1998 =

Services % share 1990 =

Services % share 1998 =

EXAMINER'S SECRETS

Answers that manipulate the data will receive higher marks than those that merely restate their findings, e.g. you could calculate the difference in employment between the years.

(b) What does the trend indicate? How will this affect the workforce?

First summarize the changes, then explain what they indicate. What type of economy exists in the UK?

Now say what the effect on the workforce will be.

Stakeholders and their objectives

Organizations today must recognize the objectives of their stakeholders. To disregard them is to risk losing customers and goodwill. The importance attached to the views of these groups depends on their relative strength in the market place.

THE JARGON
Stakeholders are any individuals or groups who have an interest in a business activity.

Define the term 'shareholder concept'.

LINKS
For more information on business objectives see pages 23–24

SHAREHOLDER CONCEPT ○○○

This is a traditional view of a firm.

STAKEHOLDER CONCEPT ○○○

A more modern approach is to recognize the interests of all the stakeholders in a business. Some management theorists believe that in the long run it is more beneficial for firms to recognize the views of these groups and to include their objectives in the decision making process. Some of these groups include:

Each stakeholder group has many objectives and goals. In this exercise, one possible objective has been identified for each group.
In each case say what action the business could take to satisfy the objective and show what benefit it might bring to the business.

Employees
Objective	Improved working conditions
Action	
Benefit	

Suppliers
Objective	Gain more regular orders and payments
Action	
Benefit	

Customers
Objective	Products tailored more closely to the customer's needs
Action	
Benefit	

Local community
Objective	Improve local services
Action	
Benefit	

CONFLICT OF OBJECTIVES ○○○

THE JARGON
'Satisficing' is the acceptance of a strategy that is satisfactory for all instead of pursuing a policy that is in the interests of only one group.

All the groups are competing for a slice of the rewards generated by the business. Conflict appears inevitable as more for one group appears only possible with less for another. The stakeholder view, however, believes that the total rewards can be increased through 'cooperation' and that all stakeholders can benefit. This strategy is known as 'satisficing'.

19

BUSINESS STUDIES

Turn the page for some exam questions on this topic ➤

EXAM EXERCISE

● ● ●

A local hospital is reviewing its objectives for the next five-year development plan. As part of the process it wants to identify all its stakeholders and to estimate their possible needs. For each of the identified stakeholders state an objective.

Write possible objectives in the table.

DON'T FORGET

Individuals within each group may also have different interests and priorities. This mixture of objectives makes it extremely difficult for a business to satisfy all its stakeholders.

Stakeholders	Objectives
Management	
Doctors	
Nursing staff	
General employees	
Patients	
Relatives of patients	
Local community	
Government	
Suppliers	

EXAM QUESTION 1

● ● ●

The reaction of a firm to consumer pressure groups will depend on a number of factors. For each of the factors below, explain why it might be important, and give an example.

Explain the importance of each factor, then add the most appropriate example from this list.
• Some banks stopped charging for use of cash machines.
• British Airways has banned smoking on all its flights.
• The attempt to ban all blood sports.
• At the time of the Brent Spar controversy, Shell's petrol sales were damaged.

EXAMINER'S SECRETS

Answers that are able to quote a relevant example are always preferable to mere descriptions. Make sure you know several examples of pressure groups such as ASH, Friends of the Earth, Greenpeace, CAMRA, etc.

1. The purchasing power of the pressure group:

2. The reaction of competitors:

3. Access to politicians:

4. The relative costs and benefits of adopting the demanded changes:

Types and size of business

There are many types of business in the commercial world each with their own benefits and drawbacks. You need to know how they are financed, who is in control and who makes the decisions.

BUSINESS ORGANIZATIONS

○○○

DON'T FORGET
99.2% of all businesses in the UK are classified as small.

In the tables provided list three advantages and three disadvantages of each form of business organization. Some of the factors you should think about are listed below.
- How easy is it to establish the organization?
- Is the organization's liability unlimited?
- Who keeps the profits?
- Are there any divisions of labour?
- Are there economies of scale?
- Does the organization issue shares? If so, who owns them? Are they offered privately or publicly?
- Do accounts have to be made public?

Sole trader: is the simplest form of business unit as it is easy to establish with only a small amount of capital. In general, the sole trader provides the capital for the business, bears all the risk and makes all the decisions.

Advantages	Disadvantages

Partnership: a common form of business in professional areas such as law, accountancy, medicine and insurance. A Partnership Agreement details the rights and responsibilities of each partner including each partner's capital input, share of profits and losses and voting rights.

Advantages	Disadvantages

DON'T FORGET
Doctors and dentists are often in partnerships.

Private Limited Companies: limited liability means that the owners are financially responsible only for the amount invested in the company and do not risk their own personal wealth. Shares can only be offered on a private basis.

Advantages	Disadvantages
limited liability	hard to sell shares
greater economies of scale	public have access to

THE JARGON
Private limited companies must have the designation 'Limited' at the end of their name, often abbreviated to 'Ltd'.

Public Limited Companies (plcs): although they are small in number, plcs account for the majority of output, capital investment and employment in the UK. They are owned by the shareholders but are controlled and managed by salaried directors.

Advantages	Disadvantages

IF YOU HAVE TIME
Make a list of five public limited companies that you know and that can be used to illustrate exam questions.

Turn the page for some exam questions on this topic ➤

EXAM QUESTION 1 ●●●

DON'T FORGET!
Public limited companies are in the private sector. It is easy to confuse these terms!

The economy can be divided into two sectors, the private **sector** and the public sector. The private sector is made up of sole traders, partnerships and limited companies. Explain what is meant by a public sector organization, and give examples.

Identify who owns, controls and finances such organizations. Provide at least three examples.

EXAMINER'S SECRETS
Many students fail to distinguish between public limited companies and public sector organizations. Accuracy with terminology will avoid losing marks.

EXAM QUESTION 2 ●●●

Rachel Wrigley has been a sole trader for five years and has **built up a highly successful internet café on a London high street. She believes the concept can be profitably extended to other parts of the country but is unwilling to risk any more of her own financial capital. She wants to concentrate on finding new locations and developing new business. Outline three advantages and three disadvantages that Rachel would face if she decided to expand by becoming a limited company, then evaluate the choices facing Rachel.**

Make sure that you write in context by referring to Rachel's current position and her future plans.

Advantages
1.

2.

3.

Disadvantages
1.

EXAMINER'S SECRETS
It is more likely that the higher order skills of analysis and evaluation will be displayed when answers are written with reference to the context of the question, in this case addressing the concerns of Rachel.

2.

3.

Evaluation requires you to balance the two arguments and to express an opinion.

Evaluation

Business objectives

It is important that an organization has a common purpose and direction that is understood by all – owners, management and workforce. This formal statement of aims is often phrased in a mission statement. From this statement, a hierarchy of objectives can be formed both long term and short term.

THE JARGON
A mission statement is a document detailing the long-term goals of an organization. It is often expressed in qualitative terms concentrating on quality and customer service.

Define these objectives in terms of time scale, importance and who formulates them. Provide an example of each type of objective.

THE JARGON
Long and short-term objectives are sometimes referred to as strategic and tactical objectives.

IF YOU HAVE TIME
Examine a number of annual reports to compare the mission statements of a diverse group of companies. Is there a common theme?

DON'T FORGET
Markets are dynamic therefore the goals of a business are likely to change with continual developments in the market.

List three reasons why profit is important to a business.

Explain two ways in which growth reduces risk.

LINKS
For more information on stakeholders and their objectives see pages 19–20.

LONG-TERM AND SHORT-TERM OBJECTIVES   ○○○

Objectives are goals that the organization aims to achieve. They must be measurable and attainable otherwise they will have a demotivating effect on the employees. Each organization will have different objectives depending on its size, its age, its market and the resources available. What is common to all organizations, however, is that they will have a series of long-term and short-term objectives.

Long-term or strategic objectives:

Short-term or tactical objectives:

COMMON OBJECTIVES OF AN ORGANIZATION   ○○○

Three objectives commonly associated with all organizations are:

Survival: All new firms strive to survive as they attempt to build a customer base in the market. Even established businesses can feel threatened by new competitors or new products. In these circumstances survival may necessitate the offering of goods and services at highly competitive prices in order to reach a sustainable level of sales that guarantees break-even.

Profit: For most businesses profit making is the major concern of the organization. Profit is an important objective because it:

Growth: Once established, many firms pursue growth as their main objective. Growth is seen not only as a means of increasing profits but also as a means of limiting risk. This is because:

Turn the page for some exam questions on this topic ➤

EXAM QUESTION 1

●●●

The objective of survival is most commonly associated with newly formed businesses as they strive to gain sufficient market share. There are, however, circumstances when established concerns feel the need to adopt survival strategies. For each of the situations below, identify strategies the business could adopt, and outline the dangers associated with each.

(a) A business facing falling sales during a recession.

> Think about each of these possible areas: advertising, costs and pricing. Each time, say what the dangers might be if the business changed its policy in the relevant area.

(b) A business threatened by a takeover.

DON'T FORGET
A change in objectives can be forced upon an organization with very little time for planning and execution.

EXAM EXERCISE

●●●

For each of the following ten activities, say whether you think they are short-term (tactical) or long-term (strategic).

> Tick the correct columns.

	Long-term	Short-term
Place extra advert in local paper		
Expand into Europe		
Employ four more sales people		
Diversify into a new market		
Create a research department		
Offer a limited period sales promotion		
Introduce new technologies		
Complete a customer order		
Expand by a series of takeovers		
Build links with the local area		

Government and business

All market-led economies accept the need for government intervention in the workings of the economy. The key question is not whether the government should intervene but what should be the purpose of that intervention. Within the UK it is generally agreed that this role should be to create a stable business environment where firms and people are not disadvantaged.

THE JARGON
The public sector consists of organizations owned or financed by the government.

Add some further examples of public-sector goods and services.

Now explain briefly how the education system, health services and transport infrastructure help business.

CREATING AN ECONOMIC FRAMEWORK ○○○

Although the privatization of the 1980s and 1990s has removed many industries from direct government control, the government is still a major user of resources and supplier of goods and services. These include:

education, health services, transport infrastructure,

Many of these goods and services help business. For example:

THE GOVERNMENT AS REGULATOR ○○○

There are many areas where the government has intervened in the world of business, for example, by introducing competition legislation. Other areas include:

State at least two other areas where the government has intervened.

State one advantage and one disadvantage of this legislation to the firm.

THE GOVERNMENT AS PROMOTER ○○○

Many opportunities are provided for firms by the government's activities as promoter. Government activities include research and development (R&D), international trade, employment training and regional policy. Small firms' assistance is especially important.

State at least two ways in which the government has assisted small firms.

Why would it want to do this?

Turn the page for some exam questions on this topic ➤

EXAM QUESTION 1

● ● ●

Despite its many advantages privatization may still be criticized. Discuss this statement.

An ideal answer would include a brief definition of 'privatization'. Write two or three sentences explaining the term. Give examples of industries often affected.

EXAMINER'S SECRETS
Try to give some context to the term, e.g. when did it start, what sort of industries are usually involved, where is it happening now.

Here are some of the advantages claimed for privatization:
1. a reduction in the size of the public sector
2. an increase in efficiency by introducing competition
3. reduced public sector borrowing to finance investment
4. reduced dependence on the state (e.g. to finance losses)
5. provides funds to develop a better infrastructure
6. widens share ownership
7. improves customer choice and quality of provision.

Look at the list of advantages claimed for privatization. Write a brief explanation of points 2 and 3.

EXAMINER'S SECRETS
To get high marks you do not have to use all these points – but you are expected to explain the ones you do use!

Here are some of the problems associated with privatization:
1. it is still difficult to bring competition into some industries
2. in some cases the productivity gains have not materialized
3. complaints about fat cat pay rises awarded to directors
4. regulation of privatized utilities is not robust enough
5. there have been problems with the share issues.

Write two or three sentences explaining point 5. Point 1 has already been done as an example.

1. Where the privatized firm was a state monopoly it has sometimes been difficult to introduce competition into that area. Both the rail companies and the water utilities come into this category. In each case it is left to the government appointed regulator to try and get some efficiency gains.

Marketing objectives

The objectives that managers set for a firm depend on many factors including the competitive environment, the nature of the market and the state of the economy. Objectives will also be determined by internal factors such as the resources the firm has available.

MARKETING ORIENTATION ○○○

There are several different 'orientations' that a firm could adopt. For example, a production-led firm will use techniques to maximize production and minimize cost. Products will be standardized to achieve this objective.

Alternatively, businesses might have a sales orientation or a marketing orientation.

Write a paragraph to explain what you understand by the term 'marketing orientation'.

THE JARGON
A sales-orientated firm will emphasize the varying product features and advertising to create and retain market share without considering the needs of its customers.

TYPES OF MARKETING OBJECTIVES ○○○

There are a number of marketing objectives that may be pursued by an organization. Most apply to not for profit organizations as well.

List at least three marketing objectives that a company might have.

WATCH OUT!
Remember that marketing objectives must fit in with the wider objectives of the business.

In practice, firms sometimes fail to achieve their marketing objectives. The reasons for this may be either external or internal to the firm. Factors within the firm might be getting the right employees, problems with the quality of raw materials or the production process. The size of the marketing budget may also be a constraint.

External factors relate to the environment in which the firm works. Many of these factors can be categorized as political (or legal), social, economic or technological.

Here are four external factors that may interfere with marketing objectives. For each one, say whether it is social, technological, political, or economic.

- Legislation may prevent a firm from making extravagant claims about the product.
- A recession could reduce sales activity.
- Attitudes to a product may change.
- A product may become outdated.

Turn the page for some exam questions on this topic ➤

EXAM QUESTION 1 ● ● ●

Heath Printing Ltd has decided that its key marketing objective for the coming year is short-term profit maximization. What are the possible implications of this for the firm's marketing mix?

To answer this question well, you need to be clear what is meant by the phrase 'short-term profit maximization'. Write two sentences to explain this here.

The implications for the marketing mix are as follows.

The marketing mix will now focus on increasing sales. Write one sentence about the impact on each of these:
• price
• promotion
• place (distribution).

EXAMINER'S SECRETS
This is another example of a question where it is useful to consider both the short and the long-term implications for the firm.

Write two sentences explaining the possible long-term implications of pursuing this objective.

EXAM QUESTION 2 ● ● ●

Agbrigg Tents Ltd is a firm that has specialized in the production of standardized tents and marquees. At a recent board meeting the decision was taken to become more marketing orientated by developing a wider range of products more closely reflecting customer needs. What are the possible implications for the firm?

State at least three ways the firm might benefit from being more marketing orientated.

Suggest ways the relationship between the marketing and production departments might change now that the firm is more marketing orientated.

The market and its segmentation

Most markets today are segmented in some way. However, because segmentation limits the size of the market, some firms consider developing products that have mass appeal within either the European or the global market.

MASS MARKETING

○○○

Mass marketing has many benefits for firms.

Think of some benefits that mass marketing might have for businesses.

THE JARGON
Mass marketing is based on the idea that an undifferentiated product will be popular to everyone within a country or even in other countries.

Now give at least two examples of products that might have a global appeal.

Products that might have a global appeal include:

SEGMENTATION

○○○

THE JARGON
Segmenting a market implies it is made up of lots of individuals who can be grouped in many different ways .

Segmentation is interesting to the marketeer if the buying behaviour of one group is different to other groups. Common ways of segmenting a market include by age, gender, income, ethnicity and interests. Here are some examples:

Look at the products listed here. State four ways you might segment each product market. Think about age, income, ethnic origin, interests and gender.

WATCH OUT
You can't always segment the markets in the ways suggested.

Food: *income, ethnic origin,*

Holidays: *income,*

Magazines: *gender, interests*

Dress: *age-*

Sometimes markets are more effectively segmented by usage. Take the case of toothpaste. The most common method of segmentation for toothpaste is to look at how or why it is used. For example, we can classify users on the basis of:

Smokers/non smokers, heavy users/light users, reason for use (sparkling teeth, mouth odour, flavour, decay prevention, price), loyalty of consumer.

The restaurant market could also be segmented by usage.

Give two or more examples of how you could segment the restaurant market by usage.

Once a product market has been broken down into its different segments the firm is then able to develop a different marketing mix for each individual segment. This is often termed differentiated marketing.

Turn the page for some exam questions on this topic ➤

EXAM QUESTION 1 ● ● ●

While most firms target a market segment, Marty Lodge has made his money from a market niche. A motor car fanatic, Marty's enthusiasm for rebuilding saloon cars to higher specifications gave him the idea for a business.

Marty Lodge Motors was founded in 1984 to take new saloon cars and rebuild (customize) them to the owner's higher specifications.

Despite working in a very specialist market Marty has found that he has been able to charge very high prices and earn profits that are far higher than in the wider market segment.

Over the years demand has increased and with it the size of Marty Lodge Motors. He now employs ten men in a newly built garage. Even so, Marty has found that over the last few years prices and profits have fallen. More recently, he has also heard that a major motor car manufacturer plans to customize its own cars.

Discuss the situation Marty faces.

Before you start to answer the question, make sure you can distinguish between a market segment and a market niche. Write a short explanation of each here.

Now explain why prices and profits may be higher in the niche market that Marty works in.

REVISION EXPRESS
For more on elasticity of demand see page 71 in the *Revision Express A-level Study Guide*.

Explain why, with growth in the market, prices and profits may have fallen.

Now explain why a large car manufacturer would want to enter a small segment of the car market.

Product

The term 'product' is used by marketeers to refer to both goods and services. Marketeers are interested in the management of the firm's products so as to ensure the firm's objectives are achieved.

THE PRODUCT LIFE CYCLE ○○○

Most products have a limited life during which they can be marketed profitably. Each product will pass through four recognizable stages: **introduction**, **growth**, **maturity** and **decline**. All products will have a different life cycle as the period of time spent in each stage varies. By identifying where the product is in its life cycle, marketeers can devise the best possible marketing mix.

R&D

Introduction
High failure rate of products, little competition, frequent modifications, informative advertising, loss making.

Growth
increase in sales – people become more aware.

Maturity
high market share –

Decline
need extension strategies 2 keep it going.

> List the characteristics associated with each stage of the product life cycle (the first one has been done for you!).

REVISION EXPRESS
For more on advertising see page 72 in the *Revision Express A-level Study Guide*.

EXTENSION STRATEGIES ○○○

It is often possible to extend the life of a product beyond its maturity by the use of an extension strategy.

> Here are some extension strategies. Draw a line to match each strategy to an example.

THE JARGON
Extension strategies may be *defensive* where they are trying to postpone the decline of a product or *offensive* where the aim is to reposition the product and give it a long-term future.

1 More frequent use — Changes made to physical appearance, image or packaging.

2 Extend product range — Baby toiletries promoted to adults, ladies' electric shavers.

3 Modify product — Frozen turkeys or chocolate crème eggs sold all year not just at Christmas or Easter.

4 Identify new uses — A food product extended by diet, slimline, low fat, low calorie versions.

Turn the page for some exam questions on this topic ➤

EXAM QUESTION 1

● ● ●

These data relate to Caretours, a highly profitable company operating in four segments of the holiday market. Read the data and answer the questions that follow.

Holiday	Market growth 1997–2000(%)	Market share 1999(%)	Sales revenue (£ 000)			
			1997	1998	1999	2000
Overseas package	3	10	2 180	2 237	2 132	2 146
Cruises	4	7	560	1 030	1 300	1 410
Holiday camps	−6	5	1 350	1 110	810	720
Children's activity	9	2	–	252	487	487

Using the concept of the product life cycle analyse the sales prospects for each product.

EXAMINER'S SECRETS
When you are analysing data always ask yourself 'what is the trend?'

The revenue figures for the overseas package suggest that it is in the maturity stage of the product life cycle. It is unlikely that there will be much sales growth in this area and eventually sales may decline.

It is difficult to make any firm judgement based on three years' results for children's activity holidays. However, in the absence of other information, it would seem that the company is having difficulty breaking into this market so this could imply a mature segment.

Critically examine the company's product portfolio using the Boston matrix.

THE JARGON
The Boston matrix is an attempt to analyse a company's portfolio of products in terms of market growth and market share. Products are classified as question marks, stars, cash cows or dogs.

It is likely that overseas package holidays and cruises are cash cows because market growth seems to have slowed into maturity. The strong cash flows associated with cash cows probably account for the company being highly profitable.

Price

Pricing decisions are crucial to the success of the business. Consumers often have a perception of the right price. Price your product too high and customers think they are being cheated. Charge too low a price and they question the quality. Clearly the marketeer has to be careful when setting the price.

PRICING THE PRODUCT: A CASE STUDY ○ ○ ○

DG Ltd is a small local double glazing firm which uses cost plus pricing. It is facing competition from a new company, Bestglass. Bestglass is using a number of price promotions (a form of competitive pricing) that are now affecting DG Ltd's sales.

Now answer these questions on pricing the product.

Explain the term cost plus pricing. Why is it used by DG?

Explain 'competitive pricing'. Why is it used by Bestglass?

WATCH OUT
In an undifferentiated product market it is likely that firms will be forced into some form of competitive pricing policy.

If DG Ltd adopts a competitive pricing policy what impact is this likely to have on consumers and the firms themselves?

EXAMINER'S SECRETS
Here is another example of where it is useful to think of both the short term and the long term.

PRICE SENSITIVITY ○ ○ ○

Price changes affect some products far more significantly than others. Thus a cut in the price of potatoes is likely to have little impact upon demand but a cut in the price of crisps may raise demand and total revenue significantly. This relationship between price and demand is referred to as the Price Elasticity of Demand (PED).

WATCH OUT
Make sure you can give some examples of products with price elastic or inelastic demand curves.

Complete the table indicating whether total revenue rises or falls.

Price change	Type of price elasticity	Impact on total revenue
Increase	Elastic demand	
	Inelastic demand	
Decrease	Elastic demand	
	Inelastic demand	

If a firm wanting to increase total revenue faces a price elastic demand curve what would you recommend it should do?

Turn the page for some exam questions on this topic ➤

EXAM QUESTION 1

● ● ●

BC Unisex Hairsalon recently introduced a 10% price rise as a consequence of increases in costs. Now, demand for women's haircuts has fallen by 5% but demand for men's haircuts has fallen by 20%.

(a) Calculate the price elasticity of demand for men's and women's haircuts.

> The formula is:
> % Change in quantity demanded
> ─────────────────────────────
> % Change in price

(b) Explain why the price elasticity of demand for men and women's haircuts may be different.

> Describe the PED for men's haircuts.

> Describe the PED for women's haircuts.

> Now try to explain why the PEDs are different.

EXAM QUESTION 2

● ● ●

(a) What pricing strategies for new products are available to a firm?

> There are two possibilities – price skimming and penetration pricing. Price skimming has been done for you. Now write a paragraph about penetration pricing.

Price skimming is charging the highest price that buyers will pay. It is used when demand is price inelastic and competition is low. This price will gradually be reduced as the market at that price becomes saturated. A skimming policy has the advantage that it enables the firm to recoup some of its high R&D costs.

WATCH OUT
The key words here are 'for new products'. In practice the firm might consider other pricing policies as well, for example full cost or psychological pricing.

EXAMINER'S SECRETS
Make sure you can give examples of firms using these different methods.

(b) Which pricing strategy would you select for an innovative product?

Promotion

Promotion refers to the communication process between seller and buyer. There are four major methods of promotion – advertising, sales promotion, personal selling and publicity. Firms will use a range of these in their promotional strategy.

ADVERTISING

Write one or two sentences describing each of these forms of advertising:
• institutional
• informative
• persuasive.

THE JARGON
Advertising is defined as purchased, non-personal communication using mass media.

LINKS
For more information on the product life cycle see pages 31–32.

Institutional advertising

Informative advertising

Persuasive advertising

PERSONAL SELLING

Fill the blank spaces in the text from this list:
expensive, person to person, market intelligence, consumer, cost, salesperson, complaints, recruitment.

This takes place when promotion is on a _____ basis. The major advantage is the consumer has the opportunity to ask questions about the product while the _____ gains the confidence of the _____.
Apart from giving advice, salespeople may also demonstrate goods, take orders, collect payment, deliver goods and deal with _____. The _____ gathered by the sales force can also provide the organization with valuable information on consumers and their requirements. The major disadvantage of personal selling is its _____. The _____, training and payment of a sales force may be very _____.

PROMOTIONAL MIX

Organizations often use more than one form of promotion to create a promotional mix. For instance, a double glazing company might use:

What might a manufacturer of double glazed windows include in its promotional mix? Give at least three examples.

Turn the page for some exam questions on this topic ➤

EXAM QUESTION 1   ● ● ●

The government is considering a ban on the advertising of tobacco products. Assess the implications of this.

First write two sentences saying what advertising is and why it is important.

What are the short and long-term implications for the tobacco industry?

Now outline the effect on other industries.

What would be the effect on the government?

What about the consumer?

EXAM QUESTION 2   ● ● ●

Give two examples of how the following businesses should advertise to reach their consumers.
1. Local DIY firm
2. Expensive computer equipment supplier
3. National bridal retailer

EXAMINER'S SECRETS
Your choice should be based on reaching the largest number of potential customers at the lowest cost.

Number 1 has been done for you. Have a go at 2 and 3.

1. The DIY firm must advertise locally. It could use local newspapers or radio. It might also consider posters in the locality.

Place

'Place' is concerned with the way a product is made available to the consumer in a particular place. It is sometimes also referred to as distribution or marketing channels. The place element in the marketing mix is often considered to be unimportant but effective and efficient distribution channels may be the key to competitive advantage for a firm!

CHANNELS OF DISTRIBUTION ○○○

The initial decision a firm has to take is whether to use intermediaries or sell direct to the public. Direct selling removes all market intermediaries, maximizes control of distribution and reduces loss of revenue. Factors that suggest direct selling is preferable include:

State at least two factors encouraging the use of direct selling.

Factors encouraging the use of intermediaries include:

State at least two factors encouraging the use of intermediaries.

WATCH OUT
Remember a firm can use more than one distribution channel!

If a firm decides to sell indirectly through intermediaries one possibility is to sell directly to the retailer **(producer to retailer)**. Thus a supermarket may purchase most of its products direct from the manufacturer. It is possible for the manufacturer and the retail outlet to liaise over point of sale display and sales promotions.

Another approach adopted by firms is **'producer to wholesaler'**. Advantages of this include:

Give two advantages of dealing with wholesalers.

FRANCHISING ○○○

Franchising is an agreement between the owner of patents for goods or services (the franchiser) to give another person (the franchisee) the right to produce or sell those goods or services. Examples include:

Give three examples of franchise firms.

Give four likely terms in the franchise agreement.

Turn the page for some exam questions on this topic ➤

EXAM QUESTION 1   ● ● ●

A British manufacturer of paper products is launching a new range of paper tissue. What factors might affect the firm's selection of distribution channel?

Write an introductory paragraph listing the options available to the firm.

In practice there are many factors you could consider including:

1. the extent of market coverage needed
2. distribution costs increase with longer distribution channels
3. could the existing distribution channels be used?
4. distribution decisions must be consistent with other elements of the marketing mix.

Write one or two sentences on points 2 and 4.

REVISION EXPRESS
For more on pricing methods see pages 70–71 of the *Revision Express A-level Study Guide*.

EXAM QUESTION 2   ● ● ●

What benefits and problems would business owners face from franchising their business idea to other people?

State at least two benefits a business owner would gain from franchising a business idea.

State at least two problems a business owner would face as a result of franchising a business idea.

Market research

Market research is the collection, collation, analysis and evaluation of data relating to the marketing and consumption of goods and services. Successful marketing enables organizations to reduce the risks associated with launching new products, entering new markets or developing existing products. It will not, however, entirely eliminate the risk.

DON'T FORGET
Initial market research by Sony indicated that the Walkman would not sell. Fortunately the Chairman refused to believe the results and launched what became one of the most successful products of modern times.

THE JARGON
A market is anywhere that buyers and sellers can come together to exchange goods and services.

THE JARGON
Secondary research is also referred to as desk research.

> **List at least two more internal and external sources of data.**

THE JARGON
Primary research is also referred to as field research.

> **For each of the five methods of collecting primary data briefly state either an advantage or disadvantage associated with the method.**

ROLE OF MARKET RESEARCH ○○○

Market research is an attempt to gather information about a market and to analyse it in a scientific manner in order to:
Make sales predictions: in order to determine future output levels and to design new products and services.
Understand the market: to determine the extent of the market, to identify existing customers, to identify potential customers and to determine what influences consumer buying habits.
Identify new opportunities: exploring the market either to test newly designed products or to identify new wants and desires among the customers.

SECONDARY AND PRIMARY RESEARCH ○○○

Secondary research involves the unearthing of data that already exists either from within the business or from outside agencies:

Internal: sales figures,

External: government publications,

Primary research is the process of gathering data direct from the target market. The main methods of collecting field research are:

Personal interviews:
Telephone interviews:

Postal surveys:

Direct observation:

Test marketing:

EXAMINER'S SECRETS
Make sure you can accurately define and explain the differences between the different sampling techniques. Many candidates struggle with this, so it's a good way of impressing the examiner!

> **List three forms of sampling.**

DON'T FORGET
Sampling introduces uncertainty into the findings as only a fraction of the population is asked.

SAMPLING ○○○

In order to obtain a full picture of the market it would be necessary to ask all of the customers (known as the population). As this is prohibitively expensive only a small number are asked (a sample).
There are a number of sampling methods such as:

Turn the page for some exam questions on this topic ➤

EXAM QUESTION 1   ● ● ●

Many research methods use questionnaires as the basis of their information gathering. In the formulation of a questionnaire:

(a) What type of questions can be asked?

Mention the two main types of questions.

DON'T FORGET
Questionnaires should be pre-tested on a small sample group before being used on a wider basis. In this way any errors or ambiguities can be identified and removed.

(b) How should it be designed so that it is effective?

Now have a go at part (b).

EXAM QUESTION 2   ● ● ●

John-Paul Associates build and manage leisure centres on a national basis throughout the UK. They are considering opening their first centre in the Lake District area close to the market town of Kendal.

The board of directors has requested market research be done on the proposal.

In the table provided identify three advantages and three disadvantages of John-Paul Associates using desk and field research in order to build information on the proposed project.

EXAMINER'S SECRETS
Choosing between field and desk research is always a question of balancing time and cost against accuracy of results. Consideration of these problems will show evidence of evaluation.

	Advantages	Disadvantages
Desk		
Field		

Workforce planning

Workforce planning is the process of anticipating the organization's future labour requirements. It reflects the organization's future strategy. This not only requires the human resource function to look at the numbers employed but also the mix of skills. Workforce planning is also affected by changes in technology, law and social and demographic factors.

THE WORKFORCE PLAN ○○○

The workforce plan is a form of supply and demand management. It aims to reduce the risk of either a future shortage or a surplus of labour. You should be aware that either situation is costly to the firm.

Where the workforce plan indicates the likelihood of a shortage or surplus of labour, action should be taken to ensure that situation does not develop. Thus a predicted shortage of computer technicians could be overcome by recruitment of new employees with the right skills. Other strategies to address a shortage of labour include:

REVISION EXPRESS
See the *Revision Express A-level Study Guide* pages 14–20 for more on these influences.

List at least four other ways in which a shortage of labour might be overcome.

List at least four ways in which a surplus of labour might be overcome.

RECRUITMENT ○○○

Recruitment is an important part of the work of any human resource department. In many organizations you will find that this work has been centralized. This has various advantages.

Give three reasons why an organization might want to centralize recruitment.

Internal promotion and external recruitment both have advantages:

Here are some arguments for internal promotion (I) and external recruitment (E). Indicate which the argument is in favour of by putting (I) or (E) after each sentence.

provides new blood

reduced recruitment costs

internal promotion may cause friction amongst other workers

it can improve employee motivation

the person is known to the firm

internal promotion merely transfers the recruitment problem elsewhere.

Turn the page for some exam questions on this topic ➤

EXAM QUESTION 1 ●●●

THE JARGON
A person is made redundant when the employer can show that the type of work offered by the employee is no longer required or that demand for that kind of labour has fallen.

Due to improvements in its computerized management information system, Bramhope Insurance is considering making 50 people redundant at its Head Office.

Discuss the problems the firm might face as a result of making people redundant.

Write at least two sentences on each of the following: morale, cost, and image of the firm.

REVISION EXPRESS
People often resist change. For more on this area see pages 46–47 of the *Revision Express A-level Study Guide.*

Now say what steps the firm could take to limit these problems. The first is done for you.

- The best way of maintaining the morale of the workforce is to keep them informed of what is going to happen, give guarantees where possible and let those being made redundant know what help they are going to be given by the firm.

EXAM QUESTION 2 ●●●

What arguments would you use to persuade a manager that although training may be seen as costly and time-consuming, it has benefits that outweigh these factors?

Try to think of at least three arguments.

THE JARGON
Span of control refers to the number of subordinates responsible to and reporting directly to a manager.

IF YOU HAVE TIME
Write a list of the benefits the employee gains through training.

Organization structure

Early management writers were concerned to find the one best form of organization structure. Today it is accepted that there is no one best organization structure and that what works for one firm may be disastrous for another. You will also find that an organization will change its structure over time as it grows, or in response to periodic crises.

We trained hard, but it seemed that every time we were beginning to form up into teams we would be reorganized.
I was later to learn that we tend to meet any situation by reorganizing and a wonderful method it can be for creating an illusion of progress, while producing confusion, inefficiency and demoralization.
GAIUS PETRONIUS AD 56

> Here are some key terms that are used when talking about organization structure. Draw a line linking each term to the correct definition.

ORGANIZATION STRUCTURE ○○○

The formal organization is the deliberately planned structure of roles within the organization. It is the means by which the activities of many people are coordinated so as to achieve organizational objectives. It is often presented pictorially in an organization chart.

1. Chain of command	The number of subordinates directly reporting to and controlled by a manager.
2. Informal organization	The policy of delegating decision-making power to lower levels in the organization.
3. Span of control	An organization based on rules, procedures and hierarchical authority. Weber argued it was an efficient rational organization.
4. Bureaucracy	The vertical line of authority within an organization. It enables orders to be passed down through the organization.
5. Decentralization	The removal of one or more layers of management from an organization's hierarchy.
6. Delayering	The network of social relationships developed by people while at work.

DELEGATION ○○○

Delegation means passing decision-making power down through the hierarchy from manager to subordinate. Delegation allows the manager to concentrate on more important parts of his job. It also helps train the next generation of managers. There are three important aspects to delegation: responsibility, authority and accountability.

> Write one sentence explaining each of these terms.

Turn the page for some exam questions on this topic ➤

EXAM QUESTION 1 ●●●

Outwood Construction Ltd is a house building firm. The firm has adopted a functional structure with five departments: Purchasing, Construction, Sales, Personnel and Finance. The firm is owner-managed and the owner has tended to use a narrow span of control together with an autocratic management style. Despite growing rapidly over the last decade profits have not increased proportionately. A firm of management consultants has suggested that a functional structure is inappropriate and recommended the firm adopt a matrix organizational structure.

(a) What problems may arise from adopting a functional structure?

> Write a paragraph outlining problems that may arise with a functional structure, then have a go at question (b).

(b) Explain the possible link between a narrow span of control and an autocratic management style.

(c) Complete the diagram below and use it to explain the matrix structure, and how it relates to a departmental structure. What are the advantages of the matrix structure?

> Complete the diagram opposite and use it to explain the term matrix structure.

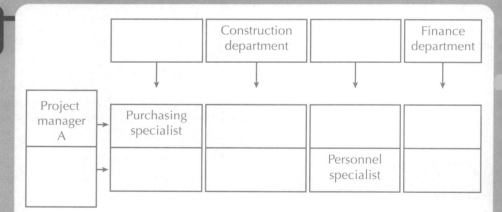

> First explain how the departmental structure and matrix structure relate to one another.

> Now mention some advantages of the matrix structure.

Motivation in theory

An organization is interested in the motives behind people's behaviour because it wants to know what makes them perform well at work. It can then use that knowledge to maximize its employees' effectiveness.

SCIENTIFIC MANAGEMENT AND HUMAN RELATIONS APPROACHES   ○○○

> The passage has some words missing. Use the following list to complete the gaps:
> social, work, 'scientific', incentive, manual, money, dehumanized, work study,

F W Taylor established what became known as the   school of management. Taylor believed that   workers were motivated primarily by   and were not interested in   . The role of the manager therefore was to devise the best way of doing the job through   and to motivate workers through the use of high   payments. The major criticism of this approach was that work is   and the   influences on employee behaviour are ignored.

The human relations school's understanding of employee motivation was entirely different. It relied heavily on the work of Mayo and his 'Hawthorne Plant' experiments, which concluded:

> What are the major conclusions of the Hawthorne Plant experiments?

The human relations school was criticized though for not recognizing the conflict of interest within industry. Paying attention to workers' social needs would not necessarily improve motivation or productivity.

MASLOW AND HERZBERG   ○○○

> Complete the diagram, which relates to Maslow's hierarchy of needs.

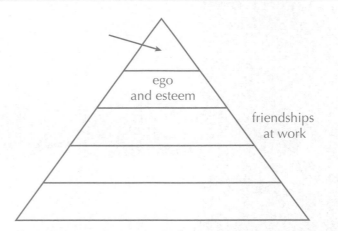

> **WATCH OUT**
> Make sure you can distinguish between the content and context of the job and relate this to both Maslow's and Herzberg's work.

Herzberg's two-factor theory looks at factors that make a manager feel good or bad about his job. Hygiene factors cause dissatisfaction when absent but little satisfaction when present.

> Explain what you understand by the term 'motivator' factors.

Motivator factors are those which

Turn the page for some exam questions on this topic ➤

EXAM QUESTION 1

● ● ●

As a university student John Cooke was very pleased to land a job stacking shelves one night a week at the supermarket. £45 for ten hours' work wasn't bad, he thought. On his first night the supervisor gave each of the five workers a list of aisles to fill up and told them to 'get on with it'. Everyone seemed too busy to help so John learnt the job by watching others. It was a pretty lonely job with no one to talk to. In addition lighting was poor and it was cold. The rest break that night was interesting. John learnt that the supervisors were generally unhelpful, slow to praise and quick to blame. He also learnt that labour turnover on the nightshift was high and that the workers never completed filling the aisles allocated to them. These were left for the day staff to complete.

(a) Use Herzberg's two factor theory to analyse the situation facing the workers.

Part of the answer has already been done for you.

> According to Herzberg there are five motivating factors: achievement, recognition, the work itself, responsibility and advancement. From the information given it is difficult to see how the workers could be motivated. Certainly, they have responsibility but the actions of the supervisors suggest that this isn't valued and the other motivating factors are absent.

Now write at least three sentences about the hygiene factors and the workers.

(b) The text suggests that productivity is not as high as it should be. How do you think that F W Taylor would have dealt with the situation?

Part of this has been done for you. Add a paragraph about pay.

> To maximize the worker's efforts Taylor would have first analysed their jobs and the equipment they used. He would have found the best way of doing the job and insisted the workers worked this way. This would be the supervisor's responsibility.

(c) Unlike Taylor, Herzberg did not believe that pay was a motivating factor. Why was this?

THE JARGON

In Herzberg's terms an incentive scheme may result in *movement* but not *motivation*.

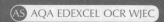
Motivation in practice

Motivating its employees is important to any organization. Motivated employees are less likely to leave the organization or be absent from work. They are also likely to produce work of a higher quality and are willing to take on greater responsibilities. Yet there is no simple answer to the question of how to motivate employees because every person and every situation is different.

SYMPTOMS AND CAUSES OF POOR MOTIVATION   ○ ○ ○

A symptom is the outward sign of a problem. A cause is the reason the problem exists. Thus labour absenteeism may be the symptom while the cause behind the symptom may be poor conditions of work.

> Here are some symptoms and causes of poor motivation. Place S against those you consider to be symptoms and C against those that are causes.

Poor quality work	Job insecurity
Poor pay	Failure to meet deadlines
Monotonous work	Disciplinary problems
Not part of social group	Changes to work groups
Poor communication	Sullen attitudes

JOB DESIGN AND MOTIVATION   ○ ○ ○

It is important that employees enjoy their work yet many jobs are dull and uninteresting because they are repetitive.

> State at least two problems that may arise for the firm as a result of repetitive work.

Job rotation, enlargement and enrichment are all ways to make work less monotonous.

> Explain what each term means. (The first has been done for you.)

Job rotation is a situation in which staff are trained in a number of different jobs. Staff are then rotated through these jobs so as to reduce monotony. The employer also benefits through greater staff flexibility. However workers may object if it disturbs social groups.

Job enlargement

THE JARGON
Both job rotation and enlargement are examples of 'horizontal extension of the job'. This means that the extra tasks are of the same level of difficulty and do not give the employee any more responsibility.

Job enrichment

Turn the page for some exam questions on this topic ➤

EXAM QUESTION 1 ○○○

Between 1995 and 2000, Ossett plc has been transformed. A loss-making washing machine company with a history of poor labour relations, by June 2000 it had doubled output, increased profits and improved labour relations. Wages had increased but only in line with inflation. So what had happened? The assembly line technology had been replaced by work groups who built a unit from scratch. Three-man teams were responsible for planning, organizing and controlling their own work. They also decided what jobs each team member would do. Three management levels had disappeared and the remaining managers empowered to take on wider challenges. In several ways the firm has found empowerment to be a valuable intrinsic reward.

THE JARGON
The removal of management levels throughout an organization is often referred to as 'delayering'.

(a) Why might a firm want to replace the 'assembly line technology'?

> In these sorts of questions, the examiner will not be impressed if you only write one short sentence – always try to develop your answer, rather than giving just the most basic information.

(b) State at least two benefits the workers get from working in teams.

THE JARGON
Assembly line technology involves part-finished goods moving from one work station to another by means of conveyor belts.

(c) Explain what is meant by 'the firm has found empowerment to be a valuable intrinsic reward'.

(d) The case tends to suggest that money is not important as a motivator. How far do management writers agree?

> Two points have been made for you.

Taylor regarded money, particularly when in the form of an incentive scheme, to be a very effective way of motivating individuals to work hard (but Herzberg might argue this was movement not motivation).

Mayo

Herzberg

Vroom suggested that motivation was determined by the worker's expectations as to whether their efforts would receive just rewards.

Leadership

Leadership may be defined as the means by which individuals or groups are persuaded to work towards the achievement of organizational goals. A leader is, therefore, any person who has the power to exercise control over others.

CLASSIFYING LEADERS   ○○○

Leaders are sometimes classified as autocratic, democratic or laissez-faire. Each style has different characteristics, strengths and weaknesses.

> Draw a line linking each description to the correct leadership style.

1 autocratic   There is little direction or discipline given by the leader. The subordinates either accept or reject the responsibility.

2 democratic   Power lies in the hands of the leader who makes decisions alone. Communication is one way with little opportunity for feedback from subordinates.

THE JARGON
The laissez-faire leadership style is also known as free rein.

3 laissez- faire   Although the leader retains the right to make the decisions, power is shared with the subordinates and they contribute to decision-making.

> Identify one strength and one weakness for each of the leadership styles.

Autocratic:

Democratic:

Laissez-faire:

CONTINGENCY APPROACHES TO LEADERSHIP   ○○○

A number of writers argue the best form of leadership varies according to the circumstances of the situation. To them a good leader is one who analyses the factors in the situation and chooses the appropriate style. The factors normally considered are:

> State two factors within the leader that might affect his leadership style.

The leader:

> State at least two factors within the subordinates that might affect the leader's style.

The subordinates:

> State at least two factors within the situation that might affect the leader's style.

The situation:

Turn the page for some exam questions on this topic ➤

EXAM QUESTION 1 ● ● ●

What leadership style would you use in the following situations?

(a) After higher than expected losses within the firm your department has been informed that its budget is to be reduced by 25%. Three or four members of staff will be made redundant. Full information on all the staff is available from the Human Resources Department.

In each case, you should explain your answer.

EXAMINER'S SECRETS
Think about the implications of this decision on the leader and his subordinates.

REVISION EXPRESS
For more on the impact of change on individuals see the *Revision Express A-level Study Guide* pages 46–47.

(b) The firm wishes to stagger starting and finishing work times so as to relieve traffic congestion. It doesn't matter what times each department chooses as long as everyone conforms to that decision.

EXAM QUESTION 2 ● ● ●

'You can't trust your workers these days, you know!' said one manager to a colleague. 'They're all lazy.' 'Oh I don't know,' the other replied, 'mine seem pretty keen. Indeed, I think that if you treat them as lazy and untrustworthy that's what you'll get!'

How far do you agree with these comments?

These two managers have very different attitudes to their workers. A good answer to this question would mention McGregor; how would he have described them?

Explain why treating employees as lazy and untrustworthy should mean 'that's what you'll get'.

Scale of production

Most businesses start small and expand over time. As they grow they are able to take advantage of economies of scale. This has the effect of reducing the unit costs of production making the organization more competitive. You need to know the reasons behind the desire to expand, how economies can be achieved and what limits there are to growth.

THE IMPORTANCE OF SCALE   ○○○

THE JARGON
Economies of scale are those savings and unit cost reductions gained through expanding the level of output.

Firms aim to grow in order to:
- reduce unit costs – this will improve competitiveness
- gain market share – a firm with some monopoly power can influence market prices
- reduce risk – by diversifying in terms of product and market
- survive – larger firms are more able to resist takeover bids.

ECONOMIES OF SCALE   ○○○

DON'T FORGET
Total costs are made up of fixed costs and variable costs.

As output increases, the firm's fixed costs (which must be paid irrespective of the size of output) are spread over a larger number of units, thus reducing average costs. Likewise variable costs per unit can be reduced by the following economies of scale.

For each economy of scale provide an example that illustrates how unit costs can be reduced.

- Purchasing:

- Technical:

- Specialization:

- Financial:

IF YOU HAVE TIME
Investigate economies of scale that can be achieved in marketing, administration and welfare facilities.

DISECONOMIES OF SCALE   ○○○

THE JARGON
Diseconomies of scale are factors that cause unit costs to rise when output increases due to inefficiencies.

Despite the savings to be made from growth there is a limit to the gains available. Eventually a business will reach its optimum size and expansion beyond this will result in diseconomies of scale.

Explain how each diseconomy can lead to higher unit costs.

- Co-ordination problems:

- Communication problems:

Turn the page for some exam questions on this topic ➤

EXAM EXERCISE ● ● ●

Brooke Ltd is a medium-sized firm that specializes in modernizing second-hand printing machines for resale to developing countries. Fixed costs are made up of factory premises and permanent staff. Variable costs are composed largely of spare parts and overtime working for the small group of specialist technicians. The costs for a typical month are given below. Complete the last two columns of the table by calculating the total cost and unit costs for each level of output. Then determine the output range over which economies and diseconomies of scale exist.

> **When you tackle this, remember that:**
> Total costs = Fixed costs + Variable costs
> Unit cost = Total cost / Output

Output	Fixed costs (£000)	Variable costs (£000)	Total costs (£000)	Unit/average cost
1	100	90		
2	100	170		
3	100	245		
4	100	316		
5	100	385		
6	100	452		
7	100	509		
8	100	628		
9	100	746		
10	100	880		

> **Analyse the completed table and fill in the gaps here.**

Economies of scale exist over the output range =
Diseconomies of scale begin at output =

EXAM QUESTION 1 ● ● ●

Despite the existence of potential economies of scale, many organizations prefer to remain small. The factors that influence such decisions include finance, the market, and the owner's objectives. Explain how each of these can limit the extent of business expansion.

> **Write at least two sentences for each factor.**

Finance:

The market:

The owner's objectives:

Methods of production

The choice of production method depends on the nature of the product, the total demand for it, its expected life cycle, the size of the firm, and the resources available. Different combinations of these factors will result in different production methods even for the same type of product.

THE MAIN PRODUCTION METHODS ○ ○ ○

Job production: for the manufacture of unique products to exact specifications.

For job, batch and flow production methods write a paragraph identifying:
- **the type of labour required**
- **the likely extent of demand**
- **the type of machinery needed.**
Comment on the level of productivity and give two examples of products produced in this way.

Batch production: a method where a large number (a 'batch') of identical products pass through each stage of a production process together.

EXAMINER'S SECRETS
Many candidates fail to give a good definition of batch production. 'Batch production is where items are produced in batches' is not a very revealing answer. Learn the definition given here!

Flow production: generally a mass production method where items move continuously from one production stage to another.

DON'T FORGET
The movement of the products determines whether there is batch or flow production. If the items move individually to the next stage, there is flow production.

Turn the page for some exam questions on this topic ➤

EXAM QUESTION 1 ●●●

For each of the products listed below, determine the most likely production method and explain your answer.

In each case, try to give two reasons for your choice of method.

Shirts for a football team:

A nationally popular breakfast cereal:

White paint for walls and ceilings:

Repairs to a car:

Freshly made cakes:

Visit to the dentist:

DON'T FORGET
The type of production method will depend on a variety of factors including the level of demand, the amount of standardization and the extent that mechanization can be applied.

EXAM QUESTION 2 ●●●

AJS Ltd, a manufacturer of camping equipment, has experienced rising demand for its lightweight tent favoured by backpackers and weekend hikers. For the first time the firm has received significant orders from overseas for this product. At present the tent is made using a batch production method that produces 400 tents per week. At this rate customers must wait three weeks for their orders to be completed. The firm is contemplating the introduction of a flow production system. Identify three advantages and three disadvantages of making this change.

List three advantages here.

EXAMINER'S SECRETS
Write in context by mentioning the company, the product and the specific market, e.g. introducing flow production will allow AJS Ltd to become more competitive in the camping equipment market by reducing costs and delivery time.

Now identify three disadvantages that AJS might face.

LINKS
For more information on motivation see pages 45–46.

Capacity utilization

Capacity is the maximum output that an organization can produce in a time period with a given quantity of resources. Most firms aim to produce near to or at full capacity in order to reduce the cost per unit.

LINKS
For more information on how a business determines its capacity see 'Scale of production' pages 51–52.

MEASUREMENT ○○○

Capacity utilization is a measure of the effective use of a firm's resources and is calculated using the formula:

$$\text{Capacity utilization} = \frac{\text{Actual output per period}}{\text{Full capacity output per period}} \times 100$$

Capacity use is measured as a percentage of the maximum.

For example, a business with a full capacity of 40 000 units per month is currently producing 36 800 units per month.

> **Calculate the capacity utilization, then the spare capacity in percentages.**

IMPORTANCE OF USING CAPACITY ○○○

Operating at 'under capacity' (below the maximum) is a waste of resources. The fixed assets of the business are not being used to their limit so average fixed costs will be higher than they need be.

However, operating at full capacity means it will be harder to:

> **Identify three problems of operating at full capacity.**

A high level of spare capacity will increase average costs whereas a low level might mean disappointing some customers.

DON'T FORGET
It is also possible to operate at 'above capacity' through the use of overtime working.

ADVANTAGES AND DISADVANTAGES OF FULL CAPACITY ○○○

Operating at or near to full capacity has both benefits and drawbacks for a business.

> **Identify three advantages and three disadvantages associated with working at or near to full capacity.**

Advantages:

Disadvantages:

THE JARGON
'Downtime' is when a machine is not available for scheduled work due to breakdown, lack of spares, etc.

Turn the page for some exam questions on this topic ➤

EXAM QUESTION 1

● ● ●

Brooke Bottling Ltd operates 24 hours a day, seven days a week. It uses a rotating eight-hour shift system for its four bottling lines. Each line is dedicated to the filling of a different soft drink according to container size. The results of last week's performance are given in the table below.

(a) Using the data in the table, calculate the capacity utilization rate as a percentage expressed to one decimal place.

Insert your answers in the final column.

Line number	Maximum capacity (000s bottles)	Actual performance (000s bottles)	Capacity utilization rate (%)
1	180	164	
2	130	112	
3	150	148	
4	140	139	

(b) Comment on the relative capacity utilization for the production lines. Identify any problems and suggest what might have caused them.

The answer for lines 1 and 2 has been done for you. Add your own observations for lines 3 and 4.

Lines 1 and 2: these lines appear to be operating with significant spare capacity of almost 9% and 14%. This will raise the average cost of the items being bottled on those lines. The under capacity might have been caused by machine breakdown or by lack of demand for those products.

Lines 3 and 4:

EXAM QUESTION 2

● ● ●

In an attempt to use the fixed capital to its maximum, Brooke Bottling Ltd operates a rotating shift system where employees alternate weekly between morning, afternoon and night shifts. Each shift is encouraged to perform at full capacity with rewards for the best monthly performance. Explain the human resource issues associated with trying to work at full capacity on a 24-hour basis.

Try to identify three human resource issues.

DON'T FORGET
Human resources are far more difficult to 'schedule' than machines. Operating a shift system requires the full cooperation of front-line workers.

Production control

Production is the process of organizing resources in order to satisfy the needs of customers. It is also the means for the firm to make a profit by producing an output that sells for more than the cost of the inputs used in its creation. Management must, therefore, keep an effective control on all its resources and monitor their use throughout the production process.

EFFICIENCY AND ITS MEASUREMENT ○○○

Complete the definition of efficiency.

Efficiency can be defined as

Improvements in efficiency will have a direct effect on the average costs of production and consequently on the profitability of the business. Costs and profits are, however, only indicators of efficiency. It is useful to measure the efficiency of inputs directly.

LABOUR PRODUCTIVITY ○○○

This measures the amount the workforce produces in a given time period using the equation:

$$\text{Labour productivity} = \frac{\text{Total output}}{\text{Number of employees (or man hours)}}$$

For example, in 1996 the Nissan plant produced 231 000 vehicles and employed 3 156 staff. Labour productivity was 73.19 vehicles per employee. Labour productivity can be improved in a number of ways.

Briefly explain how these changes can improve labour productivity.

Investment in new capital equipment:

Incentive schemes for workers:

Increase in staff training:

CAPITAL PRODUCTIVITY ○○○

This measure is increasingly more important as firms invest in more capital-intensive production systems. Capital productivity can be measured using the equation:

$$\text{Capital productivity} = \frac{\text{Total output}}{\text{Capital employed}}$$

Example: a business produced 3 000 units per week using eight old machines. These have been replaced by six new ones without any loss of output.

Calculate the capital productivity for both the old machines and the new ones. Comment on the change.

Turn the page for some exam questions on this topic ➤

EXAM QUESTION 1

○ ○ ○

North Engineering Ltd design and manufacture propellers for a wide range of boats. They have a small factory employing 20 workers using five machines. The results from the production department for August are given in the table below. Using the data provided, calculate (a) the capital productivity in units per machine and (b) the labour productivity in units per man hour. Comment on the results.

Add your answers to the table.

Period	Output (units)	Labour (man hours)	Capital productivity (units per machine)	Labour productivity (units per man hour)
Week 1	21 000	800		
Week 2	22 000	830		
Week 3	24 000	860		
Week 4	24 600	860		

Now comment on the results giving at least one reason for the identified trend in capital and labour productivity during August.

EXAMINER'S SECRETS
When faced with trend data it is best to calculate percentage changes to show the trend. Manipulation of the data demonstrates the skill of analysis and will be rewarded more highly than simple descriptions.

EXAM QUESTION 2

○ ○ ○

Improvements in capital productivity are often achieved with the replacement of outdated machinery. This modernization can have beneficial effects for the workforce but can also cause human resource problems. Explain three benefits for labour and three drawbacks for labour associated with improvements in capital.

Remember to concentrate just on human resources issues.

Benefits

Drawbacks

Stock control

Effective stock control is essential to any business especially those involved in manufacturing. Any stock control system must ensure that there are sufficient raw materials and work in progress to supply the production line as well as ensuring finished goods for the end consumer. Understocking will result in lost sales or production 'downtime'. Overstocking will tie up valuable capital as well as increasing the risk of stock damage and deterioration.

TERMS YOU NEED TO KNOW   ○○○

Define each of the terms.

THE JARGON
Stock control is often referred to nowadays as 'materials management'.

DON'T FORGET
The reorder level is calculated using the equation:
Reorder level = (usage rate × lead time) + buffer stock

Lead time

Work in progress
Buffer stock

Reorder level

EOQ (the economic order quantity)

Just-in-time (JIT) manufacturing

STOCK CONTROL CHARTS   ○○○

Stock control charts provide a quick visual image of the usage and current level of stock. Exam questions often require you to either construct or interpret a chart.

On the stock control chart diagram label the items marked A to D. Indicate the lead time and label it point E. What is its duration?

LINKS
Stock is part of an organization's working capital and is an important item in the balance sheet. For more information on balance sheets see pages 65–66.

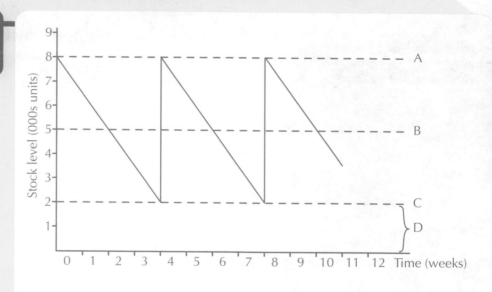

Turn the page for some exam questions on this topic ➤

EXAM QUESTION 1 ● ● ●

Milner Ltd is a musical instruments manufacturer. One of its key raw materials is brass. Average usage is 400 kg per week. Opening stock at the beginning of January was 1 600 kg, which is the maximum stock held at any one time. As a buffer stock they wish to have one week's supply in reserve. The lead time is one week. In weeks 1 to 4 usage was normal at 400 kg but in weeks 5 and 6 it increased to 800 kg and 600 kg respectively. Weeks 7 and 8 were normal. Three deliveries of 800 kg, 1400 kg and 900 kg were received in this period.

(a) Calculate the reorder level and mark on the diagram.
(b) On the diagram below draw the stock control chart using the information provided.

Plot your answers on the diagram to get a picture of the fluctuation in stock usage over a two month period.

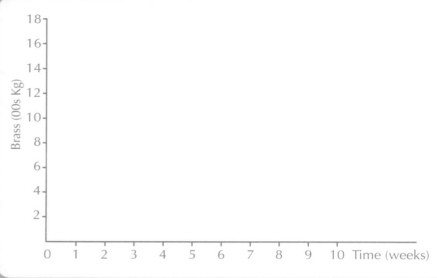

(c) Determine the closing stock figure.

EXAMINER'S SECRETS
Most mistakes involve poor plotting of the stock usage. Remember that a delivery is shown as a straight vertical line. Marks are allocated for correctly drawn diagrams.

EXAM QUESTION 2 ● ● ●

Identify the benefits and costs of holding stock.

Add the benefits and costs to the table.

Benefits of holding stocks	Costs associated with stock

DON'T FORGET
Determination of a firm's stock policy depends on:
• the resources of the firm
• the availability and size of discounts
• the speed of change in the market
• the financial effect of 'downtime'.

Quality control

Quality is difficult to define. Consumers are forever demanding higher levels of quality and it is what they perceive as 'quality' that really matters. An organization must ensure that its processes guarantee the production of items to the specification required. They must also, however, seek to constantly improve the current standards in order to keep up with customer expectations.

Quality is defined by the customer.
W EDWARD DEMING (AMERICAN QUALITY GURU)

Add three more measures of quality that consumers might seek from a product or service.

MEASURES OF QUALITY

○○○

Quality is a subjective matter that will vary from customer to customer. Some of the measures of quality include:

- reliability
- appearance

QUALITY CONTROL

○○○

In the past quality control meant 'inspecting' the product at the end of the production line prior to despatch to the consumer. In other words it was a fault-finding exercise. Problems with this system are as follows.

Identify and explain three problems of a quality control system based on inspection.

LINKS
For quality control to be effective the workforce must be adequately trained. For more information on training see Exam question 2 on page 62.

TOTAL QUALITY MANAGEMENT (TQM)

○○○

There have been a number of new approaches to quality issues in recent years. One of the first was Total Quality Management. TQM is really a philosophy as it attempts to change the culture of a company so that all employees become part of the quality system. The basic features of TQM are:

List five basic features of a TQM system.

LINKS
For TQM to work effectively the employees must be well-motivated. For more information on motivation see 'Motivation in theory' and 'Motivation in practice' on pages 45–48.

Turn the page for some exam questions on this topic ➤

For more on this topic, see pages 128–129 of the *Revision Express A-level Study Guide*

EXAM QUESTION 1

● ● ●

TQM is just one of many quality initiatives that have been tried in recent years to improve the delivery of goods and services. Some of the others are listed below. Explain each one and outline an advantage for an organization in adopting its use.

Add your responses after each heading.

Quality circles:

Kaizen:

EXAMINER'S SECRETS

In questions relating to quality it is useful to include specific references to bodies that promote quality such as The British Standards Institution, The Consumers Association, The Association of British Travel Agents (ABTA), etc.

Benchmarking:

BS 5750 (ISO 9000):

THE JARGON

Quality assurance is an attempt to ensure that quality standards are met throughout the organization. This includes the design stage, raw material and component procurement, production, delivery and after sales service.

EXAM QUESTION 2

● ● ●

Explain each of the following terms, and state why it is important to a firm for quality purposes.

Add your answer after each heading.

Induction:

On-the-job training:

Off-the-job training:

Multiskilling:

Use and preparation of accounts

Accounting is the process of recording a firm's financial transactions in a suitable format and of summarizing this in the form of accounting reports. Accounting can be divided into two types, financial accounting and management accounting. Together the two forms of information provide insights into the success or failure of past decisions and operations. The information also enlightens management as to the opportunities and difficulties of future plans.

USERS OF ACCOUNTING INFORMATION ○○○

There are two groups of users of accounting information, internal users and external users. You need to know who they are and what their interests are.
Internal users

> **Identify two more internal users and briefly state their interest in having access to accurate accounting information.**

- Management: to plan courses of action, to control the use of scarce resources and to analyse and evaluate past actions and decisions.

External users

> **State the main interest of each group of external users.**

These groups only have access to published accounts.
- Suppliers
- Banks:
- Government:

IF YOU HAVE TIME
Investigate the interests of four more external users: potential investors, competitors, consumer pressure groups and the local community.

THE JARGON
'True and fair view' is the term used by auditors to confirm that the accounts of a business are accurate.

ACCOUNTING CONCEPTS AND CONVENTIONS ○○○

The accounting process must produce statements that show a 'true and fair view' of the business's financial position. To achieve this a series of accounting concepts and conventions are used to deliver information in a standard common language. You need to be able to define the terms and, in some cases, apply them.

> **Define the following concepts and conventions.**

THE JARGON
Financial accounting is concerned with the production of the principal accounting statements (balance sheet, profit and loss statement, etc.). Management accounting generates information for internal use to aid the analysis, planning and control of the firm's activities (budgets, cash flow forecasts, etc.).

Matching concept (accruals):

Going concern:

Consistency:

Prudence (conservatism):

Double entry:

Turn the page for some exam questions on this topic ➤

EXAM QUESTION 1

Peter Harley is a sole trader supplying safety equipment to the building industry. At the end of his second year of trading he has created sales of £100 000. In his store he has £28 000 of unsold stock. On 1 January he had £20 000 of stock and his purchases throughout the year totalled £75 000. His accountant has emphasized that the accounts must be drawn up on the basis of the matching principle so that only the stock used during the year is included in that year's accounts.

(a) Calculate, using the matching principle, the actual stock used during the year.

> Add your calculations here, then have a go at part (b).

LINKS
For more information on accounts see page 65.

(b) Explain why it would be misleading to charge all £95 000 worth of stock against the sales made in the year.

EXAM QUESTION 2

Shar Ltd imports tropical plants for resale to specialist outlets. At the end of the financial year the accountant is presented with the following situations:

(a) At the beginning of the year a car was bought for £12 000 which will be sold in two years for an estimated £4 000. How much of the cost of the van should be allocated to this year's accounts?

> Explain how each situation should be treated according to the appropriate accounting concepts and conventions.

(b) 100 plants bought for £1 000 have developed some form of leaf mould and probably will fetch only £200. What value should be placed on this stock?

(c) Last year all machinery was depreciated at 20% of its original value. As sales have not been as good the manager wants to reduce the depreciation charge to 10%.

EXAMINER'S SECRETS
Definitions of concepts and conventions are often best done using an example.

Final accounts

The final accounts of a business provide a systematic way of presenting the financial history of the organization over a period of time. The main components are the profit and loss account, the balance sheet and the cash flow statement (see page 67 for a treatment of cash flow). The role of these accounts is to provide an accurate view of the business's financial position.

THE PROFIT AND LOSS ACCOUNT ○○○

In exam questions you might be required to construct or interpret a simple profit and loss account. Therefore it is important that you understand the basic components and can calculate them.

Define each term of the profit and loss account and show how it is calculated.

Sales revenue (or sales turnover):

Less cost of goods sold (or cost of sales):

Gross profit:

Less overheads:

Operating or net profit:

DON'T FORGET
Interest and tax must be deducted from net profit to arrive at 'profit after tax'. This amount can be distributed to shareholders in the form of dividends, used to repay loans or kept in the business as 'retained profits'.

THE BALANCE SHEET ○○○

DON'T FORGET
The balance sheet is a snapshot of the business taken on one particular day, normally the last day of the trading period. The title of the balance sheet should reflect this by being in the form of 'Balance sheet *as at* (date)'.

The balance sheet is a 'snapshot' of the business's financial situation at a given point in time. It shows the 'use of funds' and the 'source of funds'. It also lists the resources that the business owns (its assets), the resources that it owes (liabilities) and the capital belonging to the owners. You must be able to define these terms.

Distinguish between these balance sheet terms.

Assets – fixed and current

Liabilities – long-term and current

IF YOU HAVE TIME
Make a list of at least five fixed assets that might be associated with:
• an airline
• a school
• a retail outlet.

Turn the page for some exam questions on this topic ➤

EXAM EXERCISE ●●●

Dominic's is a fashion retail outlet preparing for its year-end accounts. The following figures apply to this year's trading:
Cost of goods sold £54 000, sales revenue £125 000, overheads £21 000 and a bank loan of £100 000 at 10% interest. The tax rate is 20%. It is proposed to repay £10 000 of the loan and to distribute £8 000 as dividends to the shareholders. Complete the profit and loss account and determine the retained profit.

Add your answers to the table here.

Profit and loss account for the year ending

	£000s
Sales revenue	
Less cost of goods sold	
Gross profit	
Less overheads	
Net profit	
Less interest	
Less tax	
Profit after interest and tax	
Loan repayment	
Dividends	
Retained profit	

DON'T FORGET
Tax is imposed only on the profit remaining after interest has been deducted.

EXAM EXERCISE ●●●

The following figures relate to BAB plc for the year ending on 31 December (all figures are in £m): Buildings 120; Cash 15; Creditors 25; Stock 30; Machinery 45; Debtors 20. There are no long-term liabilities. Complete the balance sheet below.

Insert the six items in the correct position in the balance sheet. Calculate the final figure for:
(a) net current assets
(b) assets employed
(c) reserves
(d) total capital employed.

BAB plc: Balance sheet as at 31 December

	£m	£m
Fixed assets		
1.		
2.		165
Current assets		
3.		
4.		
5.		
Less current liabilities		
6.		
Net current assets		
Assets employed		
Financed by:		
Share capital	160	
Reserves		
Total capital employed		

DON'T FORGET
The formula you need is:
net current assets = current assets − current liabilities (also referred to as working capital).

Cash flow management

It is crucial for all firms to manage their cash flow effectively. Without adequate liquid resources a firm will be unable to settle its bills, reward its workforce or pay its suppliers. The effective control of working capital, therefore, is essential for survival.

THE IMPORTANCE OF CASH   ○○○

Firms require cash for three reasons.

> **Explain the three reasons for holding cash and provide an example of each.**

1. **For transaction purposes:**

2. **For precautionary purposes:**

3. **For speculative purposes:**

CASH FLOW PROBLEMS   ○○○

Each time a sale is made it should generate a profit and eventually increase the cash holdings of the business. Most transactions are not for cash but are done on credit. This creates a delay in the cash inflow to the business and is one of the causes of cash flow problems.

Any of the following could cause a problem for cash flow:

> **Explain how each factor could cause a cash flow problem.**

Stockpiling

Poor credit control

Market changes

DON'T FORGET
70% of businesses that fail in their first year do so because of cash flow problems.

IF YOU HAVE TIME
Liquidity problems can be identified through the use of liquidity ratios. Learn the equations for the current ratio, the acid test ratio and the gearing ratio.

Turn the page for some exam questions on this topic ➤

EXAM QUESTION 1 ●●●

The management of Desai Construction wants to identify any future cash problems and to plan appropriate remedial action.

(a) Complete the cash flow forecast based on the notes detailed below the table.

Add your answers to the table.

DON'T FORGET
The usefulness of a cash flow forecast is only as good as the accuracy of the estimated cash movements.

EXAMINER'S SECRETS
Candidates who stress that forecasts are merely estimates and rarely accurate over along period of time will score highly.

Cash flow forecast (£m)

	J	A	S	O	N	D
Opening balance	12	5	1			
Cash sales	82	88	100			
Rental income	4	4	4			
Total inflows	86	92	104			
Total cash	98	97	105			
Payments						
Materials	41	44	50			
Production costs	52	52	52			
Total outgoing	93	96	102			
Closing cash balance	5	1	3			

Notes: Cash sales are expected to be £94m in October and then to increase by £10m in each of the next two months. Rental income is constant. Materials are always 50% of sales. Production costs are to rise to £56m in October, then stay constant.

(b) Identify the timing and size of Desai Construction's cash flow problem.

Now answer questions (b), (c) and (d).

(c) What remedial action might Desai take?

(d) Calculate the cost of funding the shortfall if borrowing costs are 2% per month on the balance outstanding.

EXAM QUESTION 2 ●●●

What are the disadvantages of the following solutions to a temporary cashflow problem?

Each of the solutions mentioned will reduce cash outflow in the short term. What are the disadvantages?

Delaying payments to suppliers:

Cutting prices to boost sales:

Reducing current expenditure particularly on stock:

Costs and revenue

In order to make effective decisions and to calculate profit, a firm needs accurate cost information. Different accounting costs behave in different ways. Some costs are fixed for a period of time while others change as output increases. Costs can also be classified according to the product being made. You need to understand the terms, how costs behave and their impact on profits.

THE JARGON
Accounting cost is the value of the resources used up in production.

Write down the differences between the two terms.

DON'T FORGET
The exact length of the short and long runs will depend on the type of business. For example, a retail outlet can change its stock levels and product range quite quickly but a farmer needs much longer as production must be planned well in advance.

CLASSIFICATION ACCORDING TO TIME AND OUTPUT   ○○○

This type of classification is used to calculate the financial impact of changing the level of output.

Fixed costs and **variable costs**

Short run and **long run**

CLASSIFICATION ACCORDING TO PRODUCT   ○○○

This type of classification is used to allocate costs to individual products. This allows the organization to measure its efficiency by comparing costs of production over time. It also helps in determining a price that will cover the product's costs.

Write down the differences between the two terms.

Direct costs and **indirect costs**

LINKS
For more information on costs see page 71.

TOTAL COST, REVENUE AND PROFIT   ○○○

Total cost and total revenue enable the business to calculate its profit. To earn more profits the firm must either boost revenue or reduce costs. Revenue can be improved by selling more or by increasing prices. Total costs can be reduced either by improving efficiency or by obtaining cheaper inputs.

Write down the equation for each of the terms.

Total cost

Total revenue

Profit

Turn the page for some exam questions on this topic ➤

EXAM QUESTION 1 ●●●

Hindmarch Plastics Ltd produces a range of storage boxes for industrial use in batches of 10 000. The variable costs are labour (£1 per box), materials (£2 per box) and packaging (£0.20 per box). Fixed costs are £100 000. The boxes are sold for £8 each and current production is 40 000 boxes.

(a) Complete the cost and revenue schedule using the information given.

> Add your answers to the table, then answer parts (b) and (c).

No. of boxes	10 000	20 000	30 000	40 000	50 000
Fixed costs					
Labour					
Materials					
Packaging					
Total costs					
Total revenue					
Profit					

(b) What is the profit level of the current output level?

(c) If cheaper raw materials at £1.80 per unit could be purchased how would this affect: (i) total costs (ii) profit at the current output level?

EXAM QUESTION 2 ●●●

In order to improve the control of costs Armidale Ltd, a manufacturer of agricultural equipment, has introduced cost and profit centres. Define these terms (using examples) and explain the benefits for Armidale.

> Define the terms 'cost centre' and 'profit centre' and give an example of each.

A cost centre is

A profit centre is

> Identify four benefits for Armidale Ltd that might result from the introduction of cost and profit centres.

Break-even analysis

Break-even analysis is used to determine the level of output where profit begins to be earned. Sales beyond the break-even output will result in profits. If firms do not break-even in the long run they will not survive.

DEFINING KEY BREAK-EVEN TERMS ○○○

These are the key terms and definitions associated with break-even.

Define the key terms given here.

DON'T FORGET
At break-even output:
Total revenue = Total costs.

EXAMINER'S SECRETS
'Low price special orders' may still be acceptable to businesses as long as they generate a positive contribution.

Total revenue:
Fixed costs:

Variable costs:

Total costs:
Contribution per unit:

THE IMPORTANCE OF BREAK-EVEN ○○○

All firms need to calculate the following:

Define the terms given here. Say why they are important and give the equation.

Break-even output:

DON'T FORGET
Margin of safety can also be expressed as a percentage of current output in which case use the equation:
$$\frac{\text{Margin of safety}}{\text{current output}} \times 100\%$$

Margin of safety:

ADVANTAGES AND DISADVANTAGES OF BREAK-EVEN ANALYSIS ○○○

Break-even is a simple model that helps the management decision-making process.

How can the break-even model be used to reflect changes in prices and costs?

Identify one assumption of the simple break-even model.

Turn the page for some exam questions on this topic ➤

EXAM QUESTION 1 ●●●

Techno Ltd is a manufacturer of electronic calculators. It has fixed costs of £300 000; variable costs are £4 per calculator and it sells the calculators for £10 each. Draw the break-even graph and determine:

(a) the break-even level of output

(b) the margin of safety assuming a sales level of 80 000 units.

Complete the graph.

EXAMINER'S SECRETS
Remember to label the axes correctly, to choose a suitable scale and to draw the revenue and cost lines accurately. Examiners will look for these qualities in a diagram.

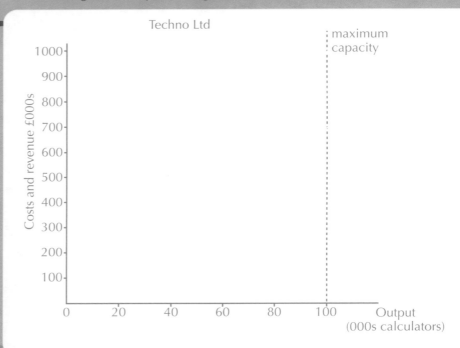

EXAM QUESTION 2 ●●●

Sandal Logistics is a transport company specializing in the delivery of raw materials to footwear manufacturers. Its average cost of delivery is £500 per load for which it charges £600. A large international producer has requested a special delivery of 200 loads of materials to its factory in Leeds for which it is only prepared to pay £400 per load. Variable costs per load are £350.

Jot down note-form answers to this multi-part question.

(a) Identify a variable cost associated with the mileage driven.

(b) Calculate the total contribution associated with this order.

DON'T FORGET
Contribution is the key factor for 'special orders'.

(c) Under what circumstances should this order be accepted?

(d) What qualitative factors should Sandal Logistics take into account before accepting or rejecting this order?

EXAMINER'S SECRETS
Critical comment on the impact of accepting the special order will demonstrate 'evaluation' and earn top marks. For example, delaying orders for regular clients might damage the long-term business for the sake of a short-term gain.

Budgeting

The main purposes of a budget are to plan the activities of the next accounting period, to help control the business as it progresses through the period and to analyse any variations from the plan. Remedial action can then be taken before any problems become too serious.

THE PURPOSE OF BUDGETS ○○○

Budgets act as both a planning tool and a control mechanism.
The budgeting process helps planning by:

> **Identify three ways that budgets can help to plan a business organization's activities.**

THE JARGON
A budget is a financial plan quantified in monetary terms, prepared and agreed in advance, showing the expected revenue and expenses over a given period of time.

The budget acts as a control mechanism by:

> **Identify two ways that budgets can help to control a business organization's activities.**

THE BUDGETING PROCESS ○○○

The budgeting process should be a combination of 'top down' target setting by senior management and 'bottom up' resource planning by departments. The final outcome is an 'agreed' budget that is demanding but at the same time realistic and attainable. A typical budget is compiled in stages.

> **Briefly state five main stages in the budget process.**

THE JARGON
Differences between planned and actual budget outcomes are referred to as 'variances'.

VARIANCE ANALYSIS ○○○

Variance analysis involves the comparison of planned outcomes in the budget with 'actual' outcomes. The differences are known as 'variances' that can be either favourable or adverse.

> **Define the two types of variance.**

A favourable variance is

An adverse variance is

DON'T FORGET
Variances act as alarm bells to warn management that current outcomes are not going according to plan.

Turn the page for some exam questions on this topic ➤

EXAM QUESTION 1 ● ● ●

SLB Furnishings Ltd is a fast growing business designing and supplying stylish office furniture. Management wish to introduce a more effective method for planning and controlling expansion in the future and have decided to introduce a more formal budget process. The advantage of budgets is recognized by the board but the managing director is not convinced that it will solve the firm's control problems. Identify and explain three possible drawbacks of budgetary control that the managing director might be concerned about.

Jot down a note-form response to this question.

DON'T FORGET
'A budget is a tool not a master'. This expression emphasizes that a budget is an aid to decision-making and not a plan that must be slavishly followed.

EXAM QUESTION 2 ● ● ●

SLB Furnishings Ltd have implemented budgetary control and the first figures for the manufacturing section for January are given below.

(a) Calculate the variances and complete the table stating in the 'comment' column whether the variance is favourable or adverse.

Add your answers to the table.

January Budget (£000s)

	Budget	Actual	Variance	Comment
Sales revenue	150	180		
Less material cost	(75)	(90)		
Less labour	(15)	(21)		
Gross profit	60	69		
Less overheads	(20)	(22)		
Net profit	40	47		

EXAMINER'S SECRETS
The use and manipulation of data presented in questions is evidence of analysis and will score more highly than simple descriptive answers.

(b) Suggest and explain a possible reason for the variance in: (i) sales revenue (ii) labour cost.

Now think about these more analytical questions.

Answer section

Answer section

SEE HOW YOU GOT ON BY CHECKING AGAINST THE ANSWERS GIVEN HERE.

Have you remembered to fill in the self-check circles? Do this to track your progress.

For more detail on the topics covered in this book, you can check the *Revision Express A-level Study Guide*, your class notes or your own textbook. You can also find exam questions and model answers at www.revision-express.com.

Don't forget, tear out these answers and put them in your folder for handy revision reference!

The market

(AS) EDEXCEL OCR WJEC

When buyers and sellers of a product meet, a market is created. The idea of the market is important because it is through the interaction of buyers and sellers that prices are determined.

DEMAND

Demand refers to the quantity of a product that consumers will buy at a given price. The demand curve normally slopes down from left to right. This is because:

as the price falls, the product becomes relatively more attractive to consumers.

SUPPLY

The supply curve slopes upwards from left to right. This is because:

as prices rise, existing producers are encouraged to produce more, and less efficient producers enter the market.

THE DETERMINANTS OF SUPPLY AND DEMAND

Where there is a shift in the position of either a supply or a demand curve it means that a factor other than price has changed – this factor is the determinant.

Factor changed	Shift in demand curve	Shift in supply curve
Consumer income	✓	
Prices of other goods	✓	
Consumer tastes	✓	
Cost of production inputs		✓
Technological advances		✓
Social or cultural attitudes	✓	✓
Tax changes		✓
Substitute prices	✓	

THE JARGON
Aggregate demand refers to the total quantity of a product demanded by consumers within a country.

Why does the demand curve slope down from left to right?

Why does the supply curve slope upwards from left to right?

THE JARGON
Supply refers to the quantity of a product that producers are capable of supplying at a given price.

Here are some of the factors that may cause a shift in a supply or a demand curve. Which do they affect – or is it both? (Tick the relevant columns.)

WATCH OUT
Some of these factors may affect both supply and demand.

PRICE DETERMINATION

The diagram below shows how the interaction of supply (S) and demand (D) determine price.

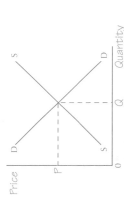

Identify and label the vertical axis 'Price'. Identify and label the Quantity axis. Draw a horizontal line to identify the equilibrium price. Label this P. Draw a vertical line to identify the equilibrium quantity. Label this Q.

Turn the page for some exam questions on this topic ▶

For more on this topic, see pages 4–5 of the *Revision Express A-level Study Guide*

EXAM QUESTION 1

House prices have sometimes risen sharply in the south-east of England.
(a) What factors might have contributed to this situation?

Some of the factors listed helped cause the rise in prices. In each case you are given a choice. Highlight the correct word.

Fall/increase in price of rented accommodation

Difficulties in obtaining building land in south/north

Rise/fall in numbers of jobs available in south

Rise/fall in mortgage interest rates

Fall/rise in building society lending

Lower/higher paid jobs in the south

Availability/non-availability of council houses for purchase

Increases/decreases in prices of building materials

(b) Give one way the government might be affected by the rise in house prices.

There will be pressure on the government to release more land for housing developments.

(c) Give one way that rising house prices might affect businesses based in the south-east.

As house prices rise, firms will find it more difficult to attract workers from other parts of the country.

Now have a go at parts (b) and (c).

EXAM QUESTION 2

From time to time governments intervene in the market to control prices. The diagram below illustrates a situation where minimum wage legislation has been imposed.

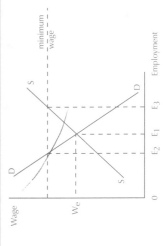

(a) What is the market equilibrium wage and employment level?
The equilibrium wage is 'We' and equilibrium employment level is 'E1'.

(b) How has the imposition of a minimum wage affected employment?
Total employment has fallen from the equilibrium employment level of 'E1' to 'E2'. Some employees who were willing to work for less than the minimum wage may now find themselves out of work. This is because some firms will not pay the higher wage (price).

EXAMINER'S SECRETS
Examiners are impressed if you can use supply and demand analysis to explain why prices have changed.

Answer these two questions with reference to the graph.

EXAMINER'S SECRETS
Some firms, in the longer term, may seek to replace the more expensive labour with labour-saving capital machinery.

Markets and competition

Competition refers to the degree of rivalry between firms in a market to sell you their products and services. **Where a firm is in a competitive situation the consumer is likely to get a better deal in terms of price and quality.**

THE SPECTRUM OF COMPETITION

The degree of competition in a market varies. At one end there is the perfectly competitive market and at the other end monopoly where there is no competition. In between these extremes are monopolistic competition and oligopoly. These are the forms of competition that exist in most markets.

The characteristics of monopolistic competition are:

- undifferentiated product
- free entry
- many sellers
- price takers
- low profits.

An oligopoly has different characteristics from those listed above. Its characteristics are:

- barriers to entry instead of free entry
- few sellers instead of many sellers
- high profits instead of low profits.

Here are some characteristics of different market structures. List those that relate to monopolistic competition in the space provided:

- **many sellers**
- **single seller**
- **free entry**
- **low profits**
- **price makers**
- **price takers**
- **undifferentiated product**

List three characteristics of an oligopoly that makes it different.

THE IMPACT OF COMPETITION: CASE STUDY

The holiday package industry is very competitive, and this is reflected in what firms offer the consumer. For example, one might offer free child places, another discounts for booking two holidays in a year. Other enticements include:

- use of different forms of transport
- many starting points for holidays
- free insurance
- tour packages in the resort
- representative services in the resort
- extension packages for second or third weeks.

List other ways holiday companies seek to attract customers. Try to think of at least three.

EXAMINER'S SECRETS
Governments encourage competition because it means the consumer gets a better quality product at a lower price. You will often find that it also means the business will provide a product or service closer to what the consumer wants.

FIXING THE MARKET

There are various forms of unfair competition:

- selling below cost so as to drive a competitor out of the market
- agreements between firms to limit output and raise prices
- supplier forcing retailers to stock the supplier's full range of products rather than selected popular brands.

List at least three forms of unfair competition.

THE JARGON
Sometimes firms try to manipulate the market to their own advantage. This is termed fixing the market. They try to do this to protect their prices and profits.

Turn the page for some exam questions on this topic ▶

For more on this topic, see pages 6–7 of the Revision Express A-level Study Guide

EXAM QUESTION 1

In some exam papers you may be given a press cutting to read. You are then required to answer some questions based on that material. The questions below are typical and would be based on a press cutting about OPEC. The press cutting might start 'OPEC is a cartel created by some of the oil exporting countries...'.

(a) Give one reason why OPEC wants to regulate the supply of oil.

By limiting the quantity of oil being produced, the cartel can increase the price. Higher revenue is obtained for producing a smaller quantity!

(b) OPEC is able to do this because oil has an inelastic demand curve. Explain this statement.

Oil is a necessity. Although higher prices will reduce demand it will still be bought in large quantities.

(c) What impact does this have on consumers?

The consumers' cost of living will rise.
The consumer has less to spend on other goods.

THE JARGON
OPEC is shorthand for Organization of Petroleum Exporting Countries. A cartel is a group of businesses that come together to agree selling area, exchange information or agree prices.

Answer the questions in the spaces here.

THE JARGON
A necessity is a product that many consumers are unable to do without.

IF YOU HAVE TIME
Draw an inelastic demand curve!

Give two points in response to this question.

EXAM QUESTION 2

Both the UK government and the EU are keen to ensure competition exists in all markets. Think of three things that have been used to achieve this aim and write a short paragraph about each.

Article 86 of the Treaty of Rome (1956) bans 'abuse of a dominant position'. This would occur where a firm uses its power to impose unfair terms on suppliers, retailers or customers.

Under the Fair Trading Act (1973) and Competition Act (1990, 1998) a merger of two companies that control more than 25% of a market can be referred to the Competition Commission to see whether that merger is in the public interest. Less than 3% of all mergers were referred in the period 1950–1995 though.

Articles 92–94 of the Treaty of Rome (1956) prohibit the use of state aid to distort competition, for example, where a loss-making firm receives a subsidy from a government.

An answer to this question might mention Article 86 of the Treaty of Rome. Write one or two sentences about this here.

You could also write about the Fair Trading Act, and Competition Act. Remember to give the dates of the Acts when you mention them.

WATCH OUT
Legislation passed by the UK government applies to situations that occur within the UK. EU legislation applies to situations where more than one member state is involved.

Finally, you could write about Articles 92–94 of the Treaty of Rome.

Macro-economic factors

(AS) AQA EDEXCEL OCR WJEC

The macro-economic environment refers to the part of the economic environment over which the firm has no control. Firms must try to understand these economic processes to best guess future developments and thus protect their interests and exploit opportunities.

INFLATION

Inflation may be caused by cost push or demand pull influences. It may also be imported.

1 Cost push	Increases in the prices of raw materials or components from abroad force British manufacturers to raise the prices of their products.	
2 Demand pull	Rising business costs, such as wages or interest payments, force firms to increase prices so as to protect profit margins.	1
3 Imported	A situation where demand is growing more quickly than the ability of firms to meet that demand. It often arises in 'boom' conditions.	2

Draw a line to match each statement to the correct cause of inflation.

THE JARGON
Hyperinflation refers to a situation where prices rise so fast that money may cease to be used and people return to bartering.

UNEMPLOYMENT

There are various forms of unemployment including frictional, cyclical and structural. The government might use a range of strategies to reduce structural unemployment.

- Train the unemployed and give them new skills.
- Persuade new firms to move to these regions.
- Offer incentives to the unemployed to move to areas where there are jobs.

THE JARGON
Structural unemployment occurs where a region is heavily dependent upon a declining industry, e.g. mining.

Suggest three ways the government might reduce structural unemployment.

EXCHANGE RATES

Exchange rates often fluctuate and this may cause problems for businesses trading internationally. Exchange rate appreciation occurs where one currency increases in value against another (e.g. £1 might now buy 275 pesetas). Thus exchange rate appreciation might affect a British firm importing from, or exporting to, Spain as follows.

Because sterling buys more pesetas than before, importers would find that they could buy their goods from Spain for less pounds. Exporters would find it more difficult to sell into the Spanish market because the Spanish would have to pay more pesetas for the British product.

Exchange rate depreciation might affect a British firm importing from Spain, as follows.

Because sterling buys fewer pesetas than before, imports will cost more in pounds. Unless the firm can raise its selling prices, profits will fall.

THE JARGON
The exchange rate is the value of one currency in terms of another. For example, the sterling: peseta exchange rate might be £1 = 250 pesetas.

Explain the effect of exchange rate appreciation on a British firm importing from Spain. Then explain the effect if the firm is exporting to Spain.

Now explain the effect of exchange rate depreciation on a British firm importing from Spain.

Turn the page for some exam questions on this topic ▶

For more on this topic, see pages 8–9 of the *Revision Express A-level Study Guide*

EXAM QUESTION 1

What benefits and problems might a firm face from a period of rising inflation?

	Benefit	Problem
Rising prices lead to higher profits	✓	
Exchange rates may depreciate		✓
Inflation may damage business confidence		✓
Interest rates may be forced up		✓
Real value of loans less when repaid	✓	
Financial planning may be more difficult		✓
General increasing demand for goods	✓	
Exports may become uncompetitive		✓

The table lists some benefits and problems that are associated with rising inflation. Tick a column to indicate whether each statement is a problem or a benefit.

The government may put up interest rates to control inflation which will make it more expensive for people to buy goods on credit. As a result, demand for goods may fall. Higher interest rates also make it more expensive for a firm to borrow money.

Now write two or three sentences to explain why financial planning might be more difficult in a time of rising inflation.

EXAM QUESTION 2

How might a firm alter its plans if a prolonged period of heavy unemployment is predicted?

Use the instructions on the left to help you plan your answer.

EXAMINER'S SECRETS
The key to this question is to realize that it implies that a recession is imminent.

- Cut back on any investment plans.
- Reduce stock and cut production levels.
- Search for ways of cutting costs.
- Outsource peripheral activities.

What might the production department do? Give four ideas.

THE JARGON
Outsourcing arises when a firm buys in services that it previously did itself, for example, market research.

- Target other markets not affected by recession.
- Scale down plans for new product development.
- Reappraise product portfolio.
- Develop value for money promotions.

What might the marketing department do? Give four ideas.

- Take steps to reduce levels of gearing.
- Negotiate longer-term financing.
- Review and tighten credit finance arrangements.
- Sell off unwanted assets (sale and leaseback?).
- Negotiate extended credit from suppliers.

What might the finance department do?

THE JARGON
Sale and leaseback is a method of raising money by selling land and buildings. At the same time another agreement is entered into, leasing the property back from the new owner.

- Discuss potential problems with employee representatives; involve them in the change process.
- Replace permanent staff with temporary workers.
- Lay off workers.
- Redeploy/retrain surplus employees (if possible).
- Ban new recruitment.

What might the human resources (or personnel) department do?

For more on this topic, see pages 12–13 of the Revision Express A-level Study Guide

Social and demographic influences

AS AQA EDEXCEL OCR WJEC

People have always had an important influence on business. Changes in social attitudes have provided businesses with many opportunities and threats. The same may also be said for changes in population size and age structure.

EXAMINER'S SECRETS
Make sure you can quote some examples of the different ways people influence businesses.

PEOPLE AND BUSINESS

Businesses rely on people in many ways. Their attitudes and actions can influence a business, both favourably and unfavourably. There are numerous examples of businesses that have changed (or been forced to change) direction because of the influence of people. Here are some examples of the relationship people may have with business:

- as customers
- as pressure groups
- as shareholders
- as employees
- as suppliers
- as government.

The relationship between a business and its employees is important. Give at least two problems that might occur if the relationship is poor.

Businesses need highly motivated employees. If employees are demotivated, the firm may experience problems such as poor quality work, absenteeism and high labour turnover. Employees may also give the firm a bad reputation by the way they treat customers or talk about the firm.

DEMOGRAPHIC CHANGES

The UK is facing demographic changes including a reduction in the birth rate, an increase in the size of the retired population and more young people going into higher education. Various groups might be worried by these demographic changes.

Explain how the two groups mentioned here might be affected.

The government
It is likely that the government will have to raise taxes because there will be fewer people in work to pay taxes and thus support all those not working. Tax rises are never popular.

Businesses
There will be less potential employees available for recruitment. This may affect the quality and cost of labour.

There are various ways firms might avoid these problems.

Give two ways firms could avoid problems associated with demographic change.

- *Adopt more flexible work patterns, e.g. jobshare or flexitime (particularly important to women).*
- *Replace labour through the use of technology.*

These trends provide both opportunities and threats to a firm or industry. For instance, there might be more demand for academic textbooks and pensioner holidays (often out of season), but there will be less demand for products such as baby goods and toys.

Turn the page for some exam questions on this topic ▶

EXAM QUESTION 1

One major trend during the twentieth century has been the increasing use of cars by people in their everyday lives. Assess the possible implications of this for business and society.

Here are some of the points you could make:

	Benefit	Problem
1. Car fumes a major pollutant		✓
2. Cuts journey times	✓	
3. The car industry provides much employment	✓	
4. Increased road congestion		✓
5. Car taxes are source of government revenue	✓	
6. Major cause of accident and injury		✓
7. Improved social and work mobility	✓	
8. Health problems caused by lack of exercise		✓
9. Forces government to invest heavily in roads		✓

Indicate whether you think each point is a benefit or a problem (with some of these points you might be able to argue that it is both a benefit and a problem).

EXAMINER'S SECRETS
In an exam you would not be expected to use all these points. You would be required to select what you consider to be the most important and develop a short paragraph round each of those points.

Develop the statement in point 3.

The car industry provides a livelihood for many people, including workers in car plants, showrooms and petrol stations. People are also employed in repairing cars, valeting and car insurance.

List some jobs that are created by the car industry.

Explain point 9.

Many families have two cars and some have more. Cars are used to take people to work, children to school and for social purposes. As a result, the government has had to invest heavily in road building schemes. In many cases the improvements just encourage more people to use their cars rather than public transport.

Write a short paragraph giving the reasons why the government has had to invest in road building schemes. You could mention what effect this investment has had.

EXAM QUESTION 2

Female employment rates have grown throughout the twentieth century. Women now form nearly 50% of the workforce. However, their weekly earnings are only 75% of their male counterparts'.

Explain these trends.

Here are some points you could use to explain the rise in female employment rates.
- Women can control family size.
- Growth of tertiary sector jobs.
- Social attitudes have changed.
- More highly educated women.
- Gender discrimination unlawful.

Write a paragraph explaining how social attitudes have changed.

Social attitudes towards women have changed. It is now acceptable for women to work and look after a family at the same time. It is also now accepted that women may be employed in senior managerial posts or in the professions (for example, the legal profession).

Women take career breaks; there is still sex discrimination; women may refuse to work hours that cause problems with their childcare arrangements; many women want part-time jobs, and these offer few career paths.

Now explain why women's earnings are so much lower than men's. Try to think of up to four points.

Technological influences

When we use the term 'technology' we are referring to the application of existing knowledge and skills to create and use materials, processes and products. Technology is often seen as determining the products made, the processes by which they are made and the organizational structure. Technology may also affect an individual's motivation and attitude to work.

TECHNOLOGY – SOME IMPORTANT TERMS ○○○

Draw lines matching each term or phrase with the correct definition.

REVISION EXPRESS
For more on CAD/CAM see pages 132–133 of the *Revision Express A-level Study Guide*

1 Information technology	The process by which an interesting job is replaced by a more monotonous one through the use of machinery.	④
2 Management information system	A computer based system used to produce a detailed product design. Designs can be modified or refined using a computer based system.	③
3 Computer aided design	The use of robots in the production process, particularly where work is hazardous or monotonous.	⑤
4 Deskilling	The acquisition, processing, storage and dissemination of information using computers.	①
5 Robotics	Any system of production where manufacturing equipment is controlled by a computer.	⑥
6 Computer aided manufacturing	A computerized system which provides management with the information with which to plan, organize, coordinate and control.	②

INFORMATION TECHNOLOGY (IT) ○○○

Strategies for managing IT involve the whole organization. Here are some of the issues to be considered:

- selecting staff to set up and run IT-based management systems
- identifying changes to products, processes and administrative systems to take advantage of IT
- ensuring all departments recognize the importance of IT
- deciding whether to develop a customized system or purchase a standard commercial package.

In addition, IT can change the organizational structure.

How might the organizational structure be changed by the introduction of new information technology?

IT introduction tends to encourage the centralization of administrative procedures. You will find that:

- senior managers can handle more work
- less work is delegated
- managers have a wider span of control
- some managerial levels may disappear
- 'local' management may not be required.

EXAMINER'S SECRETS
The implications of adopting new technology' are an important exam topic.

Turn the page for some exam questions on this topic ▶

For more on this topic, see pages 14–15 of the *Revision Express A-level Study Guide*

EXAM QUESTION 1

The benefits arising from the introduction of new technology far outweigh the problems. How far do you agree with this statement?

Write an introductory paragraph, setting the scene for an answer to this question. You might want to begin by saying something about the term 'new technology'. What exactly does it mean?

New technology is a very broad term that encompasses the idea of applying computerization to products, production processes and administrative procedures. As with any change there are both benefits and problems.

Here are some of the points that could be made. Highlight those points that you consider to be problems.

- The cost is often high and the firm may have to compromise in order to stay within budget.
- There is an opportunity to reduce staffing levels.
- Improved communication may result within the organization.
- There is the likelihood of employee resistance to change.
- Better management control as a result of more accurate information.
- Change will mean that some staff find it difficult to adjust.
- In the short term costs are going to outweigh benefits.
- Embracing new technology prevents other firms using this as a means of gaining competitive advantage over you.

Now write a concluding paragraph, summing up the arguments. You might want to distinguish between the short-term impact and the long-term impact.

There are many benefits from introducing new technology into the firm. However, the benefits are longer term and in the short term the firm is going to have to accept that problems may arise. Indeed in the short term, profits may even fall as a result of the introduction of new technology.

EXAM QUESTION 2

Mountbatten Estates is a property company that has just introduced a new Management Information System into its office. As a result some employees have left, absenteeism is higher and morale is lower. To what extent could these problems have been avoided?

Briefly state why employees might react unfavourably to change.

Employees are concerned as to how the change will affect them. In particular, will they lose their jobs? Can they do the new ones? Do they lose status or pay? Are social groups going to be broken up?

Now write at least two sentences to summarize the points you would make in the main part of your answer.

There will always be resistance to change among employees, particularly if information is mainly spread through the grapevine. However, by giving guarantees on items such as redundancy, retraining, status and work groups and also by involving people in the change process, the resistance can be significantly reduced.

© Pearson Education Limited 2001

AS AQA EDEXCEL OCR WJEC

Business, law and society

Increasingly, businesses are being expected to act in a socially responsible manner, particularly in relation to the environment, employees and consumers. You will also find that the law often intervenes to protect these groups' interests.

Social responsibility and ethics

A firm's profit might increase as a result of being socially responsible.

Give one reason to explain a rise in profits. Then give a reason for a fall in profits.

Consumers may be attracted by such a policy and employees motivated more.

However, it is equally likely that a firm's profits will fall, since...

... the cost of being socially responsible may be greater than the benefits obtained.

THE JARGON
Business ethics are the moral principles that guide a manager's behaviour. Business ethics are greatly influenced by the corporate culture of the firm.

Firms often face ethical dilemmas.

Think of an ethical dilemma for firms working with suppliers in developing countries.

Should a UK firm producing goods abroad use child labour where this is within the law and culture of that country?

It is important to distinguish between a firm behaving legally and behaving ethically.

Explain the difference.

The legal standard is often the minimum level of acceptable behaviour. In many situations members of society expect far more.

The most ethical behaviour can be difficult to identify. For instance:

Explain why the management of a polluting factory might face a dilemma due to the conflicting interests of stakeholders.

the costs of controlling pollution at a factory may be so high as to make production unprofitable. But closing the factory would result in the loss of many jobs. The firm may be seen as acting irresponsibly whatever it does.

THE JARGON
The shareholder approach to social responsibility argues that a firm is responsible only to its shareholders. The stakeholder approach acknowledges a responsibility to many other groups as well as shareholders.

Consumer protection law

The rights of the consumer are protected by a number of Acts. These include:

Draw a line linking these statements to the correct Act.

1 Trade Descriptions Act 1968/72	This act requires that goods should be of merchantable quality, fit for their purpose and as described.	2
2 Sale of Goods Act 1979	This act requires retailers and manufacturers to provide safety advice and instructions for all dangerous goods.	4
3 Consumer Credit Act 1974	This act makes it illegal for a trader to give false or misleading descriptions of goods on offer.	1
4 Consumer Protection Act 1989	This act ensures that the customer gets the quantity of a product asked for or stated on a label.	5
5 Weights and Measures Act 1985	This act requires the true cost of borrowing to be disclosed.	3

EXAMINER'S SECRETS
You will not be required to know these Acts in great detail. You will be expected to know about the impact on the firm and the consumer.

Turn the page for some exam questions on this topic ➤

For more on this topic, see pages 16–21 of the *Revision Express A-level Study Guide*

Exam question 1

In the twenty-first century we have a right to expect firms to act in a socially responsible manner.
To what extent do you agree with this statement?

Here are some arguments for and against the statement.

Tick to indicate which statements are for and which are against.

	For	Against
1. Acting responsibly may reduce a firm's competitiveness.		✔
2. Acting responsibly creates a favourable image.	✔	
3. Directors have a legal duty to shareholders.		✔
4. The prime task of business is to maximize profits.		✔
5. The interests of stakeholders may conflict with each other.		✔
6. Acting responsibly may attract good employees.	✔	

EXAMINER'S SECRETS
In an exam you would not have time to develop all these points, so highlight those you consider to be the most important and concentrate on these. Also make sure that you choose arguments both for and against.

Now write a short paragraph developing point 5 above.

Pleasing one stakeholder may annoy another so there is no point in trying to be socially responsible. For example, expansion of a local airport may benefit the local business community but annoy local residents.

Exam question 2

Identify and illustrate the different kinds of law that affect management. What problems can these cause for management?

Write at least two sentences explaining how the law affects the marketing function within a firm.

The marketing function is affected by many pieces of consumer legislation such as the Sale of Goods Act and Trade Descriptions Act. These Acts are designed to ensure the consumer gets what they want and is not confused by misleading descriptions of goods or services.

Now write a short paragraph about the effects of the Companies Acts on information that must be given to investors. Also mention the responsibilities of directors if a business becomes insolvent.

There are many Companies Acts that affect the firm. Many relate to the amount of information that must be given to investors in the final accounts. Directors are also responsible, personally, if the business continues trading whilst insolvent.

Think about problems that legal controls give management. What is the impact on costs, time and freedom of action?

- The firm incurs extra costs complying with legislation. This is important where the firm is competing with firms from other countries that have lower standards.
- Managers have to give time to these legal issues and this diverts them from other issues.
- Legal controls act as a constraint on what action the manager is allowed to take but also act as a guide to what action needs to be taken in a situation.

EXAMINER'S SECRETS
To get a good mark you would have to identify legislation that also affects the human resources and production function. You could talk about 'equality' legislation as well as health and safety legislation.

© Pearson Education Limited 2001

Nature of business

Business involves the transformation of inputs into an output that is designed to satisfy a customer's needs. For a business to be profitable it must 'add value' during the transformation stage so that a price can be charged that is higher than the cost of the inputs.

THE JARGON

'Value added' is the difference between the cost of materials and the price customers are prepared to pay for the finished product.

> Define each of the types of output and give at least two examples of each.

IF YOU HAVE TIME

Make a list of the goods and services that you consume in a typical week classifying them into the different kinds.

INPUTS AND OUTPUTS

Inputs are the resources needed to produce goods or a service. They will include a combination of the four factors of production: land, labour, capital and enterprise. These resources are transformed into the following outputs:

Consumer durable goods: goods that are long-lasting, e.g. TV, radio, washing machine.

Consumer non-durable goods (consumables): items that can only be used once, e.g. food, petrol, paper.

Capital goods: products used by a business to make further goods, e.g. machinery, tools, factory.

Services: activities that assist firms and individuals, e.g. insurance, transport, banking.

PRIVATE AND PUBLIC SECTOR

Goods and services are provided for consumers and firms by either the private sector or the public sector.

Private sector: the section of the economy consisting of privately owned firms ranging from sole traders to multinational companies.

Public sector: the part of the economy consisting of organizations owned and/or financed by local and central government.

> Put the following organizations, services or products in the correct part of the table: local authority leisure centre, Post Office, British Telecom, libraries, McDonalds, BBC, local hairdresser, Asda, NHS, Virgin rail services.

Private sector	Public sector
British Telecom	NHS
McDonalds	BBC
local hairdresser	local authority leisure centre
Asda	Post Office
Virgin rail services	libraries

THE CHAIN OF PRODUCTION

The production chain is the entire sequence of activities required to turn raw materials into a consumer product. These activities can be classed by the type of production that takes place.

> In each case, after the words 'Activities include', write the relevant examples from this list: transport, mining, insurance, refining, communications, oil exploration, construction, farming, manufacturing.

Primary sector: the extraction or harvesting of basic raw materials.
Activities include mining, oil exploration and farming.

Secondary sector: the conversion of raw materials into finished goods.
Activities include construction, manufacturing and refining.

Tertiary sector: the provision of services for firms and individuals.
Activities include insurance, transport and communications.

Turn the page for some exam questions on this topic ▶

For more on this topic, see pages 32–33 of the Revision Express A-level Study Guide

EXAM EXERCISE

For each of the activities listed, indicate the relevant economic sector.

> In each case, tick the relevant column.

	Primary	Secondary	Tertiary
Retailing			✓
Nursing			✓
Mining and quarrying	✓		
Construction		✓	
Energy and water supplies	✓		
Engineering		✓	
Banking			✓
Teaching			✓
Farming	✓		
Steel fabrication		✓	
Forestry	✓		
Motor assembly		✓	
Dentistry			✓

DON'T FORGET

The sectors are interdependent. For example, the produce from farming in the primary sector is processed by the secondary sector and distributed and sold by the tertiary sector.

EXAM QUESTION 1

Economies are dynamic in that they are constantly changing and adapting to new technologies, new material and new consumer demands. Organizations and workers must adapt to these changes if they are to remain in business or employment.

(a) Using the following data, calculate the percentage share of total employment for the manufacturing and service sectors for each year.

Employment in UK industries (000s)

	1990	1998
All employment	22 920	23 237
Manufacturing	4 708	4 056
Service industries	16 350	17 664

> Write your calculations in the spaces provided.

Manufacturing % share 1990 = $\dfrac{4\,708}{22\,920} \times 100 = 20.54\%$

Manufacturing % share 1998 = $\dfrac{4\,056}{23\,237} \times 100 = 17.45\%$

Services % share 1990 = $\dfrac{16\,350}{22\,920} \times 100 = 71.34\%$

Services % share 1998 = $\dfrac{17\,664}{23\,237} \times 100 = 76.02\%$

EXAMINER'S SECRETS

Answers, that manipulate the data will receive higher marks than those that merely restate their findings, e.g. you could calculate the difference in employment between the years.

(b) What does the trend indicate? How will this affect the workforce?

> First summarize the changes, then explain what they indicate. What type of economy exists in the UK?

Manufacturing's share of employment has fallen by just over 3% with 652 000 fewer people employed in the sector. Services, on the other hand, have increased their share of employment by nearly 5% with 1 314 000 more people employed in the sector. It appears that the UK is predominantly a service economy.

> Now say what the effect on the workforce will be.

The workforce, especially new entrants such as school leavers and university graduates, must recognize that different skills will be needed to secure employment, predominantly in services.

© Pearson Education Limited 2001

Stakeholders and their objectives

AS AQA EDEXCEL OCR WJEC

Organizations today must recognize the objectives of their stakeholders. To disregard them is to risk losing customers and goodwill. The importance attached to the views of these groups depends on their relative strength in the market place.

THE JARGON
Stakeholders are any individuals or groups who have an interest in a business activity.

Define the term 'shareholder concept'.

LINKS
For more information on business objectives see pages 23–24

SHAREHOLDER CONCEPT

This is a traditional view of a firm.

All the actions of a firm are designed to increase the wealth of the business for the benefit of the owners or shareholders. Management's main task is to maximize profits.

STAKEHOLDER CONCEPT

A more modern approach is to recognize the interests of all the stakeholders in a business. Some management theorists believe that in the long run it is more beneficial for firms to recognize the views of these groups and to include their objectives in the decision making process. Some of these groups include:

Each stakeholder group has many objectives and goals. In this exercise, one possible objective has been identified for each group.

In each case say what action the business could take to satisfy the objective and show what benefit it might bring to the business.

Employees

Objective	Improved working conditions
Action	Higher wages, longer holidays
Benefit	More loyal staff, reduced absenteeism

Suppliers

Objective	Gain more regular orders and payments
Action	Guarantee orders (perhaps in exchange for better discounts)
Benefit	Long-term partnership and cooperation

Customers

Objective	Products tailored more closely to the customer's needs
Action	Consultation through market research
Benefit	Increased consumer loyalty

Local community

Objective	Improve local services
Action	Support local community projects
Benefit	Less local opposition and more local customers

CONFLICT OF OBJECTIVES

All the groups are competing for a slice of the rewards generated by the business. Conflict appears inevitable as more for one group appears only possible with less for another. The stakeholder view, however, believes that the total rewards can be increased through 'cooperation' and that all stakeholders can benefit. This strategy is known as 'satisficing'.

THE JARGON
'Satisficing' is the acceptance of a strategy that is satisfactory for all instead of pursuing a policy that is in the interests of only one group.

Turn the page for some exam questions on this topic ►

EXAM EXERCISE

A local hospital is reviewing its objectives for the next five-year development plan. As part of the process it wants to identify all its stakeholders and to estimate their possible needs. For each of the identified stakeholders state an objective.

Stakeholders	Objectives
Management	Effective use of the hospital's scarce resources
Doctors	Sufficient medical facilities
Nursing staff	Good working conditions
General employees	Security of employment
Patients	Quality of service
Relatives of patients	Safety and comfort of patients
Local community	Standard of services offered
Government	Efficient use of tax payers' funds
Suppliers	High level of demand for goods and services

Write possible objectives in the table.

DON'T FORGET
Individuals within each group may also have different interests and priorities. This mixture of objectives makes it extremely difficult for a business to satisfy all its stakeholders.

EXAM QUESTION 1

The reaction of a firm to consumer pressure groups will depend on a number of factors. For each of the factors below, explain why it might be important, and give an example.

1. The purchasing power of the pressure group:

A campaign will be more effective when it can influence customers to abstain from buying a particular product or to switch purchases to a rival company, e.g. Shell's petrol sales were significantly affected as motorists switched to rival brands at the time of the Brent Spar controversy.

2. The reaction of competitors:

A competitor might take the opportunity to react favourably to pressure group demands as a means of winning market share, e.g. the dropping of charges to use cash machines by some UK banks.

3. Access to politicians:

Issues that politicians feel will influence voters are more likely to be supported, e.g. the attempt to ban all blood sports such as fox hunting.

4. The relative costs and benefits of adopting the demanded changes:

Some changes can be made relatively cheaply, e.g. British Airways has banned smoking on all its flights.

Explain the importance of each factor, then add the most appropriate example from this list.
- Some banks stopped charging for use of cash machines.
- British Airways has banned smoking on all its flights.
- The attempt to ban all blood sports.
- At the time of the Brent Spar controversy, Shell's petrol sales were damaged.

EXAMINER'S SECRETS
Answers that are able to quote a relevant example are always preferable to mere descriptions. Make sure you know several examples of pressure groups such as ASH, Friends of the Earth, Greenpeace, CAMRA, etc.

Types and size of business

There are many types of business in the commercial world each with their own benefits and drawbacks. You need to know how they are financed, who is in control and who makes the decisions.

BUSINESS ORGANIZATIONS OOO

Sole trader: is the simplest form of business unit as it is easy to establish with only a small amount of capital. In general, the sole trader provides the capital for the business, bears all the risk and makes all the decisions.

Advantages	Disadvantages
Easy to establish	Unlimited liability
Flexible decision making	Limited capital
Owner keeps all profit	High failure rate

Partnership: a common form of business in professional areas such as law, accountancy, medicine and insurance. A Partnership Agreement details the rights and responsibilities of each partner including each partner's capital input, share of profits and losses and voting rights.

Advantages	Disadvantages
Extra capital available	Unlimited liability
Division of labour – specialists can be used	Limited number of partners allowed
Shared responsibility	Shared profits

Private Limited Companies: limited liability means that the owners are financially responsible only for the amount invested in the company and do not risk their own personal wealth. Shares can only be offered on a private basis.

Advantages	Disadvantages
Limited liability	Shares only sold privately
Easier to raise capital	Public access to accounts
Greater economies of scale	Difficult to sell shares

Public Limited Companies (plcs): although they are small in number, plcs account for the majority of output, capital investment and employment in the UK. They are owned by the shareholders but are controlled and managed by salaried directors.

Advantages	Disadvantages
Limited liability	Costly to establish
Easier to raise large amounts of capital	Larger size might lead to slower decision making
Shares transferable	Accounts must be published

DON'T FORGET

99.2% of all businesses in the UK are classified as small.

In the tables provided list three advantages and three disadvantages of each form of business organization. Some of the factors you should think about are listed below.
• How easy is it to establish the organization?
• Is the organization's liability unlimited?
• Who keeps the profits?
• Are there any divisions of labour?
• Are there economies of scale?
• Does the organization issue shares? If so, who owns them? Are they offered privately or publicly?
• Do accounts have to be made public?

DON'T FORGET

Doctors and dentists are often in partnerships.

THE JARGON

Private limited companies must have the designation 'Limited' at the end of their name, often abbreviated to 'Ltd'.

IF YOU HAVE TIME

Make a list of five public limited companies that you know and that can be used to illustrate exam questions.

Turn the page for some exam questions on this topic ▶

For more on this topic, see pages 36–39 of the *Revision Express A-level Study Guide*

EXAM QUESTION 1

The economy can be divided into two sectors, the private sector and the public sector. The private sector is made up of sole traders, partnerships and limited companies. Explain what is meant by a public sector organization, and give examples.

A public sector organization is owned and controlled by central or local government. Such organizations are financed through taxation or in part by their own trading activities. Examples include: The Post Office, the Bank of England, the British Broadcasting Corporation (BBC), local authority services such as sports halls, swimming pools, etc., central government such as the NHS, the Department of Transport, etc.

DON'T FORGET!

Public limited companies are in the private sector. It is easy to confuse these terms!

Identify who owns, controls and finances such organizations. Provide at least three examples.

EXAMINER'S SECRETS

Many students fail to distinguish between public limited companies and public sector organizations. Accuracy with terminology will avoid losing marks.

EXAM QUESTION 2

Rachel Wrigley has been a sole trader for five years and has built up a highly successful internet café on a London high street. She believes the concept can be profitably extended to other parts of the country but is unwilling to risk any more of her own financial capital. She wants to concentrate on finding new locations and developing new business. Outline three advantages and three disadvantages that Rachel would face if she decided to expand by becoming a limited company, then evaluate the choices facing Rachel.

Advantages

1. Rachel will be able to raise more capital by persuading other interested parties to become shareholders.

2. A larger organization may be able to afford specialists such as accountants and marketing personnel. This will allow Rachel to concentrate on what she does best.

3. Rachel's liability is limited to her investment in the business. Her private wealth is not at risk.

Disadvantages

1. Rachel will have to share the profits of the business with her fellow shareholders.

2. Although Rachel might remain as the major shareholder she will have to learn how to cooperate with the new shareholders and managers. She will no longer have absolute control.

3. Financial information must be filed with the Registrar of Companies and can be inspected by the public, including Rachel's competitors.

Evaluation

Rachel's final decision will depend on whether her desire to see the business grow outweighs the loss of independence and inherent risk involved.

Make sure that you write in context by referring to Rachel's current position and her future plans.

EXAMINER'S SECRETS

It is more likely that the higher order skills of analysis and evaluation will be displayed when answers are written with reference to the context of the question, in this case addressing the concerns of Rachel.

Evaluation requires you to balance the two arguments and to express an opinion.

For more on this topic, see pages, 40–41 of the *Revision Express A-level Study Guide*

Business objectives

AQA EDEXCEL OCR WJEC

It is important that an organization has a common purpose and direction that is understood by all – owners, management and workforce. This formal statement of aims is often phrased in a mission statement. From this statement, a hierarchy of objectives can be formed both long term and short term.

THE JARGON
A mission statement is a document detailing the long-term goals of an organization. It is often expressed in qualitative terms concentrating on quality and customer service.

Define these objectives in terms of time scale, importance and who formulates them. Provide an example of each type of objective.

THE JARGON
Long and short-term objectives are sometimes referred to as strategic and tactical objectives.

IF YOU HAVE TIME
Examine a number of annual reports to compare the mission statements of a diverse group of companies. Is there a common theme?

DON'T FORGET
Markets are dynamic therefore the goals of a business are likely to change with continual developments in the market.

List three reasons why profit is important to a business.

Explain two ways in which growth reduces risk.

LINKS
For more information on stakeholders and their objectives see pages 19–20.

LONG-TERM AND SHORT-TERM OBJECTIVES   ○○○

Objectives are goals that the organization aims to achieve. They must be measurable and attainable otherwise they will have a demotivating effect on the employees. Each organization will have different objectives depending on its size, its age, its market and the resources available. What is common to all organizations, however, is that they will have a series of long-term and short-term objectives.

Long-term or strategic objectives: *these are goals to be achieved in the next three to five years. They are crucial to the organization's future and are set by senior management. An example would be to increase sales by 20% in the next four years.*

Short-term or tactical objectives: *these are goals to be achieved in the next few months in line with the business's strategic objectives. Failure to achieve an objective may not be too damaging, as these are small-scale goals. Middle management sets these, e.g. recruit 20 new sales representatives.*

COMMON OBJECTIVES OF AN ORGANIZATION   ○○○

Three objectives commonly associated with all organizations are:

Survival: All new firms strive to survive as they attempt to build a customer base in the market. Even established businesses can feel threatened by new competitors or new products. In these circumstances survival may necessitate the offering of goods and services at highly competitive prices in order to reach a sustainable level of sales that guarantees break-even.

Profit: For most businesses profit making is the major concern of the organization. Profit is an important objective because it:

- enables the business to pay its creditors
- provides finance for future investment
- provides rewards for stakeholders.

Growth: Once established, many firms pursue growth as their main objective. Growth is seen not only as a means of increasing profits but also as a means of limiting risk. This is because:

expansion leads to economies of scale that reduce unit costs and improve competitiveness. Growth allows diversification of product and diversification of market. This reduces the impact of falling sales in any one area.

Turn the page for some exam questions on this topic ▶

EXAM QUESTION 1

The objective of survival is most commonly associated with newly formed businesses as they strive to gain sufficient market share. There are, however, circumstances when established concerns feel the need to adopt survival strategies. For each of the situations below, identify strategies the business could adopt, and outline the dangers associated with each.

(a) A business facing falling sales during a recession.

- Boosting sales by increased advertising: this will increase marketing costs without necessarily increasing sales sufficiently as consumers are less willing to spend during recessionary times.
- Cutting costs by reducing staff levels: this will help protect profits but might also damage customer loyalty if the level of service falls to an unacceptable level.
- Cutting prices in an attempt to keep market share: this will reduce the profit margin and might lead to a price war if competitors adopt the same tactics.

(b) A business threatened by a takeover.

- Mount an aggressive advertising campaign to persuade current shareholders to remain loyal and not to accept the rival bid: this might be seen as defensive and only an attempt to increase the offer price.
- Seek a friendly partner who is considered more suitable: independence is still lost.
- Make a reverse takeover bid: this will involve the commitment of more capital, much of it likely to be borrowed.

Think about each of these possible areas: advertising, costs and pricing. Each time, say what the dangers might be if the business changed its policy in the relevant area.

DON'T FORGET
A change in objectives can be forced upon an organization with very little time for planning and execution.

EXAM EXERCISE

For each of the following ten activities, say whether you think they are short-term (tactical) or long-term (strategic).

Tick the correct columns.

	Long-term	Short-term
Place extra advert in local paper		✓
Expand into Europe	✓	
Employ four more sales people		✓
Diversify into a new market	✓	
Create a research department	✓	
Offer a limited period sales promotion		✓
Introduce new technologies	✓	
Complete a customer order		✓
Expand by a series of takeovers	✓	
Build links with the local area		✓

Government and business

All market-led economies accept the need for government intervention in the workings of the economy. The key question is not whether the government should intervene but what should be the purpose of that intervention. Within the UK it is generally agreed that this role should be to create a stable business environment where firms and people are not disadvantaged.

CREATING AN ECONOMIC FRAMEWORK ○○○

Although the privatization of the 1980s and 1990s has removed many industries from direct government control, the government is still a major user of resources and supplier of goods and services. These include:

THE JARGON
The public sector consists of organizations owned or financed by the government.

education, health services, transport infrastructure, police and prisons, armed forces, social services.

Many of these goods and services help business. For example:

Add some further examples of public-sector goods and services.

The education system provides a stream of young people having the skills necessary for work in industry and commerce.

The health system ensures that workers are healthy and therefore productive.

Now explain briefly how the education system, health services and transport infrastructure help business.

The transport system makes it easier for workers and goods to move throughout the country.

THE GOVERNMENT AS REGULATOR ○○○

There are many areas where the government has intervened in the world of business, for example, by introducing competition legislation. Other areas include:

- health and safety
- industrial relations law
- consumer law
- labour law.

State at least two other areas where the government has intervened.

One advantage is that all firms have to work to the same rules and regulations. A disadvantage is the extra costs and constraints imposed on firms.

State one advantage and one disadvantage of this legislation to the firm.

THE GOVERNMENT AS PROMOTER ○○○

Many opportunities are provided for firms by the government's activities as promoter. Government activities include research and development (R&D), international trade, employment training and regional policy. Small firms' assistance is especially important.

Examples include the raising of finance, tax breaks, training, advice, and reductions in red tape.

State at least two ways in which the government has assisted small firms.

The government is keen to improve the survival rates for small firms. Also, small firms are a source of innovation and may eventually go on to become the large firms of tomorrow.

Why would it want to do this?

Turn the page for some exam questions on this topic ▶

For more on this topic, see pages 48–49 of the *Revision Express A-level Study Guide*

EXAM QUESTION 1

Despite its many advantages privatization may still be criticized. Discuss this statement.

Privatization means the return of state-owned assets to private ownership. Although the trend of privatization began in the UK in the 1980s, it is now a worldwide phenomenon with billions of pounds of assets being returned to private ownership. The industries most often affected have been gas, electricity, water, rail, bus, airline and telecommunications. But in Eastern Europe many state-owned manufacturing firms are affected.

An ideal answer would include a brief definition of 'privatization'. Write two or three sentences explaining the term. Give examples of industries often affected.

EXAMINER'S SECRETS
Try to give some context to the term. e.g. when did it start, what sort of industries are usually involved, where is it happening now.

Here are some of the advantages claimed for privatization:
1. a reduction in the size of the public sector
2. an increase in efficiency by introducing competition
3. reduced public sector borrowing to finance investment
4. reduced dependence on the state (e.g. to finance losses)
5. provides funds to develop a better infrastructure
6. widens share ownership
7. improves customer choice and quality of provision.

Look at the list of advantages claimed for privatization. Write a brief explanation of points 2 and 3.

EXAMINER'S SECRETS
To get high marks you do not have to use all these points – but you are expected to explain the ones you do use!

Point 2. Many nationalized industries were not faced with competition and therefore there was no incentive to improve efficiency. It was hoped that with privatization that competition would appear; for example, electricity firms are now selling gas in the UK.

Point 3. The investment needed to keep the nationalized industries up to date was extremely high. This limited the government's ability to borrow and spend in other areas. Privatization would mean that the private sector would be raising this finance.

Here are some of the problems associated with privatization:
1. it is still difficult to bring competition into some industries
2. in some cases the productivity gains have not materialized
3. complaints about fat cat pay rises awarded to directors
4. regulation of privatized utilities is not robust enough
5. there have been problems with the share issues.

Write two or three sentences explaining point 5. Point 1 has already been done as an example.

1. Where the privatized firm was a state monopoly it has sometimes been difficult to introduce competition into that area. Both the rail companies and the water utilities come into this category. In each case it is left to the government appointed regulator to try and get some efficiency gains.

5. There have been a number of complaints that share prices have been set too low. This allowed investors to make big gains on the first day of trading. Equally, the costs of advertising and underwriting these share issues have been very high.

© Pearson Education Limited 2001

Marketing objectives

The objectives that managers set for a firm depend on many factors including the competitive environment, the nature of the market and the state of the economy. Objectives will also be determined by internal factors such as the resources the firm has available.

MARKETING ORIENTATION

There are several different 'orientations' that a firm could adopt. For example, a production-led firm will use techniques to maximize production and minimize cost. Products will be standardized to achieve this objective.

Alternatively, businesses might have a sales orientation or a marketing orientation.

When a firm has a marketing orientation it implies that the marketing function is central to the organization. The marketing function identifies suitable markets and customer requirements and communicates this information to other functions within the firm. The marketing function must work with these other functions to meet the requirements.

Write a paragraph to explain what you understand by the term 'marketing orientation'.

THE JARGON
A sales-orientated firm will emphasize the varying product features and advertising to create and retain market share without considering the needs of its customers.

TYPES OF MARKETING OBJECTIVES

There are a number of marketing objectives that may be pursued by an organization. Most apply to not for profit organizations as well.

- To increase market share
- To improve profitability
- To enhance product (or corporate) image
- To target a new market
- To develop new products or services.

In practice, firms sometimes fail to achieve their marketing objectives. The reasons for this may be either external or internal to the firm. Factors within the firm might be getting the right employees, problems with the quality of raw materials or the production process. The size of the marketing budget may also be a constraint.

External factors relate to the environment in which the firm works. Many of these factors can be categorized as political (or legal), social, economic or technological.

- Legislation may prevent a firm from making extravagant claims about the product. Political (legal)
- A recession could reduce sales activity. Economic
- Attitudes to a product may change. Social
- A product may become outdated. Technological

List at least three marketing objectives that a company might have.

WATCH OUT!
Remember that marketing objectives must fit in with the wider objectives of the business.

Here are four external factors that may interfere with marketing objectives. For each one, say whether it is social, technological, political, or economic.

Turn the page for some exam questions on this topic ▶

For more on this topic, see pages 58–59 of the *Revision Express A-level Study Guide*

EXAM QUESTION 1

Heath Printing Ltd has decided that its key marketing objective for the coming year is short-term profit maximization. What are the possible implications of this for the firm's marketing mix?

For the immediate future the firm wants to increase profits as much as possible. It will do this by limiting investment and encouraging sales.

The implications for the marketing mix are as follows.

- Prices may be discounted (unless the product sold is price inelastic – in which case they will be raised) in order to increase revenue.
- Promotions will tend to focus on encouraging sales rather than, for example, developing a brand image.
- The firm may also adopt an exclusive or selective distribution strategy rather than an extensive distribution strategy – again with the intention of increasing sales.

The focus has moved away from factors such as brand image, loyalty and new product development. With less money being devoted to these areas, future profits may fall.

To answer this question well, you need to be clear what is meant by the phrase 'short-term profit maximization'. Write two sentences to explain this here.

The marketing mix will now focus on increasing sales. Write one sentence about the impact on each of these:
- **price**
- **promotion**
- **place (distribution).**

EXAMINER'S SECRETS
This is another example of a question where it is useful to consider both the short and the long-term implications for the firm.

Write two sentences explaining the possible long-term implications of pursuing this objective.

EXAM QUESTION 2

Agbrigg Tents Ltd is a firm that has specialized in the production of standardized tents and marquees. At a recent board meeting the decision was taken to become more marketing orientated by developing a wider range of products more closely reflecting customer needs. What are the possible implications for the firm?

Responding to customer needs gives the firm greater security in the market place.
- It helps combat competition.
- It may allow the firm to raise prices (uniqueness).
- It is the marketing function that will lead in the development of new products: they will emphasize the needs of the customer.

There may be resentment within the production function over their loss of status. They now have to design a product that meets the needs of the market rather than one that is standardized and minimizes cost.

State at least three ways the firm might benefit from being more marketing orientated.

Suggest ways the relationship between the marketing and production departments might change now that the firm is more marketing orientated.

© Pearson Education Limited 2001

EXAM QUESTION 1

While most firms target a market segment, Marty Lodge has made his money from a market niche. A motor car fanatic, Marty's enthusiasm for rebuilding saloon cars to higher specifications gave him the idea for a business.

Marty Lodge Motors was founded in 1984 to take new saloon cars and rebuild (customize) them to the owner's higher specifications.

Despite working in a very specialist market Marty has found that he has been able to charge very high prices and earn profits that are far higher than in the wider market segment.

Over the years demand has increased and with it the size of Marty Lodge Motors. He now employs ten men in a newly built garage. Even so, Marty has found that over the last few years prices and profits have fallen. More recently, he has also heard that a major motor car manufacturer plans to customize its own cars.

Discuss the situation Marty faces.

Before you start to answer the question, make sure you can distinguish between a market segment and a market niche. Write a short explanation of each here.

A market segment is made up of a group of people who exhibit similar buyer behaviour. This group of people is sufficiently large for a firm to develop products specifically for their use.

A market niche is really a subsection of a segment that offers very specialist business opportunities. It is normally too small a market to attract larger firms.

Now explain why prices and profits may be higher in the niche market that Marty works in.

Marty needs to charge high prices to cover his costs. He can charge high prices because he is providing a very specialist service that is highly valued by his customers. In economic terms we can say the demand curve for his product is price inelastic. Although some people may not be willing to pay his high prices there are enough who will pay for the firm to be profitable.

REVISION EXPRESS
For more on elasticity of demand see page 71 in the *Revision Express A-level Study Guide*.

Explain why, with growth in the market, prices and profits may have fallen.

As the size of the market grows, other firms are likely to move in to satisfy the additional demand. The competition between these firms may now prevent Marty Lodge Motors from charging such high prices and making such big profits.

Now explain why a large car manufacturer would want to enter a small segment of the car market.

The segment may be small but it is growing and it is also seen as being profitable. Another possible reason is that the general market for cars is mature and it is now difficult to increase sales or market share. Additionally, technology is such that a large manufacturer can easily customize cars.

The market and its segmentation

Most markets today are segmented in some way. However, because segmentation limits the size of the market, some firms consider developing products that have mass appeal within either the European or the global market.

MASS MARKETING

Mass marketing has many benefits for firms.

Think of some benefits that mass marketing might have for businesses.

- Larger market, larger profits
- Economies in marketing, production, and management
- Larger market will reduce payback period on investment

THE JARGON
Mass marketing is based on the idea that an undifferentiated product will be popular to everyone within a country or even in other countries.

Products that might have a global appeal include:

Now give at least two examples of products that might have a global appeal.

aircraft, computers, perfume, holidays, pop stars, medications.

SEGMENTATION

Segmentation is interesting to the marketeer if the buying behaviour of one group is different to other groups. Common ways of segmenting a market include by age, gender, income, ethnicity and interests. Here are some examples:

THE JARGON
Segmenting a market implies it is made up of lots of individuals who can be grouped in many different ways.

Food: *age* (baby products), *income* (luxury foods), *ethnicity* (oriental foods), *interests* (organic food).
Holidays: *age* (18–30), *income* (budget), *interests* (cruising), *ethnic* (visits to homeland).
Magazines: *age* (children's), *gender* (women's), *ethnicity* (Asian), *interests* (fishing).
Dress: *age* (teenagers'), *gender* (men's), *ethnic* (Afro-Caribbean), *interests* (football supporters).

Look at the products listed here. State four ways you might segment each product market. Think about age, income, ethnic origin, interests and gender.

Sometimes markets are more effectively segmented by usage. Take the case of toothpaste. The most common method of segmentation for toothpaste is to look at how or why it is used. For example, we can classify users on the basis of:

Smokers/non smokers, heavy users/light users, reason for use (sparkling teeth, mouth odour, flavour, decay prevention, price), loyalty of consumer.

WATCH OUT
You can't always segment the markets in the ways suggested.

The restaurant market could also be segmented by usage.

Give two or more examples of how you could segment the restaurant market by usage.

Lunch, evening, Sunday, fast food, celebration, gourmet.

Once a product market has been broken down into its different segments the firm is then able to develop a different marketing mix for each individual segment. This is often termed differentiated marketing.

Turn the page for some exam questions on this topic ▶

Product

AS AQA EDEXCEL OCR WJEC

The term 'product' is used by marketeers to refer to both goods and services. Marketeers are interested in the management of the firm's products so as to ensure the firm's objectives are achieved.

○ ○ ○

THE PRODUCT LIFE CYCLE

Most products have a limited life during which they can be marketed profitably. Each product will pass through four recognizable stages: **introduction, growth, maturity** and **decline**. All products will have a different life cycle as the period of time spent in each stage varies. By identifying where the product is in its life cycle, marketeers can devise the best possible marketing mix.

Introduction
High failure rate of products, little competition, frequent modifications, informative advertising, loss making.

Growth
Increasing sales, emergence of competition, some product modification, informative and persuasive advertising, profit-making, new product search.

Maturity
Rate of sales increase falls, product line widened, competition grows, sales and profits fall, persuasive advertising, marginal producers leave market, development of new products.

Decline
Falling product sales, less competition as producers leave market, reduced promotional expenditure, introduction of new products.

> **List the characteristics associated with each stage of the product life cycle (the first one has been done for you).**

> **REVISION EXPRESS**
> For more on advertising see page 72 in the *Revision Express A-level Study Guide*.

EXTENSION STRATEGIES

○ ○ ○

It is often possible to extend the life of a product beyond its maturity by the use of an extension strategy.

1 More frequent use	Changes made to physical appearance, image or packaging.	③
2 Extend product range	Baby toiletries promoted to adults, ladies' electric shavers.	④
3 Modify product	Frozen turkeys or chocolate crème eggs sold all year not just at Christmas or Easter.	①
4 Identify new uses	A food product extended by diet, slimline, low fat, low calorie versions.	②

> **Here are some extension strategies. Draw a line to match each strategy to an example.**

> **THE JARGON**
> Extension strategies may be *defensive* where they are trying to postpone the decline of a product or *offensive* where the aim is to reposition the product and give it a long-term future.

Turn the page for some exam questions on this topic ▶

● ● ●

EXAM QUESTION 1

These data relate to Caretours, a highly profitable company operating in four segments of the holiday market. Read the data and answer the questions that follow.

Holiday	Market growth 1997–2000(%)	Market share 1999(%)	Sales revenue (£ 000) 1997	1998	1999	2000
Overseas package	3	10	2 180	2 237	2 132	2 146
Cruises	4	7	560	1 030	1 300	1 410
Holiday camps	–6	5	1 350	1 110	810	720
Children's activity	9	2	–	252	487	487

Using the concept of the product life cycle analyse the sales prospects for each product.

The revenue figures for the overseas package suggest that it is in the maturity stage of the product life cycle. It is unlikely that there will be much growth in this area and eventually sales may decline.

It is difficult to make any firm judgement based on three years' results for children's activity holidays. However, in the absence of other information, it would seem that the company is having difficulty breaking into this market so this could imply a mature segment.

The revenue from cruises increased significantly between 1997 and 1999. Increases after that date have not been so large. This suggests that the market is moving from growth to maturity.

Over four years the revenue from holiday camps has declined by almost half. This suggests holiday camps are in the decline stage of the life cycle.

> **Overseas package and children activity holidays have been done for you. Read the suggested answers then add your responses for cruises and holiday camps.**

> **EXAMINER'S SECRETS**
> When you are analysing data always ask yourself 'what is the trend?'

Critically examine the company's product portfolio using the Boston matrix.

It is likely that overseas package holidays and cruises are cash cows because market growth seems to have slowed into maturity. The strong cash flows associated with cash cows probably account for the company being highly profitable.

The holiday camp segment is a dog as both firm and industry are experiencing falling sales. This product may soon have to be abandoned when it moves into loss.

The children's activity holiday segment is a question mark. In a fast growing market the company may be able to turn this into a star by increasing its market share. This may require a substantial investment by the firm.

The company does not have a balanced portfolio. With no stars to replace its cash cows, profitability may soon fall. This may cause problems in financing the question mark (children's activities).

> **Package holidays and cruises have been done for you. Add your answers for holiday camps and children's activity holidays.**

> **THE JARGON**
> The Boston matrix is an attempt to analyse a company's portfolio of products in terms of market growth and market share. Products are classified as question marks, stars, cash cows or dogs.

> **An ideal answer to this question would finish by assessing the company's product mix. Write your comments here.**

Price

Pricing decisions are crucial to the success of the business. Consumers often have a perception of the right price. Price your product too high and customers think they are being cheated. Charge too low a price and they question the quality. Clearly the marketeer has to be careful when setting the price.

PRICING THE PRODUCT: A CASE STUDY

○○○

DG Ltd is a small local double glazing firm which uses cost plus pricing. It is facing competition from a new company, Bestglass. Bestglass is using a number of price promotions (a form of competitive pricing) that are now affecting DG Ltd's sales.

Explain the term cost plus pricing. Why is it used by DG?

In cost plus pricing, a profit mark-up is added to the unit cost of each product. It is used by DG Ltd to guarantee the firm is profitable.

Explain 'competitive pricing'. Why is it used by Bestglass?

Competitive pricing; prices are set so as to match or better those of competitors. This enables Bestglass to build market share and recognition.

If DG Ltd adopts a competitive pricing policy what impact is this likely to have on consumers and the firms themselves?

In the short term, consumers will gain from lower prices and the firms will experience lower profitability or even losses. In the longer term, one of the firms may leave the market. Alternatively, the firms may decide to compete in other ways. In either case the consumer will pay a higher price.

Now answer these questions on pricing the product.

WATCH OUT
In an undifferentiated product market it is likely that firms will be forced into some form of competitive pricing policy.

EXAMINER'S SECRETS
Here is another example of where it is useful to think of both the short term and the long term.

PRICE SENSITIVITY

○○○

Price changes affect some products far more significantly than others. Thus a cut in the price of potatoes is likely to have little impact upon demand but a cut in the price of crisps may raise demand and total revenue significantly. This relationship between price and demand is referred to as the Price Elasticity of Demand (PED).

Complete the table indicating whether total revenue rises or falls.

Price change	Type of price elasticity	Impact on total revenue
Increase	Elastic demand	Falls
	Inelastic demand	Rises
Decrease	Elastic demand	Rises
	Inelastic demand	Falls

To increase total revenue it will have to reduce prices.

WATCH OUT
Make sure you can give some examples of products with price elastic or inelastic demand curves.

If a firm wanting to increase total revenue faces a price elastic demand curve what would you recommend it should do?

Turn the page for some exam questions on this topic ▶

For more on this topic, see pages 70–71 of the *Revision Express A-level Study Guide*

EXAM QUESTION 1

●●●

BC Unisex Hairsalon recently introduced a 10% price rise as a consequence of increases in costs. Now, demand for women's haircuts has fallen by 5% but demand for men's haircuts has fallen by 20%.

(a) Calculate the price elasticity of demand for men's and women's haircuts.

The PED for women is $\frac{5}{10}$ or 0.5.

The PED for men is $\frac{20}{10}$ or 2.

(b) Explain why the price elasticity of demand for men and women's haircuts may be different.

The demand curve for men's haircuts is price elastic – an increase in price has led to a reduction in the demand for men's haircuts. To increase demand (and total revenue) for men's haircuts the firm would have to reduce prices.

The demand curve for women's haircuts is price inelastic with a 10% increase in price leading to a less than proportionate fall in demand.

Apart from price, the demand depends on such things as income, tastes and competing products.

Here the price inelasticity of demand for women's haircuts may be due to the reputation of the salon or the relationship built up with the customers. The price elasticity for men's haircuts may be as a result of competition in the area.

The formula is:
$$\frac{\text{% Change in quantity demanded}}{\text{% Change in price}}$$

Describe the PED for men's haircuts.

Describe the PED for women's haircuts.

Now try to explain why the PEDs are different.

EXAM QUESTION 2

●●●

(a) What pricing strategies for new products are available to a firm?

Price skimming is charging the highest price that buyers will pay. It is used when demand is price inelastic and competition is low. This price will gradually be reduced as the market at that price becomes saturated. A skimming policy has the advantage that it enables the firm to recoup some of its high R&D costs.

A penetration price is set below the prices of competing products. The aim is to gain market share quickly and discourage the growth of competition. It is likely to be used where product demand is price elastic and competition could develop quickly. Penetration pricing might be used by a firm after first having skimmed the market.

(b) Which pricing strategy would you select for an innovative product?

For an innovative product, price skimming is best because demand is likely to be inelastic and competition low. This maximizes revenue.

There are two possibilities – price skimming and penetration pricing. Price skimming has been done for you. Now write a paragraph about penetration pricing.

WATCH OUT
The key words here are 'for new products'. In practice the firm might consider other pricing policies as well, for example full cost or psychological pricing.

EXAMINER'S SECRETS
Make sure you can give examples of firms using these different methods.

For more on this topic, see pages 72–73 of the *Revision Express A-level Study Guide*

Promotion

Promotion refers to the communication process between seller and buyer. There are four major methods of promotion – advertising, sales promotion, personal selling and publicity. Firms will use a range of these in their promotional strategy.

ADVERTISING

Institutional advertising is designed to improve the standing of the organization with the general public. If an organization is respected by the public they are more likely to buy its products.

Informative advertising conveys information and raises consumer awareness of a product. It can be used in the early stages of the product life cycle or after modifications.

Persuasive advertising is often used in the mature stage of the product life cycle where there are several similar products on the market. The aim is to persuade consumers to buy this firm's product rather than another firm's.

> Write one or two sentences describing each of these forms of advertising:
> • institutional
> • informative
> • persuasive.

> **THE JARGON**
> Advertising is defined as purchased, non-personal communication using mass media.

> **LINKS**
> For more information on the product life cycle see pages 31–32.

PERSONAL SELLING

This takes place when promotion is on a *person to person* basis. The major advantage is the consumer has the opportunity to ask questions about the product while the *salesperson* gains the confidence of the *consumer*. Apart from giving advice, salespeople may also demonstrate goods, take orders, collect payment, deliver goods and deal with *complaints*. The market intelligence gathered by the sales force can also provide the organization with valuable information on consumers and their requirements. The major disadvantage of personal selling is its *cost*. The recruitment, training and payment of a sales force may be very expensive.

> Fill the blank spaces in the text from this list:
> expensive, person to person, market intelligence, consumer, cost, salesperson, complaints, recruitment.

PROMOTIONAL MIX

Organizations often use more than one form of promotion to create a promotional mix. For instance, a double glazing company might use:
• a salesforce and possibly teleseales team
• sales literature promoting products
• internet site promoting firm's products
• product advertising
• sales promotions (for consumers or sales force)
• sponsor sports events
• point of sale displays in DIY shops
• publicity via press releases.

> What might a manufacturer of double glazed windows include in its promotional mix? Give at least three examples.

Turn the page for some exam questions on this topic ▶

EXAM QUESTION 1

The government is considering a ban on the advertising of tobacco products. Assess the implications of this.

Advertising is one of the ways a firm may promote its product to the consumer: In many cases the aim of advertising is to create brand loyalty.

In the short term, brand loyalty probably means that there will be little impact upon a tobacco firm's revenue and profits. In the longer term, the inability to advertise may mean fewer people smoke, thus reducing revenue and profits. However, firms may find other ways to promote products without advertising. An alternative is price competition.

Advertising and media firms would lose revenue and profits. Some other sales promotion firms may benefit, though. In the long term, if less people smoke then many other firms in different industries may benefit from the diverted consumer expenditure.

The government raises a lot of money through taxes on tobacco products. In the longer term this may be reduced by a ban on advertising. The government will have to find other ways to raise this lost revenue or reduce spending.

In the longer term, the consumer may have a healthier lifestyle and more money to spend on other products.

> First write two sentences saying what advertising is and why it is important.

> What are the short and long-term implications for the tobacco industry?

> Now outline the effect on other industries.

> What would be the effect on the government?

> What about the consumer?

EXAM QUESTION 2

Give two examples of how the following businesses should advertise to reach their consumers.
1. Local DIY firm
2. Expensive computer equipment supplier
3. National bridal retailer

> **EXAMINER'S SECRETS**
> Your choice should be based on reaching the largest number of potential customers at the lowest cost.
> Number 1 has been done for you. Have a go at 2 and 3.

1. The DIY firm must advertise locally. It could use local newspapers or radio. It might also consider posters in the locality.

2. People who are interested in expensive computer equipment will often buy specialist magazines. As they are interested in computers it is also likely they will use the internet. The supplier should consider advertising in these magazines and on selected websites on the internet.

3. Having a national presence, the bridal retailers might consider bridal or other magazines aimed at the 18–30 market. Advertising in these magazines could be reinforced by advertising in local papers and cinemas near their branches.

Place

'Place' is concerned with the way a product is made available to the consumer in a particular place. It is sometimes also referred to as distribution or marketing channels. The place element in the marketing mix is often considered to be unimportant but effective and efficient distribution channels may be the key to competitive advantage for a firm!

CHANNELS OF DISTRIBUTION   ○○○

The initial decision a firm has to take is whether to use intermediaries or sell direct to the public. Direct selling removes all market intermediaries, maximizes control of distribution and reduces loss of revenue. Factors that suggest direct selling is preferable include:

State at least two factors encouraging the use of direct selling.

- the need for an expert sales force to demonstrate products
- the need for specialist transport requirements
- buyers are geographically concentrated in one area.

Factors encouraging the use of intermediaries include:

State at least two factors encouraging the use of intermediaries.

- insufficient marketing expertise
- insufficient resources to finance sales force
- product range too small to justify sales force
- sales force costs too high because buyers spread over a wide area.

If a firm decides to sell indirectly through intermediaries one possibility is to sell directly to the retailer (**producer to retailer**). Thus a supermarket may purchase most of its products direct from the manufacturer. It is possible for the manufacturer and the retail outlet to liaise over point of sale display and sales promotions.

Another approach adopted by firms is '**producer to wholesaler**'. Advantages of this include:

Give two advantages of dealing with wholesalers.

Wholesalers sell in smaller lots. Firms' stockholding costs reduced. Wholesalers have more contacts than the firm. Greater likelihood of prompt payment.

FRANCHISING   ○○○

Franchising is an agreement between the owner of patents for goods or services (the franchiser) to give another person (the franchisee) the right to produce or sell those goods or services. Examples include:

Give three examples of franchise firms.

Kwikprint, Body Shop, Dynorod, Burger King, Pronuptia.

Give four likely terms in the franchise agreement.

The franchiser agrees to

- assign an exclusive sales territory
- allow the use of the trade name
- provide training and advice
- sell goods to the franchisee.

Turn the page for some exam questions on this topic ▶

For more on this topic, see pages 74–75 of the *Revision Express A-level Study Guide*

EXAM QUESTION 1   ●●●

A British manufacturer of paper products is launching a new range of paper tissue. What factors might affect the firm's selection of distribution channel?

Write an introductory paragraph listing the options available to the firm.

There are a variety of distribution channels that are available to this firm. It is possible for the firm to sell direct to the customer (this is becoming more important because of the internet). Another possibility is to sell to the retailer who then sells on to the consumer (approximately 60% of consumer goods use this channel). The third method is to sell to a wholesaler who sells on smaller quantities of these goods to smaller retailers.

In practice there are many factors you could consider including:
1. the extent of market coverage needed
2. distribution costs increase with longer distribution channels
3. could the existing distribution channels be used?
4. distribution decisions must be consistent with other elements of the marketing mix.

Write one or two sentences on points 2 and 4.

Point 2. Each link in the distribution chain has to add something to the price of the product in order to make a profit. In long chains distribution costs can exceed the production costs.
Point 4. In deciding what distribution channels are to be used the firm must look at how the product is priced and promoted. For example, if the product is priced and promoted for exclusivity then the firm must be selective in its use of outlets.

REVISION EXPRESS
For more on pricing methods see pages 70–71 of the *Revision Express A-level Study Guide.*

EXAM QUESTION 2   ●●●

What benefits and problems would business owners face from franchising their business idea to other people?

State at least two benefits a business owner would gain from franchising a business idea.

Rapid expansion can take place without high capital costs. The franchiser also benefits from the initial fee and royalties paid by the franchisee. Franchisees may be also more committed to making the new outlet succeed than salaried managers.

State at least two problems a business owner would face as a result of franchising a business idea.

As the franchisees are self-employed it is difficult to control their activities and ensure operational uniformity. This may reflect badly on the whole franchise operation. Longer term, the franchisee often wishes to terminate the agreement to avoid paying royalties to the franchiser.

WATCH OUT
Remember a firm can use more than one distribution channel!

Market research

Market research is the collection, collation, analysis and evaluation of data relating to the marketing and consumption of goods and services. Successful marketing enables organizations to reduce the risks associated with launching new products, entering new markets or developing existing products. It will not, however, entirely eliminate the risk.

DON'T FORGET
Initial market research by Sony indicated that the Walkman would not sell. Fortunately the Chairman refused to believe the results and launched what became one of the most successful products of modern times.

THE JARGON
A market is anywhere that buyers and sellers can come together to exchange goods and services.

ROLE OF MARKET RESEARCH

Market research is an attempt to gather information about a market and to analyse it in a scientific manner in order to:
Make sales predictions: in order to determine future output levels and to design new products and services.
Understand the market: to determine the extent of the market, to identify existing customers, to identify potential customers and to determine what influences consumer buying habits.
Identify new opportunities: exploring the market either to test newly designed products or to identify new wants and desires among the customers.

SECONDARY AND PRIMARY RESEARCH

Secondary research involves the unearthing of data that already exists either from within the business or from outside agencies:

THE JARGON
Secondary research is also referred to as desk research.

Internal: sales figures, previous market reports, sales representatives' reports, stock movements, etc.
External: government publications, reports from trade associations, trade journals, commercial data specialists, e.g. Dun and Bradstreet, Mintel.

List at least two more internal and external sources of data.

Primary research is the process of gathering data direct from the target market. The main methods of collecting field research are:

THE JARGON
Primary research is also referred to as field research.

Personal interviews: expensive and time consuming.
Telephone interviews: cheap to conduct and easy to cover a wide geographical area.
Postal surveys: cheap to conduct but suffers from poor response rates, often well below 10%.
Direct observation: gives insights into how customers react to certain displays.
Test marketing: good for assessing market reaction before launching a product on a wider basis.

For each of the five methods of collecting primary data briefly state either an advantage or disadvantage associated with the method.

EXAMINER'S SECRETS
Make sure you can accurately define and explain the differences between the different sampling techniques. Many candidates struggle with this, so it's a good way of impressing the examiner!

SAMPLING

In order to obtain a full picture of the market it would be necessary to ask all of the customers (known as the population). As this is prohibitively expensive only a small number are asked (a sample).
There are a number of sampling methods such as:

- random sampling
- quota sampling
- stratified sampling.

List three forms of sampling.

DON'T FORGET
Sampling introduces uncertainty into the findings as only a fraction of the population is asked.

Turn the page for some exam questions on this topic ▶

EXAM QUESTION 1

Many research methods use questionnaires as the basis of their information gathering. In the formulation of a questionnaire:
(a) What type of questions can be asked?

Questions can be:
- closed questions that only allow a limited response, often from a predetermined list of alternatives
- open questions that allow a more detailed investigation of the interviewees' attitudes.

(b) How should it be designed so that it is effective?

For the questionnaire to be effective it must:
- have clear, unambiguous questions
- not rely on calculation or the subject's memory
- be easy to understand and avoid jargon
- not contain leading questions that suggest a particular answer or opinion
- be reasonably short
- be easy to complete and tabulate
- be conducted in a polite and thankful manner.

Mention the two main types of questions.

DON'T FORGET
Questionnaires should be pre-tested on a small sample group before being used on a wider basis. In this way any errors or ambiguities can be identified and removed.

Now have a go at part (b).

EXAM QUESTION 2

John-Paul Associates build and manage leisure centres on a national basis throughout the UK. They are considering opening their first centre in the Lake District area close to the market town of Kendal.
The board of directors has requested market research be done on the proposal.

	Advantages	Disadvantages
Desk	Cheap to obtain Based on actual data about the leisure industry Samples can be much larger	Data might be out of date Data not specific to the Kendal area Data was originally collected for another purpose
Field	Designed to answer specific objectives Research findings only available to J-P Data is current and specific to the area	Expensive to design and collect It is a time-consuming task Unless professionally designed it is easy to introduce bias

In the table provided identify three advantages and three disadvantages of John-Paul Associates using desk and field research in order to build information on the proposed project.

EXAMINER'S SECRETS
Choosing between field and desk research is always a question of balancing time and cost against accuracy of results. Consideration of these problems will show evidence of evaluation.

Workforce planning

(AS) AQA OCR WJEC

Workforce planning is the process of anticipating the organization's future labour requirements. It reflects the organization's future strategy. This not only requires the human resource function to look at the numbers employed but also the mix of skills. Workforce planning is also affected by changes in technology, law and social and demographic factors.

REVISION EXPRESS
See the Revision Express A-level Study Guide pages 14–20 for more on these influences.

THE WORKFORCE PLAN OOO

The workforce plan is a form of supply and demand management. It aims to reduce the risk of either a future shortage or a surplus of labour. You should be aware that either situation is costly to the firm.

Where the workforce plan indicates the likelihood of a shortage or surplus of labour, action should be taken to ensure that situation does not develop. Thus a predicted shortage of computer technicians could be overcome by recruitment of new employees with the right skills. Other strategies to address a shortage of labour include:

- training and development of existing staff
- use of temporary contracts or agency workers
- reducing labour turnover (look at pay and conditions of work)
- encourage overtime working
- productivity bargaining and/or automation.

List at least four other ways in which a shortage of labour might be overcome.

- Restricting recruitment
- Early retirement
- Redeployment and retraining
- Redundancies
- Eliminate overtime

List at least four ways in which a surplus of labour might be overcome.

RECRUITMENT OOO

Recruitment is an important part of the work of any human resource department. In many organizations you will find that this work has been centralized. This has various advantages.

- There is one focal point for all communications and applications from outside the organization.
- Centralization ensures that recruitment procedures are followed all the time.
- Recruitment law is complex and line managers may not have sufficient knowledge of it.

Give three reasons why an organization might want to centralize recruitment.

Internal promotion and external recruitment both have advantages:

Here are some arguments for internal promotion (I) and external recruitment (E). Indicate which the argument is in favour of by putting (I) or (E) after each sentence.

provides new blood (E)
reduced recruitment costs (I)
internal promotion may cause friction amongst other workers (I)
it can improve employee motivation (I)
the person is known to the firm (I)
internal promotion merely transfers the recruitment problem elsewhere. (E)

Turn the page for some exam questions on this topic ▶

For more on this topic, see pages 86–87 of the Revision Express A-level Study Guide

EXAM QUESTION 1 •••

THE JARGON
A person is made redundant when the employer can show that the type of work offered by the employee is no longer required or that demand for that kind of labour has fallen.

Due to improvements in its computerized management information system, Bramhope Insurance is considering making 50 people redundant at its Head Office.

Discuss the problems the firm might face as a result of making people redundant.

- The morale and motivation of the workforce may fall. This may result in reduced quality and output. Some valuable staff may leave even though not directly affected by the redundancy situation.
- Redundancy is costly. It could be even more costly if opposed by trade unions that disrupt operations. This might limit finance for projects.
- The image of the firm could suffer. This might affect future sales or recruitment.

Write at least two sentences on each of the following: morale, cost, and image of the firm.

REVISION EXPRESS
People often resist change. For more on this area see pages 46–47 of the Revision Express A-level Study Guide.

- The best way of maintaining the morale of the workforce is to keep them informed of what is going to happen, give guarantees where possible and let those being made redundant know what help they are going to be given by the firm.
- Compulsory redundancies can be reduced to a minimum by freezing recruitment, inviting people to volunteer, redeploying people (with retraining). The firm may also rely on natural wastage.
- All that has been said above would help the image of the firm. It may also be necessary to spend more money promoting the image it wants to project.

Now say what steps the firm could take to limit these problems. The first is done for you.

EXAM QUESTION 2 •••

What arguments would you use to persuade a manager that although training may be seen as costly and time-consuming, it has benefits that outweigh these factors?

- Well-trained workers need less supervision. This reduces costs and allows the manager to have a wider span of control.
- Well-trained workers are more profitable because they are faster and more accurate.
- Training can also reduce costs arising from accidents.
- If a firm has a good training programme this may improve the image of the firm and may attract good quality applicants to positions in the firm.

Try to think of at least three arguments.

THE JARGON
Span of control refers to the number of subordinates responsible to and reporting directly to a manager.

IF YOU HAVE TIME
Write a list of the benefits the employee gains through training.

Turn the page for some exam questions on this topic ▶

Organization structure

(AS) AQA EDEXCEL OCR WJEC

Early management writers were concerned to find the one best form of organization structure. Today it is accepted that there is no one best organization structure and that what works for one firm may be disastrous for another. You will also find that an organization will change its structure over time as it grows, or in response to periodic crises.

> We trained hard, but it seemed that every time we were beginning to form up into teams we would be reorganized.
> I was later to learn that we tend to meet any situation by reorganizing and a wonderful method it can be for creating an illusion of progress, while producing confusion, inefficiency and demoralization.
> GAIUS PETRONIUS AD 56

ORGANIZATION STRUCTURE

The formal organization is the deliberately planned structure of roles within the organization. It is the means by which the activities of many people are coordinated so as to achieve organizational objectives. It is often presented pictorially in an organization chart.

1. Chain of command — The number of subordinates directly reporting to and controlled by a manager. (3)
2. Informal organization — The policy of delegating decision-making power to lower levels in the organization. (5)
3. Span of control — An organization based on rules, procedures and hierarchical authority. Weber argued it was an efficient rational organization. (4)
4. Bureaucracy — The vertical line of authority within an organization. It enables orders to be passed down through the organization. (1)
5. Decentralization — The removal of one or more layers of management from an organization's hierarchy. (6)
6. Delayering — The network of social relationships developed by people while at work. (2)

Here are some key terms that are used when talking about organization structure. Draw a line linking each term to the correct definition.

DELEGATION

Delegation means passing decision-making power down through the hierarchy from manager to subordinate. Delegation allows the manager to concentrate on more important parts of his job. It also helps train the next generation of managers. There are three important aspects to delegation: responsibility, authority and accountability.

• Responsibility: in accepting a task the employee accepts the duty to see it is carried out properly.
• Authority: the subordinate must be given the necessary authority to carry out their responsibilities.
• Accountability: having been given the authority and responsibility to carry out a task the subordinate is accountable for their efforts.

Write one sentence explaining each of these terms.

For more on this topic, see pages 90–91 of the *Revision Express A-level Study Guide*

EXAM QUESTION 1

Outwood Construction Ltd is a house building firm. The firm has adopted a functional structure with five departments: Purchasing, Construction, Sales, Personnel and Finance. The firm is owner-managed and the owner has tended to use a narrow span of control together with an autocratic management style. Despite growing rapidly over the last decade profits have not increased proportionately. A firm of management consultants has suggested that a functional structure is inappropriate and recommended the firm adopt a matrix organizational structure.

(a) What problems may arise from adopting a functional structure?

As decision-making is normally concentrated at the top, functionally structured organizations tend to be slow in responding to external change. Moreover, the specialization of departments and their narrow perspective leads to communication and coordination problems.

Write a paragraph outlining problems that may arise with a functional structure, then have a go at question (b).

(b) Explain the possible link between a narrow span of control and an autocratic management style.

An autocratic leadership style implies that all major decisions are made at the top of the firm. The manager therefore has little time to deal with subordinates and so has a narrow span of control.

A wider span of control forces superiors to delegate more to subordinates and is associated with a democratic management style.

(c) Complete the diagram below and use it to explain the matrix structure, and how it relates to a departmental structure. What are the advantages of the matrix structure?

Complete the diagram opposite and use it to explain the term matrix structure.

The departmental structure still exists but acts as a resource bank for the project managers to draw on. Thus, a project manager will go to each of the departments and request staff to help complete the project. After the project is completed, team members return to their parent department until another project team is formed.

First explain how the departmental structure and matrix structure relate to one another.

Departmental barriers are broken down and a teamwork approach is encouraged. There is also tighter control of the project through the coordinating role of the project leader.

Now mention some advantages of the matrix structure.

Motivation in theory

An organization is interested in the motives behind people's behaviour because it wants to know what makes them perform well at work. It can then use that knowledge to maximize its employees' effectiveness.

SCIENTIFIC MANAGEMENT AND HUMAN RELATIONS APPROACHES

○○○

F W Taylor established what became known as the 'scientific' school of management. Taylor believed that *manual* workers were motivated primarily by *money* and were not interested in *work*. The role of the manager therefore was to devise the best way of doing the job through *work study* and to motivate workers through the use of high *incentive* payments. The major criticism of this approach was that work is *dehumanized* and the *social* influences on employee behaviour are ignored.

> The passage has some words missing. Use the following list to complete the gaps:
> social, work, scientific, incentive, manual, money, dehumanized, work study.

The human relations school's understanding of employee motivation was entirely different. It relied heavily on the work of Mayo and his 'Hawthorne Plant' experiments, which concluded:

* people are motivated by social needs not money
* division of labour destroys enjoyment of work
* work groups have a bigger impact on worker behaviour than money or organizational controls.

> What are the major conclusions of the Hawthorne Plant experiments?

The human relations school was criticized though for not recognizing the conflict of interest within industry. Paying attention to workers' social needs would not necessarily improve motivation or productivity.

MASLOW AND HERZBERG

○○○

> Complete the diagram, which relates to Maslow's hierarchy of needs.

self actualization

challenging work

ego and esteem — status symbols

social — friendships at work

safety — employment security

physiological — pay

> WATCH OUT
> Make sure you can distinguish between the content and context of the job and relate this to both Maslow's and Herzberg's work.

Herzberg's two-factor theory looks at factors that make a manager feel good or bad about his job. Hygiene factors cause dissatisfaction when absent but little satisfaction when present.

Motivator factors are those which create *satisfaction* and cause an employee to work harder. Possible factors include a sense of achievement on completing work or promotion prospects.

> Explain what you understand by the term 'motivator' factors.

Turn the page for some exam questions on this topic ▶

●●●

EXAM QUESTION 1

As a university student John Cooke was very pleased to land a job stacking shelves one night a week at the supermarket. £45 for ten hours' work wasn't bad, he thought. On his first night the supervisor gave each of the five workers a list of aisles to fill up and told them to 'get on with it'. Everyone seemed too busy to help so John learnt the job by watching others. It was a pretty lonely job with no one to talk to. In addition lighting was poor and it was cold. The rest break that night was interesting. John learnt that the supervisors were generally unhelpful, slow to praise and quick to blame. He also learnt that labour turnover on the nightshift was high and that the workers never completed filling the aisles allocated to them. These were left for the day staff to complete.

(a) Use Herzberg's two factor theory to analyse the situation facing the workers.

According to Herzberg there are five motivating factors: achievement, recognition, the work itself, responsibility and advancement. From the information given it is difficult to see how the workers could be motivated. Certainly, they have responsibility but the actions of the supervisors suggest that this isn't valued and the other motivating factors are absent.

> Part of the answer has already been done for you.

Hygiene factors cause dissatisfaction when absent but little satisfaction when present. From the text it seems that many hygiene factors are absent. Supervision is poor, relationships with the supervisors are poor, there is only limited social contact and working conditions are poor. This probably explains the high labour turnover.

> Now write at least three sentences about the hygiene factors and the workers.

(b) The text suggests that productivity is not as high as it should be. How do you think that F W Taylor would have dealt with the situation?

To maximize the worker's efforts Taylor would have first analysed their jobs and the equipment they used. He would have found the best way of doing the job and insisted the workers worked this way. This would be the supervisor's responsibility.

Taylor would also have made changes to the way the workers were paid by introducing an incentive system. For example, a low rate could be given for finishing the first four aisles but a much higher rate for finishing the fifth or even the sixth aisle.

> Part of this has been done for you.

(c) Unlike Taylor, Herzberg did not believe that pay was a motivating factor. Why was this?

Herzberg believed pay is a hygiene factor that causes dissatisfaction if absent. Thus if an employee is underpaid this will be a cause of dissatisfaction. Where an employee's pay is good this will soon be taken for granted and so will not motivate.

> THE JARGON
> In Herzberg's terms an incentive scheme may result in *movement* but not *motivation*.

Motivation in practice

Motivating its employees is important to any organization. Motivated employees are less likely to leave the organization or be absent from work. They are also likely to produce work of a higher quality and are willing to take on greater responsibilities. Yet there is no simple answer to the question of how to motivate employees because every person and every situation is different.

SYMPTOMS AND CAUSES OF POOR MOTIVATION ○○○

A symptom is the outward sign of a problem. A cause is the reason the problem exists. Thus labour absenteeism may be the symptom while the cause behind the symptom may be poor conditions of work.

Poor quality work	S	Job insecurity	C
Poor pay	C	Failure to meet deadlines	S
Monotonous work	C	Disciplinary problems	S
Not part of social group	C	Changes to work groups	C
Poor communication	S	Sullen attitudes	S

Here are some symptoms and causes of poor motivation. Place S against those you consider to be symptoms and C against those that are causes.

JOB DESIGN AND MOTIVATION ○○○

It is important that employees enjoy their work yet many jobs are dull and uninteresting because they are repetitive.

- Inattention may result in mistakes being made or accidents.
- Stress is often related to 'high workload, low discretion' jobs, e.g. telesales.
- The relationship between the firm and its workers may suffer.

Job rotation, enlargement and enrichment are all ways to make work less monotonous.

State at least two problems that may arise for the firm as a result of repetitive work.

Job rotation is a situation in which staff are trained in a number of different jobs. Staff are then rotated through these jobs so as to reduce monotony. The employer also benefits through greater staff flexibility. However workers may object if it disturbs social groups.

Job enlargement is an attempt to make a job less boring by adding a number of different tasks to it. It has the effect of lengthening the time before the cycle is repeated.

Job enrichment involves the worker being given greater responsibilities and challenges in the work undertaken. This could be introducing new tasks, removing controls or increasing accountability. It is therefore a 'vertical extension of the job'.

Explain what each term means. (the first has been done for you.)

THE JARGON
Both job rotation and enlargement are examples of 'horizontal extension of the job'. This means that the extra tasks are of the same level of difficulty and do not give the employee any more responsibility.

Turn the page for some exam questions on this topic ▶

For more on this topic, see pages 94–95 of the *Revision Express A-level Study Guide*

EXAM QUESTION 1

Between 1995 and 2000, Osett plc has been transformed. A loss-making washing machine company with a history of poor labour relations, by June 2000 it had doubled output, increased profits and improved labour relations. Wages had increased but only in line with inflation. So what had happened? The assembly line technology had been replaced by work groups who built a unit from scratch. Three-man teams were responsible for planning, organizing and controlling their own work. They also decided what jobs each team member would do. Three management levels had disappeared and the remaining managers empowered to take on wider challenges. In several ways the firm has found empowerment to be a valuable intrinsic reward.

(a) Why might a firm want to replace the 'assembly line technology'?

Assembly line technology is a good example of a 'high workload, low discretion' job where workers have little control over their working lives. It may cause stress and/or poor labour relations.

THE JARGON
The removal of management levels throughout an organization is often referred to as delayering.

In these sorts of questions, the examiner will not be impressed if you only write one short sentence – always try to develop your answer, rather than giving just the most basic information.

(b) State at least two benefits the workers get from working in teams.

The workers are more in control of their working lives. The jobs are more interesting and there is likely to be more social interaction.

(c) Explain what is meant by 'the firm has found empowerment to be a valuable intrinsic reward'.

Empowerment means giving workers more control over their working lives. Empowerment is thought to improve motivation because the worker now finds the job more interesting, challenging or significant. These are what Herzberg calls the motivators and as the drive comes from within the person it is an example of intrinsic motivation as opposed to extrinsic motivation (wages and fringe benefits).

THE JARGON
Assembly line technology involves part-finished goods moving from one work station to another by means of conveyor belts.

(d) The case tends to suggest that money is not important as a motivator. How far do management writers agree?

Taylor regarded money, particularly when in the form of an incentive scheme, to be a very effective way of motivating individuals to work hard (but Herzberg might argue this was movement not motivation).

Mayo argued that the key to employee motivation was attention to their social needs.

Herzberg regarded money as a hygiene factor rather than a motivator. If money was considered unsatisfactory the worker would be dissatisfied but where it was satisfactory it would be taken for granted rather than motivate. Vroom suggested that motivation was determined by the worker's expectations as to whether their efforts would receive just rewards.

Two points have been made for you.

Leadership

Leadership may be defined as the means by which individuals or groups are persuaded to work towards the achievement of organizational goals. A leader is, therefore, any person who has the power to exercise control over others.

CLASSIFYING LEADERS

Leaders are sometimes classified as autocratic, democratic or laissez-faire. Each style has different characteristics, strengths and weaknesses.

1 autocratic — There is little direction or discipline given by the leader. The subordinates either accept or reject the responsibility. ③

2 democratic — Power lies in the hands of the leader who makes decisions alone. Communication is one way with little opportunity for feedback from subordinates. ①

3 laissez-faire — Although the leader retains the right to make the decisions, power is shared with the subordinates and they contribute to decision-making. ②

Autocratic: *Quick decisions can be made. Does not encourage initiative or commitment.*

Democratic: *Can be highly motivating for subordinates. Decision-making might take a long time.*

Laissez-faire: *Can be motivating for some employees. Often results in high frustration and low productivity.*

CONTINGENCY APPROACHES TO LEADERSHIP

A number of writers argue the best form of leadership varies according to the circumstances of the situation. To them a good leader is one who analyses the factors in the situation and chooses the appropriate style. The factors normally considered are:

The leader: *the leader's feelings on sharing decisions, their interest in subordinates' personal growth, their confidence in the subordinates' training.*

The subordinates: *their need for independence and responsibility; their confidence in their ability to deal with the problem.*

The situation: *the importance and complexity of the decision; time or money constraints; organizational values, e.g. emphasis on results or developing people.*

Turn the page for some exam questions on this topic ▶

Sidebar notes (left page):

- Draw a line linking each description to the correct leadership style.

- **THE JARGON** The laissez-faire leadership style is also known as free rein.

- Identify one strength and one weakness for each of the leadership styles.

- State two factors within the leader that might affect his leadership style.

- State at least two factors within the subordinates that might affect the leader's style.

- State at least two factors within the situation that might affect the leader's style.

For more on this topic, see pages 96–97 of the *Revision Express A-level Study Guide*

EXAM QUESTION 1

What leadership style would you use in the following situations?

(a) After higher than expected losses within the firm your department has been informed that its budget is to be reduced by 25%. Three or four members of staff will be made redundant. Full information on all the staff is available from the Human Resources Department.

This is a decision that must be taken by the manager alone in an autocratic manner. It is likely that staff, throughout the firm, are already worried about the situation. To involve departmental staff in deciding who should be made redundant would be very unproductive. Instead of concentrating on the work of the department they would be completely focused on who should go. Social relationships may also be so damaged that certain members of the department would never be able to work together again.

(b) The firm wishes to stagger starting and finishing work times so as to relieve traffic congestion. It doesn't matter what times each department chooses as long as everyone conforms to that decision.

This decision affects everyone in the department. It is a decision where everyone's view is as valuable and important as the next person's. To make the decision without consulting the subordinates is likely to damage the leader's relationships with staff. It is also unlikely that the leader would get the commitment to the decision that is required. A democratic approach is needed.

EXAM QUESTION 2

'You can't trust your workers these days, you know!' said one manager to a colleague. 'They're all lazy.' 'Oh I don't know,' the other replied, 'mine seem pretty keen. Indeed, I think that if you treat them as lazy and untrustworthy that's what you'll get!'

How far do you agree with these comments?

McGregor divided managers into two types. Theory X managers believe workers dislike work and will avoid it if they can. Theory Y managers, however, believe that employees like work and want responsibility.

A Theory X manager will institute a control system that reflects his view of his subordinates and ensures that they do their work whether they want to or not. In this situation even the motivated workers are likely to give up trying and lose interest in work.

Sidebar notes (right page):

- In each case, you should explain your answer.

- **EXAMINER'S SECRETS** Think about the implications of this decision on the leader and his subordinates.

- **REVISION EXPRESS** For more on the impact of change on individuals see the *Revision Express A-level Study Guide* pages 46–47.

- These two managers have very different attitudes to their workers. A good answer to this question would mention McGregor; how would he have described them?

- Explain why treating employees as lazy and untrustworthy should mean that they do their work whether they want to or not.

Scale of production

Most businesses start small and expand over time. As they grow they are able to take advantage of economies of scale. This has the effect of reducing the unit costs of production making the organization more competitive. You need to know the reasons behind the desire to expand, how economies can be achieved and what limits there are to growth.

THE JARGON

Economies of scale are those savings and unit cost reductions gained through expanding the level of output.

THE IMPORTANCE OF SCALE   ○○○

Firms aim to grow in order to:

* reduce unit costs – this will improve competitiveness
* gain market share – a firm with some monopoly power can influence market prices
* reduce risk – by diversifying in terms of product and market
* survive – larger firms are more able to resist takeover bids.

ECONOMIES OF SCALE   ○○○

DON'T FORGET

Total costs are made up of fixed costs and variable costs.

As output increases, the firm's fixed costs (which must be paid irrespective of the size of output) are spread over a larger number of units, thus reducing average costs. Likewise variable costs per unit can be reduced by the following economies of scale.

For each economy of scale provide an example that illustrates how unit costs can be reduced.

* **Purchasing:** large firms can buy in bulk and enjoy higher discounts.
* **Technical:** large-scale modern equipment will improve efficiency especially if flow production techniques are used. This will reduce unit production costs.
* **Specialization:** larger firms can apply division of labour more effectively with the employment of specialist staff e.g. purchasing agents, technicians etc. This will improve productivity.
* **Financial:** prospective investors regard large firms as less of a risk and are willing therefore to offer loan capital at lower rates of interest.

IF YOU HAVE TIME

Investigate economies of scale that can be achieved in marketing, administration and welfare facilities.

DISECONOMIES OF SCALE   ○○○

THE JARGON

Diseconomies of scale are factors that cause unit costs to rise when output increases due to inefficiencies.

Despite the existence of potential economies of scale, many organizations prefer to remain small. The factors that influence such decisions include finance, the market, and the owner's objectives. Explain how each of these can limit the extent of business expansion.

Explain how each diseconomy can lead to higher unit costs.

* **Co-ordination problems:** larger organizations require more levels of management. Meetings of senior staff, to coordinate the increased activity, represent a considerable extra overhead cost.
* **Communication problems:** large firms have many layers of hierarchy that may result in more one-way communication. This could result in lower morale among the workforce, a fall in productivity and a subsequent rise in production costs.

Turn the page for some exam questions on this topic ▶

For more on this topic, see pages 114–115 of the *Revision Express A-level Study Guide*

EXAM EXERCISE

Brooke Ltd is a medium-sized firm that specializes in modernizing second-hand printing machines for resale to developing countries. Fixed costs are made up of factory premises and permanent staff. Variable costs are composed largely of spare parts and overtime working for the small group of specialist technicians. The costs for a typical month are given below. Complete the last two columns of the table by calculating the total cost and unit costs for each level of output. Then determine the output range over which economies and diseconomies of scale exist.

When you tackle this, remember that:
Total costs = Fixed costs + Variable costs
Unit cost = $\dfrac{\text{Total cost}}{\text{Output}}$

Output	Fixed costs (£000)	Variable costs (£000)	Total costs (£000)	Unit/average cost
1	100	90	190	190
2	100	170	270	135
3	100	245	345	115
4	100	316	416	104
5	100	385	485	97
6	100	452	552	92
7	100	509	609	87
8	100	628	728	91
9	100	746	846	94
10	100	880	980	98

Analyse the completed table and fill in the gaps here.

Economies of scale exist over the output range = 1 to 7
Diseconomies of scale begin at output = 8

EXAM QUESTION 1

Despite the existence of potential economies of scale, many organizations prefer to remain small. The factors that influence such decisions include finance, the market, and the owner's objectives. Explain how each of these can limit the extent of business expansion.

Write at least two sentences for each factor.

Finance: Investment is not available as many investors consider smaller firms to be more of a risk. Small firms have less collateral to offer as security for loans.

The market: Many markets are small by nature and can only support a small business. Examples would include local services such as a plumber, hairdresser, dentist or highly specialist fields such as art restoration.

The owner's objectives: Many businesses are owner-managed and the owner wishes to retain full control over the business. The owner might also be unwilling to take the risk associated with expansion as it often involves investing or borrowing more funds. This is often true of small family concerns where the principal objective is to provide the family members with employment.

AS AQA EDEXCEL OCR WJEC

The choice of production method depends on the nature of the product, the total demand for it, its expected life cycle, the size of the firm, and the resources available. Different combinations of these factors will result in different production methods even for the same type of product.

THE MAIN PRODUCTION METHODS

Job production: for the manufacture of unique products to exact specifications.

A highly skilled and versatile workforce is required to produce single, one-off products with little chance of a repeat order. Machinery tends to be general-purpose. Productivity is low as it is normally labour-intensive with a significant set-up time. Examples include the Channel Tunnel and your hair cut.

Batch production: a method where a large number (a 'batch') of identical products pass through each stage of a production process together.

The labour needs to be skilled only in limited tasks, as the product is more standardized, with a reasonable level of demand and the opportunity for repeat orders. The use of specialized machinery enables economies of scale to be achieved. Productivity is high as it is more capital-intensive. Examples include shoe manufacture and shirt making where each size, colour and style go through the process stages together.

Flow production: generally a mass production method where items move continuously from one production stage to another.

This is a capital-intensive method. Semi-skilled or unskilled labour can be used as the process is often highly automated. This automation results in high productivity especially when production is organized on a 24-hour continuous basis. Huge economies of scale can be achieved through bulk purchasing of materials and long production runs. Demand must be high and stable to justify the enormous capital investment required. Examples include soft drink bottling and most car manufacture.

EXAMINER'S SECRETS
For job, batch and flow production methods write a paragraph identifying:
• the type of labour required
• the likely extent of demand
• the type of machinery needed.
Comment on the level of productivity and give two examples of products produced in this way.

EXAMINER'S SECRETS
Many candidates fail to give a good definition of batch production. 'Batch production is where items are produced in batches' is not a very revealing answer. Learn the definition given here!

DON'T FORGET
The movement of the products determines whether there is batch or flow production. If the items move individually to the next stage, there is flow production.

Turn the page for some exam questions on this topic ▶

EXAM QUESTION 1

For each of the products listed below, determine the most likely production method and explain your answer.

Shirts for a football team: batch. The demand is limited in number. Shirts will only be replaced each season and the design might be altered.

A nationally popular breakfast cereal: flow. The product is standard. Demand is high and constant.

White paint for walls and ceilings: flow. This is a standard product. Demand is high as white is a basic colour used in most buildings.

Repairs to a car: job. Each job is unique to that car. Skilled labour and specific parts will be needed.

Freshly made cakes: batch. Demand is regular. A batch of cakes can move from one process to another; e.g. from baking to icing.

Visit to the dentist: job. The labour required is highly skilled. Diagnosis and treatment will be specific to each patient.

In each case, try to give two reasons for your choice of method.

DON'T FORGET
The type of production method will depend on a variety of factors including the level of demand, the amount of standardization and the extent that mechanization can be applied.

EXAM QUESTION 2

AJS Ltd, a manufacturer of camping equipment, has experienced rising demand for its lightweight tent favoured by backpackers and weekend hikers. For the first time the firm has received significant orders from overseas for this product. At present the tent is made using a batch production method that produces 400 tents per week. At this rate customers must wait three weeks for their orders to be completed. The firm is contemplating the introduction of a flow production system. Identify three advantages and three disadvantages of making this change.

List three advantages here.

1. Output will significantly increase thus allowing AJS Ltd to complete orders more quickly.
2. It can take advantage of the overseas market.
3. Significant economies of scale should reduce unit costs enabling the tents to have a higher profit margin or to become more competitive by reducing the price.

EXAMINER'S SECRETS
Write in context by mentioning the company, the product and the specific market, e.g. introducing flow production will allow AJS Ltd to become more competitive in the camping equipment market by reducing costs and delivery time.

Now identify three disadvantages that AJS might face.

1. AJS Ltd must be certain that demand will be high and constant before it commits significant financial resources to new equipment and processes.
2. Worker motivation might be affected if the new process involves change or leads to fewer jobs.
3. Breakdowns will prove more costly as the entire process will be affected.

LINKS
For more information on motivation see pages 45–46.

For more on this topic, see pages 116–117 of the *Revision Express A-level Study Guide*

© Pearson Education Limited 2001

For more on this topic, see pages 118–119 of the Revision Express A-level Study Guide

Capacity utilization

AS AQA EDEXCEL OCR WJEC

Capacity is the maximum output that an organization can produce in a time period with a given quantity of resources. Most firms aim to produce near to or at full capacity in order to reduce the cost per unit.

LINKS
For more information on how a business determines its capacity see 'Scale of production pages 51–52.

MEASUREMENT ○○○

Capacity utilization is a measure of the effective use of a firm's resources and is calculated using the formula:

$$\text{Capacity utilization} = \frac{\text{Actual output per period}}{\text{Full capacity output per period}} \times 100$$

Capacity use is measured as a percentage of the maximum.
For example, a business with a full capacity of 40 000 units per month is currently producing 36 800 units per month.

$$\text{Capacity utilization} = \frac{36\ 800}{40\ 000} \times 100 = 92\%$$

The business has 8% spare capacity.

Calculate the capacity utilization, then the spare capacity in percentages.

IMPORTANCE OF USING CAPACITY ○○○

Operating at 'under capacity' (below the maximum) is a waste of resources. The fixed assets of the business are not being used to their limit so average fixed costs will be higher than they need be.

However, operating at full capacity means it will be harder to:

- maintain and service machinery
- find time to train staff
- satisfy a sudden increase in demand.

A high level of spare capacity will increase average costs whereas a low level might mean disappointing some customers.

Identify three problems of operating at full capacity.

DON'T FORGET
It is also possible to operate at 'above capacity' through the use of overtime working.

ADVANTAGES AND DISADVANTAGES OF FULL CAPACITY ○○○

Operating at or near to full capacity has both benefits and drawbacks for a business.

Advantages:
- fixed costs per unit are minimized
- unit variable costs should be at their lowest
- lower average costs improves competitiveness as it allows the business to lower its prices.

Disadvantages:
- greater stress on the workforce
- risk of increase in machine downtime as time for maintenance is limited or reduced
- unable to meet unexpected demand, which could lead to loss of new customers to competitors.

Identify three advantages and three disadvantages associated with working at or near to full capacity.

THE JARGON
'Downtime' is when a machine is not available for scheduled work due to breakdown, lack of spares, etc.

Turn the page for some exam questions on this topic ▶

EXAM QUESTION 1 ●●●

Brooke Bottling Ltd operates 24 hours a day, seven days a week. It uses a rotating eight-hour shift system for its four bottling lines. Each line is dedicated to the filling of a different soft drink according to container size. The results of last week's performance are given in the table below.

(a) Using the data in the table, calculate the capacity utilization rate as a percentage expressed to one decimal place.

Line number	Maximum capacity (000s bottles)	Actual performance (000s bottles)	Capacity utilization rate (%)
1	180	164	91.1
2	130	112	86.2
3	150	148	98.7
4	140	139	99.3

Insert your answers in the final column.

(b) Comment on the relative capacity utilization for the production lines. Identify any problems and suggest what might have caused them.

Lines 1 and 2: these lines appear to be operating with significant spare capacity of almost 9% and 14%. This will raise the average cost of the items being bottled on those lines. The under capacity might have been caused by machine breakdown or by lack of demand for those products.

Lines 3 and 4: these are operating at almost full capacity. From a cost point of view this is good news but it might mean that basic preventative maintenance and servicing is being delayed, which will cause problems in the future.

The answer for lines 1 and 2 has been done for you. Add your own observations for lines 3 and 4.

EXAM QUESTION 2 ●●●

In an attempt to use the fixed capital to its maximum, Brooke Bottling Ltd operates a rotating shift system where employees alternate weekly between morning, afternoon and night shifts. Each shift is encouraged to perform at full capacity with rewards for the best monthly performance. Explain the human resource issues associated with trying to work at full capacity on a 24-hour basis.

Shift work is considered to be antisocial as it deprives workers, at some point in their working cycle, of contact with normal family life or social contact with peers. It might require the firm to offer higher wages as compensation.
Encouraging shifts to compete against one another might lead to a lack of cooperation between shifts. Problems occurring near the end of one shift might deliberately be left unresolved.
Operating at full capacity can be stressful for workers and can lead to increased absence.

Try to identify three human resource issues.

DON'T FORGET
Human resources are far more difficult to 'schedule' than machines.
Operating a shift system requires the full cooperation of front-line workers.

Production control

(AS) AQA EDEXCEL OCR WJEC

Production is the process of organizing resources in order to satisfy the needs of customers. It is also the means for the firm to make a profit by producing an output that sells for more than the cost of the inputs used in its creation. Management must, therefore, keep an effective control on all its resources and monitor their use throughout the production process.

EFFICIENCY AND ITS MEASUREMENT

OOO

Complete the definition of efficiency.

Efficiency can be defined as how well resources such as labour, raw materials and capital are used to produce goods and services.

Improvements in efficiency will have a direct effect on the average costs of production and consequently on the profitability of the business. Costs and profits are, however, only indicators of efficiency. It is useful to measure the efficiency of inputs directly.

LABOUR PRODUCTIVITY

OOO

This measures the amount the workforce produces in a given time period using the equation:

$$\text{Labour productivity} = \frac{\text{Total output}}{\text{Number of employees (or man hours)}}$$

For example, in 1996 the Nissan plant produced 231 000 vehicles and employed 3 156 staff. Labour productivity was 73.19 vehicles per employee. Labour productivity can be improved in a number of ways.

Briefly explain how these changes can improve labour productivity.

Investment in new capital equipment: better machinery can improve the speed, reliability and quality of the products made using the same amount of labour.

Incentive schemes for workers: financial incentives might help to motivate staff to not only produce more goods but also to improve quality.

Increase in staff training: a skilled and adaptable staff can more easily cope with production problems thus saving valuable production time.

CAPITAL PRODUCTIVITY

OOO

This measure is increasingly more important as firms invest in more capital-intensive production systems. Capital productivity can be measured using the equation:

$$\text{Capital productivity} = \frac{\text{Total output}}{\text{Capital employed}}$$

Example: a business produced 3 000 units per week using eight old machines. These have been replaced by six new ones without any loss of output.

Calculate the capital productivity for both the old machines and the new ones. Comment on the change.

Productivity of old machines = $3\,000 \div 8 = 375$ units
Productivity of new machines = $3\,000 \div 6 = 500$ units per machine.
Productivity has risen by 33% (125 units) per machine.

Turn the page for some exam questions on this topic ➤

EXAM QUESTION 1

For more on this topic, see pages 120–121 of the *Revision Express A-level Study Guide*

North Engineering Ltd design and manufacture propellers for a wide range of boats. They have a small factory employing 20 workers using five machines. The results from the production department for August are given in the table below. Using the data provided, calculate (a) the capital productivity in units per machine and (b) the labour productivity in units per man hour. Comment on the results.

Period	Output (units)	Labour (man hours)	Capital productivity (units per machine)	Labour productivity (units per man hour)
Week 1	21 000	800	4 200	26.25
Week 2	22 000	830	4 400	26.51
Week 3	24 000	860	4 800	27.91
Week 4	24 600	860	4 920	28.60

Add your answers to the table.

Capital productivity has risen from 4 200 units per machine to 4 920 per machine. This is an increase of just over 17% during the month. This is probably due to overtime working as extra hours were worked in weeks 2, 3 and 4.
Labour productivity has risen by almost 9% over the month. This might be due to longer production runs where there is less time wasted setting up the machinery for different types of propeller.

Now comment on the results giving at least one reason for the identified trend in capital and labour productivity during August.

EXAMINER'S SECRETS

When faced with trend data it is best to calculate percentage changes to show the trend. Manipulation of the data demonstrates the skill of analysis and will be rewarded more highly than simple descriptions.

EXAM QUESTION 2

Improvements in capital productivity are often achieved with the replacement of outdated machinery. This modernization can have beneficial effects for the workforce but can also cause human resource problems. Explain three benefits for labour and three drawbacks for labour associated with improvements in capital.

Remember to concentrate just on human resources issues.

Benefits

- New machinery can lead to higher labour productivity and the opportunity for improved salaries.
- New machinery might be safer to operate.
- New machinery might require further training and an improvement in the employee's skill levels.

Drawbacks

- New machinery might lead to redundancies.
- Automated machinery might lead to deskilling of the operator's function.
- New machinery might mean more monotonous working practices and greater demotivation among workers.

AQA EDEXCEL OCR WJEC

Stock control

Effective stock control is essential to any business especially those involved in manufacturing. Any stock control system must ensure that there are sufficient raw materials and work in progress to supply the production line as well as ensuring finished goods for the end consumer. Understocking will result in lost sales or production 'downtime'. Overstocking will tie up valuable capital as well as increasing the risk of stock damage and deterioration.

TERMS YOU NEED TO KNOW

Define each of the terms.

Lead time The time it takes between ordering stock, having it delivered and it being ready for use.

Work in progress Partly finished goods.

Buffer stock The stock held for unforeseen demand for finished goods or breaks in supply of raw materials.

Reorder level The level of stock when an order for new supplies is placed.

EOQ (the economic order quantity) The level of stock that minimizes the costs of holding stock and the costs of ordering stock.

Just-in-time (JIT) manufacturing A Japanese manufacturing method that schedules stock to arrive only when it is required. This method minimizes stock holding and handling costs.

THE JARGON
Stock control is often referred to nowadays as 'materials management'.

DON'T FORGET
The reorder level is calculated using the equation:
Reorder level = (usage rate × lead time) + buffer stock

STOCK CONTROL CHARTS

Stock control charts provide a quick visual image of the usage and current level of stock. Exam questions often require you to either construct or interpret a chart.

On the stock control chart diagram label the items marked A to D. Indicate the lead time and label it point E. What is its duration?

LINKS
Stock is part of an organization's working capital and is an important item in the balance sheet. For more information on balance sheets see pages 65–66.

A maximum stock level
B reorder level
C minimum stock
D buffer or safety stock
Stock level (000s units)
Time (weeks)
lead time (E) 2 weeks

Turn the page for some exam questions on this topic ▶

For more on this topic, see pages 126–127 of the *Revision Express A-level Study Guide*

EXAM QUESTION 1

Milner Ltd is a musical instruments manufacturer. One of its key raw materials is brass. Average usage is 400 kg per week. Opening stock at the beginning of January was 1 600 kg, which is the maximum stock held at any one time. As a buffer stock they wish to have one week's supply in reserve. The lead time is one week. In weeks 1 to 4 usage was normal at 400 kg but in weeks 5 and 6 it increased to 800 kg and 600 kg respectively. Weeks 7 and 8 were normal. Three deliveries of 800 kg, 1400 kg and 900 kg were received in this period.

(a) Calculate the reorder level and mark on the diagram.
(b) On the diagram below draw the stock control chart using the information provided.

Brass (00s kg) — maximum — reorder level — minimum — Time (weeks)

Plot your answers on the diagram to get a picture of the fluctuation in stock usage over a two month period.

(c) Determine the closing stock figure.
• Reorder level is 800 kg.
• Closing stock was 900 kg.

EXAMINER'S SECRETS
Most mistakes involve poor plotting of the stock usage. Remember that a delivery is shown as a straight vertical line. Marks are allocated for correctly drawn diagrams.

EXAM QUESTION 2

Identify the benefits and costs of holding stocks.

Benefits of holding stocks	Costs associated with stock
Acts as a reserve for unforeseen events such as delays from suppliers or production breakdown.	Valuable financial resources are tied up in working capital that could be better used elsewhere.
Buying in large quantities enables firms to take advantage of bulk discounts and to enjoy economies of scale.	Valuable and costly space is required as well as security to ensure stock safety.
Large stocks of finished goods enable most customer orders to be satisfied immediately thus creating goodwill.	Stock might become obsolete if kept for a long period especially for products in fast-moving markets.
There are fewer orders to research and place.	Increases the likelihood of damage or deterioration to stock.

Add the benefits and costs to the table.

DON'T FORGET
Determination of a firm's stock policy depends on:
• the resources of the firm
• the availability and size of discounts
• the speed of change in the market
• the financial effect of 'downtime'.

© Pearson Education Limited 2001

Quality control

Quality is difficult to define. Consumers are forever demanding higher levels of quality and it is what they perceive as 'quality' that really matters. An organization must ensure that its processes guarantee the production of items to the specification required. They must also, however, seek to constantly improve the current standards in order to keep up with customer expectations.

Quality is defined by the customer.
W. EDWARD DEMING (AMERICAN QUALITY GURU)

Add three more measures of quality that consumers might seek from a product or service.

MEASURES OF QUALITY

Quality is a subjective matter that will vary from customer to customer. Some of the measures of quality include:

- reliability
- appearance
- durability
- after-sales service
- functionality.

LINKS

For quality control to be effective the workforce must be adequately trained. For more information on training see Exam question 2 on page 62.

QUALITY CONTROL

In the past quality control meant 'inspecting' the product at the end of the production line prior to despatch to the consumer. In other words it was a fault-finding exercise. Problems with this system are as follows.

1. *Cost:* production has already taken place before the fault is recognized therefore expensive reworking is needed.
2. *Resentment:* line workers might feel devalued as inspectors only feel justified if they find fault with work done by the employees.
3. *Ineffective:* only a sample can be inspected, so some defective work may pass through the system to the consumer and result in complaints.

Identify and explain three problems of a quality control system based on inspection.

TOTAL QUALITY MANAGEMENT (TQM)

There have been a number of new approaches to quality issues in recent years. One of the first was Total Quality Management. TQM is really a philosophy as it attempts to change the culture of a company so that all employees become part of the quality system. The basic features of TQM are:

1. the establishment of a 'quality chain', where each receiver of work is treated as an external customer
2. emphasis on teamwork
3. empowerment of the workforce
4. 'building in' quality at each stage
5. personal responsibility for quality.

List five basic features of a TQM system.

LINKS

For TQM to work effectively the employees must be well-motivated. For more information on motivation see 'Motivation in theory' and 'Motivation in practice' on pages 45–48.

Turn the page for some exam questions on this topic ▶

For more on this topic, see pages 128–129 of the *Revision Express A-level Study Guide*

EXAM QUESTION 1

TQM is just one of many quality initiatives that have been tried in recent years to improve the delivery of goods and services. Some of the others are listed below. Explain each one and outline an advantage for an organization in adopting its use.

Add your responses after each heading.

Quality circles: a Japanese initiative that encourages small groups of workers to meet voluntarily to discuss methods of improving productivity and quality in their own work areas.

Kaizen: an approach that advocates 'continuous improvement', in small steps rather than a large-scale, 'one-off' improvement. This approach results in cheaper, more gradual change that is easier to assimilate into the working environment.

Benchmarking: identifying the best practice among the leading firms and using that as a standard against which to measure one's own performance. This ensures that the firm remains competitive with the leading businesses.

BS 5750 (ISO 9000): a British Standards certification process that guarantees that an organization sets quality targets and effectively monitors them. The ISO 9000 is the exact equivalent issued by the International Standards Organization. Purchasers using such firms can be assured of maintained standards.

EXAMINER'S SECRETS

In questions relating to quality it is useful to include specific references to bodies that promote quality such as The British Standards Institution, The Consumers Association, The Association of British Travel Agents (ABTA), etc.

THE JARGON

Quality assurance is an attempt to ensure that quality standards are met throughout the organization. This includes the design stage, raw material and component procurement, production, delivery and after sales service.

EXAM QUESTION 2

Explain each of the following terms, and state why it is important to a firm for quality purposes.

Add your answer after each heading.

Induction: this is training given to new recruits. It will ensure that all personnel understand the firm's policies including its quality systems and targets.

On-the-job training: training that takes place within the workplace. It will include skills and procedures that are specific to the firm and its particular machinery. This will ensure that all employees' skill levels are kept up to date.

Off-the-job training: training provided off-site in more general topics. This will have a good effect on the motivation of employees and may help build worker loyalty as well as improving productivity.

Multiskilling: this is training to provide a worker with several independent skills. This can reduce boredom by allowing workers to switch from one activity to another. It also reduces the need for the firm to employ several specialists.

Use and preparation of accounts

Accounting is the process of recording a firm's financial transactions in a suitable format and of summarizing this in the form of accounting reports. Accounting can be divided into two types, financial accounting and management accounting. Together the two forms of information provide insights into the success or failure of past decisions and operations. The information also enlightens management as to the opportunities and difficulties of future plans.

USERS OF ACCOUNTING INFORMATION

There are two groups of users of accounting information, internal users and external users. You need to know who they are and what their interests are.

Internal users

* Management: to plan courses of action, to control the use of scarce resources and to analyse and evaluate past actions and decisions.
* *Shareholders: to assess how their investment has been used by management.*
* *Employees: to judge the security of employment and the possibility of the award of wage increases.*

External users

These groups only have access to published accounts.

* Suppliers: *to gauge the risk of extending credit.*
* Banks: *to assess a firm's credit worthiness.*
* Government: *to assess the tax liability of a firm.*

Identify two more internal users and briefly state their interest in having access to accurate accounting information.

Slate the main interest of each group of external users.

IF YOU HAVE TIME
Investigate the interests of four more external users: potential investors, competitors, consumer pressure groups and the local community.

THE JARGON
True and fair view is the term used by auditors to confirm that the accounts of a business are accurate.

ACCOUNTING CONCEPTS AND CONVENTIONS

The accounting process must produce statements that show a 'true and fair view' of the business's financial position. To achieve this a series of accounting concepts and conventions are used to deliver information in a standard common language. You need to be able to define the terms and, in some cases, apply them.

Matching concept (accruals): relating revenues and costs with the period in which they occur.

Going concern: valuing assets on the basis that the business will continue to trade 'for the foreseeable future'.

Consistency: using the same approach to asset valuation and the allocation of costs so that comparisons can be made over time.

Prudence (conservatism): a pessimistic or cautious approach to the drawing up of accounts, e.g. only valuing stock at the lower of historic cost or net realizable value.

Double entry: all transactions have a dual nature where the source of funds is balanced by the use made of them.

Define the following concepts and conventions.

THE JARGON
Financial accounting is concerned with the production of the principal accounting statements (balance sheet, profit and loss statement, etc.).
Management accounting generates information for internal use to aid the analysis, planning and control of the firm's activities (budgets, cash flow forecasts, etc.).

Turn the page for some exam questions on this topic ▶

For more on this topic, see pages 144–147 of the *Revision Express A-level Study Guide*

EXAM QUESTION 1

Peter Harley is a sole trader supplying safety equipment to the building industry. At the end of his second year of trading he has created sales of £100 000. In his store he has £28 000 of unsold stock. On 1 January he had £20 000 of stock and his purchases throughout the year totalled £75 000. His accountant has emphasized that the accounts must be drawn up on the basis of the matching principle so that only the stock used during the year is included in that year's accounts.

(a) Calculate, using the matching principle, the actual stock used during the year.

Opening stock	£20 000
Add purchases	£75 000
Less closing stock	(£28 000)
Value of stock sold	£67 000

(b) Explain why it would be misleading to charge all £95 000 worth of stock against the sales made in the year.

Charging £95 000 of stock against the sales of £100 000 would seriously understate Peter Harley's true profits for the second year. The £28 000 of stock remaining will be used to generate sales in the third year. Only £67 000 of stock has been used to create sales in the second year giving a true gross profit of £33 000.

Add your calculations here, then have a go at part (b).

LINKS
For more information on accounts see page 65.

EXAM QUESTION 2

Shar Ltd imports tropical plants for resale to specialist outlets. At the end of the financial year the accountant is presented with the following situations:

(a) At the beginning of the year a car was bought for £12 000 which will be sold in two years for an estimated £4 000. How much of the cost of the van should be allocated to this year's accounts?

Over the two years the business will use up £8 000 of the value of the vehicle. Using the straight-line method, £4 000 should be allocated as a cost to each year. This applies the matching principle.

Explain how each situation should be treated according to the appropriate accounting concepts and conventions.

(b) 100 plants bought for £1 000 have developed some form of leaf mould and probably will fetch only £200. What value should be placed on this stock?

Applying the concept of conservatism the lower value should apply and be valued at £200.

(c) Last year all machinery was depreciated at 20% of its original value. As sales have not been as good the manager wants to reduce the depreciation charge to 10%.

The concept of consistency dictates that asset valuations and costs should be done using a consistent basis. Without this approach it would be difficult to compare one year's performance with another. The 20% rule should be maintained.

EXAMINER'S SECRETS
Definitions of concepts and conventions are often best done using an example.

Final accounts

The final accounts of a business provide a systematic way of presenting the financial history of the organization over a period of time. The main components are the profit and loss account, the balance sheet and the cash flow statement (see page 67 for a treatment of cash flow). The role of these accounts is to provide an accurate view of the business's financial position.

THE PROFIT AND LOSS ACCOUNT

○○○

In exam questions you might be required to construct or interpret a simple profit and loss account. Therefore it is important that you understand the basic components and can calculate them.

Define each term of the profit and loss account and show how it is calculated.

Sales revenue (or sales turnover):
the total value of sales in the trading period given by:
quantity sold x price
Less cost of goods sold (or cost of sales):
the direct cost of goods sold given by:
opening stock plus purchases minus closing stock
Gross profit:
the difference between sales revenue and the cost of goods sold
Less overheads:
costs that are not directly generated by the production process
Operating or net profit:
the sales revenue minus all the operating costs of the business

DON'T FORGET

Interest and tax must be deducted from net profit to arrive at 'profit after tax'. This amount can be distributed to shareholders in the form of dividends, used to repay loans or kept in the business as 'retained profits'.

THE BALANCE SHEET

○○○

The balance sheet is a 'snapshot' of the business's financial situation at a given point in time. It shows the 'use of funds' and the 'source of funds'. It also lists the resources that the business owns (its assets), the resources that it owes (liabilities) and the capital belonging to the owners. You must be able to define these terms.

DON'T FORGET

The balance sheet is a snapshot of the business taken on one particular day, normally the last day of the trading period. The title of the balance sheet should reflect this by being in the form of 'Balance sheet as at (date)'.

Distinguish between these balance sheet terms.

Assets – fixed and current
Fixed assets are those items that are to be used for more than a year. Current assets are short-term assets that are to be used up or change their form during the year.

Liabilities – long-term and current
Current liabilities are those debts that have to be paid within 12 months. Long-term liabilities comprise money owed by the firm that has more than a year to maturity.

IF YOU HAVE TIME

Make a list of at least five fixed assets that might be associated with:
• an airline
• a school
• a retail outlet.

For more on this topic, see pages 148–151 of the *Revision Express A-level Study Guide*

EXAM EXERCISE

○○○

Dominic's is a fashion retail outlet preparing for its year-end accounts. The following figures apply to this year's trading:
Cost of goods sold £54 000, sales revenue £125 000, overheads £21 000 and a bank loan of £100 000 at 10% interest. The tax rate is 20%. It is proposed to repay £10 000 of the loan and to distribute £8 000 as dividends to the shareholders. Complete the profit and loss account and determine the retained profit.

Profit and loss account for the year ending	
	£000s
Sales revenue	125
Less cost of goods sold	(54)
Gross profit	71
Less overheads	(21)
Net profit	50
Less interest	(10)
Less tax	(8)
Profit after interest and tax	32
Loan repayment	10
Dividends	8
Retained profit	14

Add your answers to the table here.

DON'T FORGET

Tax is imposed only on the profit remaining after interest has been deducted.

EXAM EXERCISE

○○○

The following figures relate to BAB plc for the year ending on 31 December (all figures are in £m): Buildings 120; Cash 15; Creditors 25; Stock 30; Machinery 45; Debtors 20. There are no long-term liabilities. Complete the balance sheet below.

BAB plc: Balance sheet as at 31 December		
	£m	£m
Fixed assets		
1. Buildings	120	
2. Machinery	45	165
Current assets		
3. Stock	30	
4. Debtors	20	
5. Cash	15	65
Less current liabilities		
6. Creditors	(25)	
Net current assets		40
Assets employed		205
Financed by:		
Share capital	160	
Reserves	45	
Total capital employed		205

Insert the six items in the correct position in the balance sheet. Calculate the final figure for:
(a) net current assets
(b) assets employed
(c) reserves
(d) total capital employed.

DON'T FORGET

The formula you need is:
net current assets = current assets – current liabilities (also referred to as working capital).

Cash flow management

It is crucial for all firms to manage their cash flow effectively. Without adequate liquid resources a firm will be unable to settle its bills, reward its workforce or pay its suppliers. The effective control of working capital, therefore, is essential for survival.

THE IMPORTANCE OF CASH

Firms require cash for three reasons.

1. For transaction purposes:
To settle daily requirements such as wages, suppliers' accounts and raw materials. Without these regular payments resources for production would be denied to the firm.

2. For precautionary purposes:
To have a reserve in case of an unforeseen expense such as a breakdown.

3. For speculative purposes:
To have some cash available to take advantage of an opportunity such as a special offer on raw materials bought for cash.

> **Explain the three reasons for holding cash and provide an example of each.**

DON'T FORGET
70% of businesses that fail in their first year do so because of cash flow problems.

IF YOU HAVE TIME
Liquidity problems can be identified through the use of liquidity ratios. Learn the equations for the current ratio, the acid test ratio and the gearing ratio.

CASH FLOW PROBLEMS

Each time a sale is made it should generate a profit and eventually increase the cash holdings of the business. Most transactions are not for cash but are done on credit. This creates a delay in the cash inflow to the business and is one of the causes of cash flow problems.
Any of the following could cause a problem for cash flow:

Stockpiling
Unnecessary high levels of stock, such as raw materials, work in progress and finished goods, tie up valuable cash resources.

Poor credit control
Allowing debtors to take longer to pay than the agreed credit period will force the firm to borrow funds in order to finance production. Short-term borrowing in the form of an overdraft is expensive and a cash drain on the business.

Market changes
Changes in taste and fashion could result in falling sales and a subsequent reduction in cash inflow. In a similar way the emergence of new competitors might threaten market share that can only be protected by price cuts or increased advertising, both of which reduce cash flow.

> **Explain how each factor could cause a cash flow problem.**

Turn the page for some exam questions on this topic ▶

EXAM QUESTION 1

The management of Desai Construction wants to identify any future cash problems and to plan appropriate remedial action.

(a) Complete the cash flow forecast based on the notes detailed below the table.

Cash flow forecast (£m)	J	A	S	O	N	D
Opening balance	12	5	1	3	(2)	(2)
Cash sales	82	88	100	94	104	114
Rental income	4	4	4	4	4	4
Total inflows	86	92	104	98	108	118
Total cash	98	97	105	101	106	116
Payments						
Materials	41	44	50	47	52	57
Production costs	52	52	52	56	56	56
Total outgoing	93	96	102	103	108	113
Closing cash balance	5	1	3	(2)	(2)	3

Notes: Cash sales are expected to be £94m in October and then to increase by £10m in each of the next two months. Rental income is constant. Materials are always 50% of sales. Production costs are to rise to £56m in October, then stay constant.

> **Add your answers to the table.**

DON'T FORGET
The usefulness of a cash flow forecast is only as good as the accuracy of the estimated cash movements.

EXAMINER'S SECRETS
Candidates who stress that forecasts are merely estimates and rarely accurate over along period of time will score highly.

(b) Identify the timing and size of Desai Construction's cash flow problem.

Desai will be overdrawn by £2m in October and by £2m in November

(c) What remedial action might Desai take?

This appears to be a short-term problem that could be easily covered by an overdraft facility.

(d) Calculate the cost of funding the shortfall if borrowing costs are 2% per month on the balance outstanding.

The total cost is £80 000 (£2m for 2 months at 2% per month).

> **Now answer questions (b), (c) and (d).**

EXAM QUESTION 2

What are the disadvantages of the following solutions to a temporary cashflow problem?

Delaying payments to suppliers:
this could damage the firm's reputation; reduce its goodwill among suppliers. Credit facilities might be withdrawn.

Cutting prices to boost sales:
this might increase cash inflow as long as the product is price sensitive. It will, however result in lower profitability.

Reducing current expenditure particularly on stock:
ordering less stock may sacrifice bulk discounts. This may raise the cost of production and reduce the profit margin. It may also result in lost sales opportunities.

> **Each of the solutions mentioned will reduce cash outflow in the short term. What are the disadvantages?**

Costs and revenue

AS AQA EDEXCEL OCR WJEC

In order to make effective decisions and to calculate profit, a firm needs accurate cost information. Different accounting costs behave in different ways. Some costs are fixed for a period of time while others change as output increases. Costs can also be classified according to the product being made. You need to understand the terms, how costs behave and their impact on profits.

THE JARGON
Accounting cost is the value of the resources used up in production.

CLASSIFICATION ACCORDING TO TIME AND OUTPUT   OOO

This type of classification is used to calculate the financial impact of changing the level of output.

Write down the differences between the two terms.

Fixed costs and variable costs

Fixed costs do not alter with changes in output in the short run whereas variable costs do.

Short run and long run

DON'T FORGET
The exact length of the short and long runs will depend on the type of business, for example, a retail outlet can change its stock levels and product range quite quickly but a farmer needs much longer as production must be planned well in advance.

Short run is the period when at least one factor of production is fixed and the scale of operations cannot be changed. In the long run, however, all factors can be varied and the scale of operation can be changed.

CLASSIFICATION ACCORDING TO PRODUCT   OOO

This type of classification is used to allocate costs to individual products. This allows the organization to measure its efficiency by comparing costs of production over time. It also helps in determining a price that will cover the product's costs.

Write down the differences between the two terms.

Direct costs and indirect costs

Direct costs can be identified with a particular process or product. Indirect costs (also known as overheads) refer to the running of the whole business and cannot be accurately allocated to individual products.

TOTAL COST, REVENUE AND PROFIT   OOO

LINKS
For more information on costs see page 71.

Total cost and total revenue enable the business to calculate its profit. To earn more profits the firm must either boost revenue or reduce costs. Revenue can be improved by selling more or by increasing prices. Total costs can be reduced either by improving efficiency or by obtaining cheaper inputs.

Write down the equation for each of the terms.

Total cost
total cost = fixed costs + variable costs
Total revenue
total revenue = quantity sold × price
Profit
profit = total revenue − total costs

Turn the page for some exam questions on this topic ▶

For more on this topic, see pages 156–157 of the *Revision Express A-level Study Guide*

EXAM QUESTION 1

Hindmarch Plastics Ltd produces a range of storage boxes for industrial use in batches of 10 000. The variable costs are labour (£1 per box), materials (£2 per box) and packaging (£0.20 per box). Fixed costs are £100 000. The boxes are sold for £8 each and current production is 40 000 boxes.

(a) **Complete the cost and revenue schedule using the information given.**

Add your answers to the table, then answer parts (b) and (c).

No. of boxes	10 000	20 000	30 000	40 000	50 000
Fixed costs	100 000	100 000	100 000	100 000	100 000
Labour	10 000	20 000	30 000	40 000	50 000
Materials	20 000	40 000	60 000	80 000	100 000
Packaging	2 000	4 000	6 000	8 000	10 000
Total costs	132 000	164 000	196 000	228 000	260 000
Total revenue	80 000	160 000	240 000	320 000	400 000
Profit	(52 000)	(4 000)	44 000	92 000	140 000

(b) **What is the profit level of the current output level?**

£92 000

(c) **If cheaper raw materials at £1.80 per unit could be purchased how would this affect: (i) total costs (ii) profit at the current output level?**

(i) Material cost would be 40 000 × £1.80 = £72 000 therefore total costs would fall by £8 000 to £220 000.
(ii) Profits would rise to £100 000.

EXAM QUESTION 2

In order to improve the control of costs Armidale Ltd, a manufacturer of agricultural equipment, has introduced cost and profit centres. Define these terms (using examples) and explain the benefits for Armidale.

Define the terms 'cost centre' and 'profit centre' and give an example of each.

A cost centre is an area of responsibility to which costs can be charged, e.g. a department or a product.

A profit centre is an area of a business for which both costs and revenue can be accurately identified, e.g. one branch in a chain of shops or one sales representative.

Identify four benefits for Armidale Ltd that might result from the introduction of cost and profit centres.

The benefits for Armidale Ltd might include:
- managers of the centres can be given targets to work towards
- different centres can be compared more easily
- cost and revenue targets can act as motivators
- problems can be identified at an early stage.

Break-even analysis

Break-even analysis is used to determine the level of output where profit begins to be earned. Sales beyond the break-even output will result in profits. If firms do not break-even in the long run they will not survive.

DEFINING KEY BREAK-EVEN TERMS

These are the key terms and definitions associated with break-even.

Total revenue: the total value of sales (price × quantity sold).
Fixed costs: costs that do not alter in the short term with changes in output or activity, e.g. rent.
Variable costs: costs that vary with output or activity in the short term, e.g. materials.
Total costs: the sum of the fixed costs and the variable costs.
Contribution per unit: the surplus left over when the unit variable costs are deducted from the price of a product.

Define the key terms given here.

DON'T FORGET
At break-even output:
Total revenue = Total costs.

EXAMINER'S SECRETS
'Low price special orders' may still be acceptable to businesses as long as they generate a positive contribution.

THE IMPORTANCE OF BREAK-EVEN

All firms need to calculate the following:

Break-even output: the output where total revenue equals total costs. It is important because any output above this earns profits. The equation is:
$$\text{Break-even output} = \frac{\text{fixed costs}}{\text{contribution per unit}}$$

Margin of safety: The amount by which current or projected sales can fall before a loss is made. It is important because it is a measure of risk. The equation is:
margin of safety = current or planned output − break-even output

Define the terms given here. Say why they are important and give the equation.

DON'T FORGET
Margin of safety can also be expressed as a percentage of current output in which case use the equation:
$$\frac{\text{Margin of safety}}{\text{current output}} \times 100\%$$

ADVANTAGES AND DISADVANTAGES OF BREAK-EVEN ANALYSIS

Break-even is a simple model that helps the management decision-making process.

The cost and revenue lines can shift their position and slope to reflect changes and to provide new break-even and margin of safety output levels.

The model assumes that the price and variable cost per unit remain constant over a wide range of output. This view is too simplistic.

How can the break-even model be used to reflect changes in prices and costs?

Identify one assumption of the simple break-even model.

Turn the page for some exam questions on this topic ▶

For more on this topic, see pages 158–159 of the *Revision Express A-level Study Guide*

EXAM QUESTION 1

Techno Ltd is a manufacturer of electronic calculators. It has fixed costs of £300 000; variable costs are £4 per calculator and it sells the calculators for £10 each. Draw the break-even graph and determine:

(a) the break-even level of output
(b) the margin of safety assuming a sales level of 80 000 units.

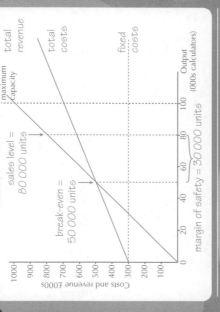

Techno Ltd
sales level = 80 000 units
break-even = 50 000 units
margin of safety = 30 000 units
Costs and revenue £000s
Output (000s calculators)
total revenue — total costs — fixed costs — maximum capacity

Complete the graph.

EXAMINER'S SECRETS
Remember to label the axes correctly, to choose a suitable scale and to draw the revenue and cost lines accurately. Examiners will look for these qualities in a diagram.

EXAM QUESTION 2

Sandal Logistics is a transport company specializing in the delivery of raw materials to footwear manufacturers. Its average cost of delivery is £500 per load for which it charges £600. A large international producer has requested a special delivery of 200 loads of materials to its factory in Leeds for which it is only prepared to pay £400 per load. Variable costs per load are £350.

(a) Identify a variable cost associated with the mileage driven.
Fuel

(b) Calculate the total contribution associated with this order.
Contribution per unit = price − variable cost
= £400 − £350 = £50
Total contribution = £50 × 200 loads = £10 000

(c) Under what circumstances should this order be accepted?
If fixed costs are already covered by existing deliveries the special order will add £10 000 to total profits.

(d) What qualitative factors should Sandal Logistics take into account before accepting or rejecting this order?
This first order might lead to further orders.
The company operates internationally which might lead to the opening of new markets abroad.
Does the company have a good payment record?
What other orders will be sacrificed in order to complete the special order? (This is known as the opportunity cost.)

Jot down note-form answers to this multi-part question.

DON'T FORGET
Contribution is the key factor for 'special orders'.

EXAMINER'S SECRETS
Critical comment on the impact of accepting the special order will demonstrate 'evaluation' and earn top marks. For example, delaying orders for regular clients might damage the long-term business for the sake of a short-term gain.

© Pearson Education Limited 2001

Budgeting

AS AQA EDEXCEL OCR WJEC

The main purposes of a budget are to plan the activities of the next accounting period, to help control the business as it progresses through the period and to analyse any variations from the plan. Remedial action can then be taken before any problems become too serious.

THE PURPOSE OF BUDGETS

Budgets act as both a planning tool and a control mechanism. The budgeting process helps planning by:

- establishing priorities and setting short-term goals for each functional area
- providing direction and coordination towards an organization's long-term objectives
- assigning responsibility to the budget holder.

The budget acts as a control mechanism by:

- requiring managers to regularly review performance, normally monthly
- identifying differences between planned and actual outcomes that can then be reviewed.

> **Identify three ways that budgets can help to plan a business organization's activities.**

> **THE JARGON**
> A budget is a financial plan quantified in monetary terms, prepared and agreed in advance, showing the expected revenue and expenses over a given period of time.

> **Identify two ways that budgets can help to control a business organization's activities.**

THE BUDGETING PROCESS

The budgeting process should be a combination of 'top down' target setting by senior management and 'bottom up' resource planning by departments. The final outcome is an 'agreed' budget that is demanding but at the same time realistic and attainable. A typical budget is compiled in stages.

1. Agree on organizational objectives
2. Collect data on past events and future trends
3. Prepare functional budgets
4. Compile a master budget
5. Monitor and review performance

> **Briefly state five main stages in the budget process.**

VARIANCE ANALYSIS

Variance analysis involves the comparison of planned outcomes in the budget with 'actual' outcomes. The differences are known as 'variances' that can be either favourable or adverse.

A favourable variance is a difference where the revenue is greater than expected or the cost is less than expected.

An adverse variance is a difference that reduces profit because costs are higher than expected or revenue is lower than expected.

> **THE JARGON**
> Differences between planned and actual budget outcomes are referred to as 'variances'.

> **Define the two types of variance.**

> **DON'T FORGET**
> Variances act as alarm bells to warn management that current outcomes are not going according to plan.

Turn the page for some exam questions on this topic ▶

For more on this topic, see pages 162–163 of the *Revision Express A-level Study Guide*

EXAM QUESTION 1

SLB Furnishings Ltd is a fast growing business designing and supplying stylish office furniture. Management wish to introduce a more effective method for planning and controlling expansion in the future and have decided to introduce a more formal budget process. The advantage of budgets is recognized by the board but the managing director is not convinced that it will solve the firm's control problems. Identify and explain three possible drawbacks of budgetary control that the managing director might be concerned about.

- Unrealistic budgets are demotivational in that staff will not attempt to achieve targets that are not feasible.
- Budgets 'imposed' by management can create resentment among the workforce, as they have not taken any part in their preparation.
- Budgets can be inflexible in times of rapid market change. They are only as good as the assumptions they are based on.

> **Jot down a note-form response to this question.**

> **DON'T FORGET**
> 'A budget is a tool not a master'. This expression emphasizes that a budget is an aid to decision-making and not a plan that must be slavishly followed.

EXAM QUESTION 2

SLB Furnishings Ltd have implemented budgetary control and the first figures for the manufacturing section for January are given below.

(a) Calculate the variances and complete the table stating in the 'comment' column whether the variance is favourable or adverse.

January Budget (£000s)

	Budget	Actual	Variance	Comment
Sales revenue	150	180	30	Favourable
Less material cost	(75)	(90)	15	Adverse
Less labour	(15)	(21)	6	Adverse
Gross profit	60	69	9	Favourable
Less overheads	(20)	(22)	2	Adverse
Net profit	40	47	7	Favourable

> **Add your answers to the table.**

> **EXAMINER'S SECRETS**
> The use and manipulation of data presented in questions is evidence of analysis and will score more highly than simple descriptive answers.

(b) Suggest and explain a possible reason for the variance in: **(i)** sales revenue **(ii)** labour cost.

(i) The higher than expected sales of £180 000 could have resulted from an effective advertising campaign or the growing popularity of the designs of the business.
(ii) The adverse labour cost variance is most likely linked to the need to fulfil the increased sales orders. Whereas sales increased by 20%, labour costs grew by 40%. This was probably the result of overtime working.

> **Now think about these more analytical questions.**

Index

Note: The page numbers in the index refer to the question section of the book. However, you may need to check the relevant answer pages for full information on a topic.

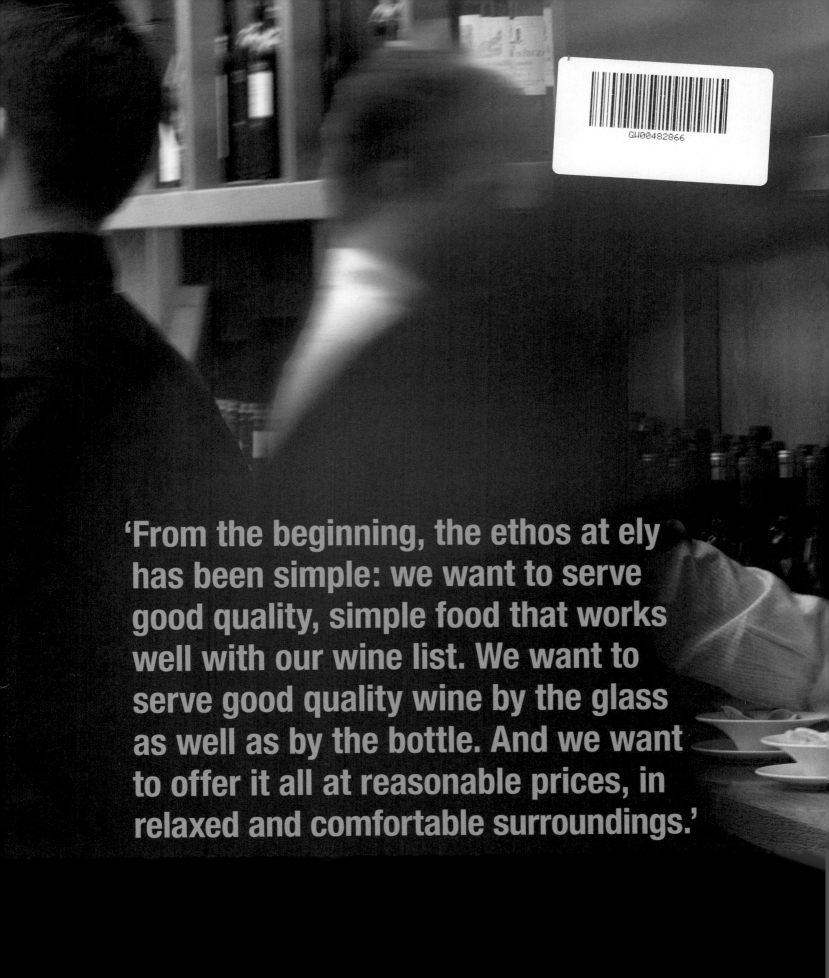

'From the beginning, the ethos at ely has been simple: we want to serve good quality, simple food that works well with our wine list. We want to serve good quality wine by the glass as well as by the bottle. And we want to offer it all at reasonable prices, in relaxed and comfortable surroundings.'

we'd like to mention...

The idea for the ely book came about soon after the opening of our third venue, ely hanover quay. We wanted to show the diversity of our venues in both design and cooking styles. Over a working lunch with Lucy, Francis and Trevor we realised how much there was to talk about. The strength of Trevor's photography came together with the sheer willingness of Francis and Lucy to be drawn in, so that what started out as a moment of madness quickly became a labour of love.
Erik and Michelle Robson

Photography by Trevor Hart, assisted by Rachel Webb

Design and art direction by Francis Curran, assisted by Xat Houatchanthara

Writing and editing by Charlotte Coleman-Smith with food and wine articles by Rionach O'Flynn

Project management by Lucy Masterson

Sarah Robson, Head Chef ely winebar; Tom Doyle, Head Chef ely hq;
Ryan Stringer, Head Chef ely chq; Franco Caparra, former Head Chef at ely chq.
Recipe testing by Ann McCarthy and Patricia Karellas

Thanks to Mary Dowey for the foreword and all her support over the years. An extra special thanks to Eamonn Moyles our business partner. And, of course, thanks to the staff at our three venues and our loyal customers, without all of whom ely would never have evolved.

ISBN 978-0-9560833. Published by ely and printed and bound in Ireland by W&G Baird Ltd.

contents

I remember feeling exuberant after my first visit to ely winebar around the end of 1999. True excitement on the Dublin wine scene at last! It was modern and relaxed but an underlying seriousness of purpose shone through in good glasses, knowledgeable but unstuffy staff and a stupendous wine list. Affordable, personality-packed wines; funky, inside-track beauties; purebred classics – they were all there in giddy profusion, a head-spinning 58 of them available by the glass.

foreword

Straight away ely became a favourite place to meet visiting winemakers from all over the world as well as wine-loving Irish friends. Champagne Bollinger's Ghislain de Montgolfier, Priorat superstar Alvaro Palacios, Peter Gago of Penfolds, Miguel Torres from Spain and his feisty winemaker sister Marimar from California... in they all piled to enjoy simple but tasty food and the opportunity to lift the lid on a Pandora's box of wine styles. Nine years on it is still that favourite place, except that now there are three elys from which to choose – all different in atmosphere but with the same focus on unfussy food and terrific wine. (You can play spot-the-winemaker in all of them.)

As you will see from the sumptuous pages that follow, ely's food has become quite sophisticated – but it is not pretentious, thank goodness, and comfort dishes from the early days like bangers and mash, fish pie and burgers made from organic Clare beef are still on the menu alongside more elaborate options.

The wine side of the business has evolved too, offering an even wider choice of tantalising bottles, every one of them hand-picked, and an expanding repertoire of adventurous food-and-wine-matches. These add a valuable extra dimension to the recipes in this book.

Like many regular customers, I look forward to enjoying the wine and food of ely through the seasons at home. The only problem is that neither is likely to taste half as good in my kitchen as in the special ambience that Erik and Michelle Robson have managed to create. So you'll probably see me in ely again soon.

Mary Dowey
Wine writer

On holiday in Seville in 1998, we did what visitors to the beautiful Spanish city love to do – enjoyed good wine by the glass, served with great tapas, wherever we went.

from seville to ely place

At the time, the only way to enjoy good wine in Ireland was by the bottle or half bottle in an expensive restaurant, or at home. And good wine by the glass was simply unheard of. In a pub, a quarter bottle was the only option. The term 'winebar' mostly conjured up images of the infamous strip of nightclubs along Dublin's Leeson Street, where cheap wine was sold at outrageous prices into the early hours of the morning.

Once back home, we decided to bring the Seville experience to Ireland. Our idea was to open an intimate, comfortable winebar where customers could enjoy finer wine by the glass, with something good to eat, in relaxed, convivial surroundings. Through a friend, we located a vacant Georgian building on Ely Place that was to become ely winebar. Many months of hard work and full skips later, ely winebar opened, offering 70 wines by the glass, including champagnes, sherries and ports.

Passionate about wine and always respectful of its traditions and culture, we prefer a relaxed style of service at ely. We are always on hand to talk to customers about the wine they like to drink, and to help educate those who are interested to learn more.

Erik and Michelle Robson

Serving finer wine by the glass is what we're all about at ely. We know that people don't always want to drink a full bottle, nor does everyone at the table necessarily want to drink the same wine.

our way with wine

That's why we've always offered wines by the glass as well as by the bottle — and use only glasses that are specifically designed to bring out the best in our wines. We serve a generous four glasses to the bottle instead of the usual five (and sometimes even six). We match our wines by the glass with the food on our lunchtime menus, so people in a hurry don't have to spend too much time deliberating over their choices. At dinner, when everyone has more time, we talk to our customers about the wines that work with the food they're ordering. Serving finer wines by the glass has never been just a sales technique at ely. We want our customers to be able to appreciate our extensive wine list, experience new and different grape varieties, and become more confident about their wine choices — all of which is made easier when they can order by the glass.

ely has always been a family affair. Erik and Michelle started the business together, along with Eamonn, financial wizard and Michelle's brother. The organic meat has always been supplied by Erik's father Hugh; and Sarah, Erik's sister, is head chef at ely winebar.

the people at ely

We try to make the family atmosphere extend to the people who work for us, too. What's essential is that they share our passion for ensuring the customer experience at ely is always a good one, and that they have an interest in wine themselves – we support any of our staff who want to use their time with us to take their wine studies further. We feel privileged to have enjoyed almost a decade of meeting truly great people from all over the world who have come to work with us. Some of our staff have been with us since the beginning, and many of those who have moved on to other things still keep in touch with us here at ely, and visit us when they are back in town. A sign, we hope, that the family atmosphere we started out with, prevails.

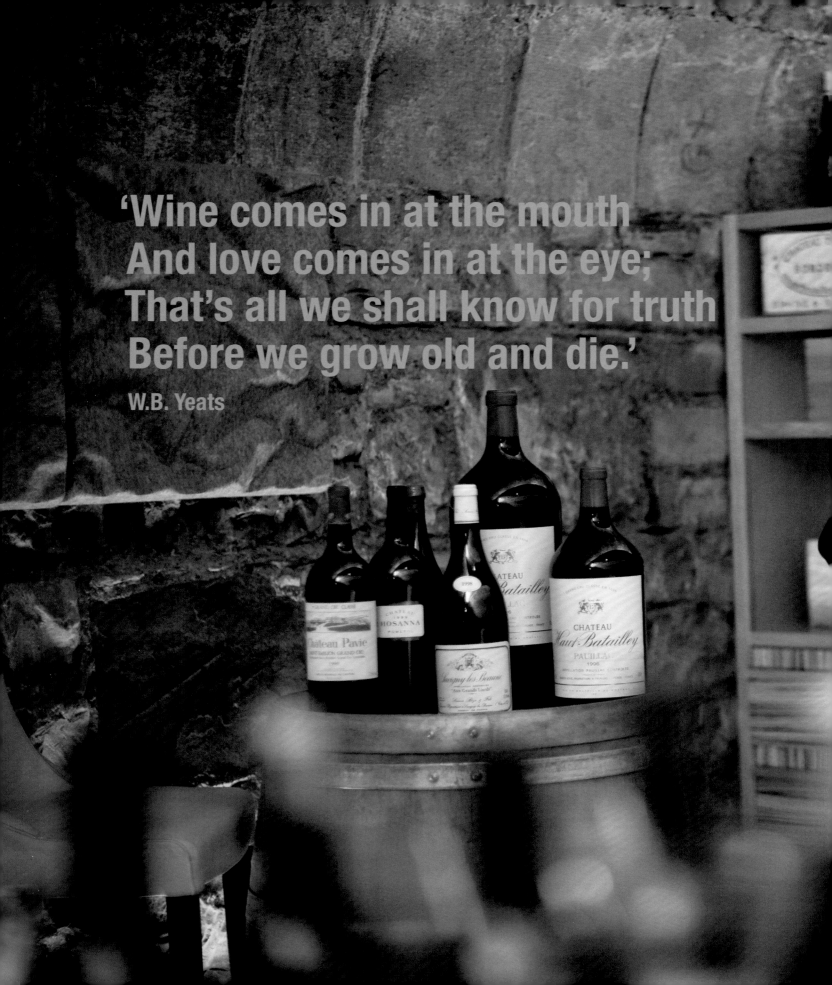

'Wine comes in at the mouth
And love comes in at the eye;
That's all we shall know for truth
Before we grow old and die.'

W.B. Yeats

When compiling our wine list, we made a conscious decision not to try and be all things to all people. We've always served wines we are passionate about – wines we like to drink ourselves.

the wines we love

Rather than fashion, it is good character and pedigree that influence the style of the wine list at ely. And these are ingredients that come from the winemakers. The winemakers we work with share the same ethos as ourselves, growing their grapes and making their wines with minimum intervention and plenty of passion. Over the years, we have built up really good relationships with our wine importers, which puts us in the privileged position of being able to cherry-pick wines of good heritage throughout the winemaking regions we love. The people who supply our wines make frequent visits to the vineyards of Europe and the New World and they choose the wines they import because they know the winemakers and trust what they do. Our ever-evolving wine list reflects the collaborative effort of all the people involved in bringing finer wines to your table at ely.

It's always worth decanting a wine, irrespective of the cost. The only exception is when it comes to a very old wine – its delicate structure may disintegrate when exposed to too much air, so it's best served straight from the bottle (and poured slowly).

be good to your wine – decant it

Otherwise, letting the air at a wine before you drink it will get the complex mix of flavours and aromas working harder. It's not unlike the way a good casserole becomes a great casserole the day after – when the different ingredients involved have had more time to develop. You don't need any special equipment to decant, and there's no great skill involved. Follow the guidelines below to make the most of your wine.

Decant your wine – ideally, for at least an hour before you want to drink, but if you just have 10 minutes before your pizza's ready, it's still worthwhile.

Either buy a decanter (you don't have to spend much), or use any good-sized glass container – a jug or a vase works fine.

Pour gently and steadily down one side.

Leave to sit somewhere cool until it's ready to drink.

Remember you can decant full-bodied white wine, too – especially if it has spent a long time in the fridge.

Corks or caps?

We believe screw caps are the way to go, even for top quality wines destined for ageing. Screw caps can help eliminate faulty wines, the most common being 'corked'. A corked bottle will have a distinctive wet, mouldy odour and lack of fruit character when tasted.

Most people have the idea that red wine should be served at room temperature. However, that really refers to the temperature in a wine cellar. In fact, the best temperature for serving wine varies according to the type of wine.

wine temperature and storage

We often serve our white wines too cold and our red wines too warm. Serving an over-chilled white minimises its flavours and aromas. Serving a red wine too warm makes it take on a soupy character and brings out too many alcoholic fumes. The table below will serve as a good guideline for how to serve your wine. Don't be afraid to chill a lighter red, either – certain gamay-based wines, for example, will benefit from an hour in the fridge before serving, especially in summer.

Serving temperature

7°C	Almost all white wines and champagnes
10°C	Full-bodied, high quality white wines, including sweet wines and rich, white Burgundies. Also the lighter reds, like Beaujolais
15°C	Red wines and ports

Storage

Keep your wine bottles stored so that:

The cork stays moist (always keep bottles on their sides)

The wines are at the lowest stable temperature possible
(make sure not to have a wine rack near a fridge, cooker or heater, for example)

The location is free of vibration

The location is not used to store other items that have a strong odour

The wine is kept out of direct sunlight and strong lighting

If you're storing a bottle of wine that's already been opened, a vacu-vin stopper (available from any good wine merchant) will keep it drinkable – but not for more than two or three days.

White wine should not be stored long-term in the fridge. Store as above, and then chill before serving.

If you're storing finer wines for a long time, it's best to ask your wine merchant's advice about how long to store it before its optimum drinking age… if it lasts that long!

It's easy to try to impress with an expensive, well-known label. People sometimes keep a special bottle of wine for, say, Christmas Day when in fact an everyday wine may be more on target.

the right wine for the occasion

The 'special bottle' may disappoint, or may not work with the kind of food that's being served. Remember, too, that all wines have a time by which it's best to drink them – so don't store your good wine for too long. If you are unsure, go online or ask your wine merchant.

The first thing to consider when choosing a wine for a special occasion is whether you are serving food. Many of the more famous French whites – Chablis, or Sancerre, for example, or a crisp New Zealand Sauvignon Blanc – are made for drinking at the table with food. So if you're hosting a party where people will be standing around drinking, but not eating, then these are not the right wines for the day. What you're looking for is a crowd-pleaser – something soft and ripe, chardonnay-based, for example (though not too heavily oaked). Or, if you're serving red, something from the Rhône Valley with a more generous fruit character, or a New World pinot noir that's suitable for drinking without food. Talk to your wine merchant, explain what kind of food you are serving, if any, and be guided by what they have to say. A good wine merchant will want to get it right just as much as you do.

Blanc de
Lynch-Bages

2004

PRODUCE OF FRANCE

BORDEAUX

APPELLATION BORDEAUX CONTROLÉE

ZES - PROPRIETAIRE A PAUILLAC - FRANCE

VIN BLANC

EAU-GRILLET

LATION CONTROLÉE

2001

BOUTEILLE AU CHATEAU

YRET-GACHET

HATEAU-GRILLET • VÉRIN 42410 • FRANCE

FRANCE

75 c

Puligny-M

La Ga

Appellation Puligny-Montra

Mis en boutei

Etienne

PULIGNY-MONTRACHET - C

Produce of F

People sometimes wonder whether the 'white wine with fish, red wine with meat' rule really matters. While we think that you should drink the wine you want, we also believe that there are reasons for the customs and traditions that have developed around wine over hundreds of years.

the wine with fish question

Like all traditions, people will be tempted to break with them – if only to make a point, or attempt to start a trend. And while there's perhaps no harm in that, the fact is that most dry white wines go with fish, and most red wines go with meat. The only exception might be a very rich fish dish, which can be complemented by a light red – maybe a pinot noir or gamay-based wine.

Which wine for foie gras?

The classic accompaniment to foie gras is Sauternes, but you should also consider a late-harvest Gewürztraminer or Tokay Pinot Gris, a rich Chardonnay or even a full-on red from Cahors.

Serve your foie gras at the same temperature as your cheese.

'In an ideal world, we would prefer if dessert wines were called sweet wines. The 'dessert wine' label has meant that people tend to drink them only with dessert.'
Simon Tyrrell

the sweeter side of things

In fact, sweet wines are quite versatile, and their sweetness can actually work better when served with something savoury. For example, Sauternes is one of a number of ideal partners for foie gras, and an Auslese works beautifully with roast goose. A good sweet wine should have a strong core of acidity — otherwise it will be too cloying and clingy. There are many different styles of sweet wines around. If you need advice, be guided by your wine waiter or your local wine merchant.

'There is no love sincerer than the love of food.'

George Bernard Shaw

At ely, we know that there is great pleasure to be had in eating and drinking according to the cycle of nature. With wine, this comes almost naturally, when a warm summer's day makes us automatically reach for a crisp Sancerre before a rich Burgundy. With food, however, it's not always so simple.

eating with the seasons

The level of choice available in recent years has made all kinds of foods available to us, all year round. But, while the supermarkets may have strawberries on their shelves in December, their taste will never compare to those that grow locally in mid-summer. Hardly surprising, when you think of the miles those strawberries have flown. Eating according to the seasons, wherever possible, takes better care of the planet, but it's also the healthiest way to live. Fruit and vegetables grown locally – especially organically – retain their goodness in a way their long-travelled, companions can never aspire to.

A visit to a local farmers' market* at any time of year makes it easy to pick the foods that grow locally, and keep the cook interested and inspired. In the following pages, we take you through ideas for eating and drinking according to the season, using some of our favourite recipes from ely winebar, ely chq and ely hq.

We don't, however, mean to make you feel guilty for reaching for a winter strawberry once in a while. At ely, while we ensure that the main elements of a recipe are always seasonal, we do, on occasion, make use of other ingredients in order to add colour or texture to a dish. We've yet to come across a homegrown pineapple, banana or kiwi fruit. Many fruits and vegetables that were previously unavailable in Ireland have added variety and taste to our diet in more recent years, and we welcome that. But we can grow our own apples, carrots, turnips and potatoes; and breed our own chickens and cows. It makes no sense to choose imported versions of these ingredients, when they're readily available to us at home. By following the flow of the seasons and eating according to what is naturally and locally available, we'll be doing what's best for the environment, and taking good care of ourselves.

*See www.irishfarmersmarkets.ie for your local farmers' market

The beef and pork at ely come from an organic farm run
by Erik's father, Hugh, in The Burren, County Clare.

down on the farm

A neighbouring organic farmer, who lives in the house used in the TV series, *Father Ted*, supplies most
of the lamb. The meat is known, for obvious reasons to fans of the show, as 'Craggy Island Lamb'.
Hugh farms roughly 450 acres of typical Burren land – plenty of rock, with wild flowers found nowhere
else in the world. The farm is home to 120 animals that are organically sourced and farmed according
to a system that's 6,000 years old and unique to the area. The animals spend summers on the lowlands,
and winters on the highlands. This is because the limestone rock acts like a huge storage heater,
absorbing the heat that comes from the Atlantic, hitting the west coast of Ireland during summer and
autumn. Even throughout winter there is little frost on the highlands, while the grasses and herbs
continue to grow.

With the meat being transferred from Co. Clare to Dublin in a matter of hours, ely lives by the
fundamental principle of the organic movement, 'Local produce for a local market'. The ely carbon
footprint is kept to a minimum, and the quality of food served is as good as it gets.

'The breeds we farm are more naturally suited to the environment in The Burren. Because of this, and the traditional, strictly organic farming methods we use, we like to think the animals have a better, more extensive life.'

Hugh Robson

The thinking at ely has always been that people want to be able to enjoy their wine with something to eat – but without the fuss and bother of a formal meal.

winebar food that works

While a plateful of tapas works perfectly in Spain, here in Ireland, we've found that the cooler climate dictates a different menu, something substantial, maybe warming, and possibly eaten as a single dish. That's why we serve good quality, fresh food that's easily managed and easily shared. Our ely cold charger – a plate of cheese with cured meats that feeds a few – has been a favourite from the early days. Other favourites include our organic beef burger, organic bangers and mash and ely fishcakes. The menus have developed and evolved considerably as we've expanded into ely chq and ely hq – where we now serve seafood and antipasta chargers too, for example, as well as some of the more sophisticated recipes you'll find in these pages. However, we believe that food should not overpower wine. The emphasis is always on the quality of the ingredients rather than bombarding the senses, and our traditional ely winebar dishes still feature in some form or other at all three ely venues.

'Fish, to taste right, must swim three times – in water, in butter, and in wine.'

Polish proverb

recipes through the seasons

As the days begin to get longer and the first daffodils appear,
those hearty winter stews start to seem a little heavy.

spring

Leafy salads, tender baby carrots, bright spring greens and succulent spring lamb all appear
to inspire the cook. That very special spring favourite, purple-sprouting broccoli, makes its
fleeting appearance – and shouldn't be missed. Late spring brings the very first asparagus,
delicious served with nothing else but melted butter. When it comes to wine, white seems the
right choice with much of what we're eating.

A note for the cook

For a more sophisticated dish, top the poached egg with a spoonful of caviar and arrange the asparagus alongside.

Locally grown, organic asparagus is one of the joys of spring.
This dish makes a great starter or a healthy snack at any time.

asparagus and poached egg on toast

What you need

16 spears green asparagus
16 spears white asparagus
rock salt, black pepper
1 small loaf bread
olive oil
1 garlic clove, halved
4 organic eggs
white wine vinegar
butter
rocket essence
(see page 224)

Serves 4

What to do

Hold each end of each asparagus spear and bend the stalk. The spear will break at the point where it becomes tough. Discard the tough ends. Blanch the spears in a large pot of boiling water with a good handful of salt to help the asparagus hold its colour. Cover and cook for 40–50 seconds then strain and submerge in iced water. When the asparagus is cold, place on kitchen paper and set aside, or refrigerate until required.

Cut 4 slices of bread, drizzle with a good quantity of olive oil and rub with the halved garlic clove. Toast or grill both sides. Poach the eggs with a pinch of salt and 1 tsp vinegar for 2 minutes in boiling water (you want the egg yolk to be runny).

Meanwhile, melt a knob of butter in a pan and add a handful of the asparagus. Season with rock salt and black pepper. Repeat this process until all spears are heated through.

Drizzle the rocket essence around the edges of each plate. Place the toast in the centre. Gently heap the asparagus over the toast (4 spears of green and 4 of white per plate). Remove the egg from the water and place on top. Pierce the egg with a fork so that it coats the asparagus and runs through the toast.

A wine that works

Château Jolys, a dry white from Jurançon, near the French Pyrénées. Fresh, with mineral and citrus notes and even a hint of asparagus. Most importantly, the flavours won't overpower the asparagus, while the acidity will cut through the poached eggs.

Also try

Cuvée Asperges, a blend of muscat, pinot gris and riesling, made with asparagus and spring in mind.

Classic winebar fare and easily prepared in advance. This recipe has been a favourite at ely winebar since the early days.

chicken liver pâté

What to do

Slowly cook the livers, butter and garlic together for 15 minutes, stirring occasionally. Add the brandy and cook for a further 10 minutes. Blend in a processor until smooth and season with salt and pepper.

Line a 450g (1lb) loaf tin with cling film and pour in the chicken liver mixture. Smooth over with a palette knife. Place in the fridge overnight.

Next day, remove from the fridge and turn the terrine out of the tin. Remove the cling film and slice with a warm knife. Serve with fingers or triangles of toast, a light chutney and some green leaves.

A wine that works

You can never have enough good sherry. It is so versatile in its many styles, and a little goes a long way. 'Peninsula' Palo Cortado by Lustau has a powerful nose, with nuts and soft oak showing through. There is a very long, warm finish with a pleasant bitterness.

Also try

Domaine des Nugues Beaujolais.

What you need

500g chicken livers
250g butter
2 cloves garlic, peeled
120ml brandy
rock salt, black pepper

Serves 8

Pesto is really easy to make at home and always worth the effort.

classic pesto

What you need

200g toasted pine nuts,
plus extra to serve

200g fresh basil leaves,
plus extra to serve

3 garlic cloves, roughly chopped

1 tsp rock salt

200ml extra virgin olive oil,
plus 1 extra tbsp

100g parmesan cheese, finely
grated, plus extra to serve

Serves 6

What to do

Put the pine nuts in a small pan and heat gently, stirring continuously, until golden brown – be careful not to burn them. Put the basil, pine nuts, garlic and a good pinch of salt with 200ml olive oil into a food processor. Pulse the mixture until it reaches a creamy consistency. Add the parmesan and pulse again. Stir into freshly cooked spaghetti, use as a dip, or spread over bruschetta – however you like your pesto! Serve with extra pine nuts, basil leaves and parmesan.

To store, spoon into a screwtop jar, or preserving jar and cover with 1 tbsp oil. The pesto will keep in the fridge for 3 days.

A note for the cook

Traditionally, pesto is made with basil leaves, but rocket works, too, and adds a bit of bite. So, when summertime brings lots of fresh rocket to your local greengrocer or farmers' market, try making it with this instead for a change.

A great way to use butternut squash and a perfect vegetarian option when you leave out the bean and bacon sauce. Simply dress with butter or a good olive oil and serve with a green leaf salad.

butternut squash ravioli
with broad beans and bacon

What to do

Dice the squash into small cubes. Heat 1 tbsp oil in a pot and sauté the shallots and garlic to colour slightly. Add the bouquet garni, then add the squash and cook for 15 minutes on medium heat until it softens. Remove from the heat and leave in the pot. The residual heat in the squash will finish the cooking process. Season to taste.

Roll out the pasta on a lightly floured surface into 2 x 30cm sheets. The width will depend on your pasta machine.

Remove the bouquet garni and form the cooled squash into 4 bundles. Evenly space these in a single row across the centre of the bottom sheet of pasta. Brush the pasta with egg and then drape the second sheet over top, working from left to right and sealing around the edges of each bundle by pressing down with your fingers. Cup your hand around each bundle of ravioli to chase the air out, making sure the pasta is level and has no creases. Then cut around each one with a round pasta or pastry cutter to make individual ravioli portions.

Bring a large pot of salted water to the boil. Drop the ravioli in gently and cook for 3-4 minutes or until they start to float. Remove with a slotted spoon and set aside.

Pop the beans out of their pods and add to a pan with the bacon and a drizzle of oil. Sauté for 2-3 minutes and season with black pepper. Spoon the beans and bacon among the serving dishes, top with the ravioli and drizzle with olive oil.

A wine that works

Pieropan 'la Rocca' Soave has to be one of the finest, most opulent Soaves available. Made from one hundred per cent garganega, it is rich with a seam of minerals and acidity, which keeps it streamlined. Lovely hints of spice, nuts and honey with a long complex finish.

Also try

Cakebread Sauvignon Blanc from Rutherford, Napa Valley, California.

What you need

200g butternut squash (peeled weight)

1-2 tbsp olive oil

50g shallots, diced (about 2 shallots)

2 cloves garlic, chopped

1 bouquet garni of thyme and bay leaf

rock salt, black pepper

200g fresh pasta dough (see recipe on page 97)

flour, for dusting

1 egg, beaten, for brushing

50g broad beans (frozen are best)

25g bacon, diced (about 2 rashers)

good quality extra virgin olive oil

Serves 4

A note for the cook
You can buy special pasta cutters for ravioli from good cookware shops.

These ravioli can easily be made in advance and placed on a floured, covered tray in the freezer until you are ready to serve. Cook them from frozen.

Traditionally, salade niçoise is made with anchovies only. Today, tuna is often included in the dish – feel free to add it to the recipe below if that's the way you like it.

salade niçoise

What to do

Poach the eggs for 3-5 minutes. Boil the potatoes and blanch the green beans until just tender. Allow the potatoes to cool and slice them.

Place all the ingredients apart from the eggs in a salad bowl and season with salt and pepper. Drizzle with olive oil, cut the eggs in half and place on top to serve.

A wine that works

Domaine du Monteillet 'Rosé d'une Nuit', is made from pure syrah in the northern Rhône. It has lively, fresh, summer fruit characters of strawberry and redcurrant, a touch of oak and nice acidity. It works really well with the anchovies and olive oil.

Also try

Domaine Stéphane Ogier 'Viognier de Rosine', from Collines Rhôdaniennes.

What you need

5 free-range or organic eggs
5 new season baby potatoes
200g extra fine green beans, tailed
20 pitted kalamata olives
1 small red onion, finely sliced
1 tin unsalted anchovies in oil, drained
250g cherry tomatoes, quartered (1 punnet)
1 cucumber, peeled, seeded and diced
rock salt, black pepper
good quality extra virgin olive oil

Serves 4

The rich, creamy wine and mushroom sauce make this a substantial dish for vegetarians and meat-eaters alike.

spinach and ricotta ravioli
with wild mushroom sauce

What you need

250-300g fresh pasta (see page 97)

For the ravioli filling

1kg spinach

1 tbsp olive oil

1 clove garlic, chopped

rock salt, black pepper

2 sprigs thyme, leaves picked

3 organic egg yolks, beaten

80g parmesan cheese

400g ricotta

For the mushroom sauce

5 tbsp extra virgin olive oil or white truffle oil

1 shallot, chopped

1 clove garlic, finely chopped

2 sprigs thyme, leaves picked

600g mixed wild or cultivated mushrooms, thinly sliced

240ml dry white wine

600ml double cream

200g grana padano (parmesan will do), grated

rock salt, black pepper

parmesan shavings, to serve

Serves 4

What to do

For the filling, steam the spinach for about 30 seconds then drop into ice-cold water. Remove and squeeze as much water out as possible. Heat the oil in a pan and add the garlic. Cook gently, then add the spinach and sauté, then season. Finely chop the spinach. Put the spinach in a bowl and add the thyme, egg yolks, parmesan and ricotta. Mix and season well.

To assemble the ravioli, divide the pasta into 4 portions. Use a pasta machine to roll into 4 sheets. Alternatively, use a rolling pin on a lightly floured work surface. Lay 1 sheet on a large baking tray. Take half of the filling and spoon it into 4 evenly spaced, separate piles across the sheet. Brush with egg and then place a second sheet on top, sealing around the edges of each bundle by pressing down with your fingers. Using a knife, cut around each one to make individual ravioli squares. Cup your hand around each ravioli to chase the air out, making sure the pasta has no creases. Repeat with the remaining 2 pasta sheets and the rest of the filling.

For the sauce, heat 2 tbsp oil in a pan and add the shallot, garlic and thyme. Cook until soft. Add the mushrooms and cook until all the liquid evaporates. Add the wine and reduce by half. Add the cream. Bring to a boil and reduce the heat, then simmer for 5 minutes and stir in the cheese. Season.

Bring a large pot of salted water to the boil. Drop the ravioli in gently and cook for 3-4 minutes or until they start to float. Remove with a slotted spoon to the serving plates. Spoon the mushroom sauce over each plate of ravioli. Drizzle with the remaining olive oil and scatter parmesan shavings over the top.

A wine that works

An unoaked Chardonnay such as Domaine Talmard from the Village of Uchizy in Mâcon, Burgundy. Ripe, fresh fruit – without the crisp acidity of a Sauvignon Blanc – rests easily with the dryness of the cheese and richness of the cream and wild mushrooms.

Also try

Domaine Sipp Mack, a Pinot Blanc from Alsace.

The preparation for this chunky, yet elegant broth may seem lengthy, but soaking beans requires no real effort. The end result is more than worth the time taken.

scallop and bean broth

What to do

Soak all the beans separately in water for 6-12 hrs.

Cook the beans and lentils in batches. Place in salted water, bring to the boil, reduce to a simmer. You'll need to do this separately because they have different sizes and cooking times – on average, 15-20 minutes for each batch.

Finely chop the shallot and sauté in a pot in a little oil until soft. Add the white wine and lime juice to deglaze, then reduce the liquid by half. Add the stock and beans and lentils. Now split the vanilla pod and place in the pot with the bay leaves. Add the cream. Season lightly and leave on a low simmer for 5-8 minutes. Make sure you don't overcook or you may end up with a bean soup.

Meanwhile, fry the scallops in a little oil until golden brown. Scallops cook very quickly so do not leave them for too long. Ideally, colour them on one side, turn over and turn off the heat.

Divide the broth evenly among 4 bowls and place 4 scallops over each. Garnish with flat-leaf parsley.

A note for the cook

You should be able to source the beans specified from most good supermarkets. If you like, you could substitute dried butter beans or broad beans, but this will alter the texture of the soup.

A wine that works

The vanilla in this dish calls for a wine with some maturity and development. Try the Vouvray Sec from Société Huet with 6-7 years in bottle. It's a Chenin Blanc that has honey and wax characters, plus the requisite acidity to balance the cream.

Also try

Clos du Papillon Savennières from Domaine des Baumard.

What you need

50g flageolet beans

50g borlotti beans

50g white coco beans

50g puy lentils

1 shallot

olive oil

½ glass white wine

juice of a lime

100ml vegetable stock (see page 224)

1 vanilla pod

2 bay leaves

100ml cream

rock salt, black pepper

16 large scallops

bunch of flat-leaf parsley

Serves 4

Most of today's salmon is farmed, so it's always worth buying organically farmed salmon. The quality has improved dramatically since the introduction of organic farming methods.

organic salmon

with pea purée, orange and fennel sauce and crispy pancetta

What you need

2 fennel bulbs, quartered,
reserving the fennel leaves
to garnish

200ml freshly squeezed
orange juice

125ml Pernod

2 star anise

½ cinnamon stick

50g butter

600g peas, fresh or frozen

75ml extra virgin olive oil

rock salt, black pepper

1kg organically farmed salmon,
skinned and cut into 4 portions

8 slices pancetta

25ml cream

Serves 4

What to do

Preheat the oven to 130°C. To make the orange and fennel sauce, place the fennel in a medium-sized saucepan with the orange juice, Pernod, star anise and cinnamon. Bring to the boil over a medium heat. Reduce the heat and allow to simmer until the fennel is tender. Remove the fennel and set aside. Reduce the cooking liquid by half and whisk in 25g of the butter.

Blanch the peas for 10-15 seconds. Blitz the peas and remaining butter in a blender.

Heat the oil in a roasting tray in the oven. Add salt and pepper to the tray then place the salmon, skin-side down, for a few seconds to colour. Turn the salmon over and return to the oven for 8-10 minutes. Remove from the tray, set aside and cover.

At the same time, cook the slices of pancetta in a frying pan. Remove and place on kitchen paper. Place the fennel bulbs in the pan and heat through in the pancetta fat until they are a light, golden brown. Heat the cream in a pot and add the pea purée, stirring all the time. Do not cover or over-cook, as this will turn it brown.

Place a portion of salmon and pea purée on each plate, add 2 pieces of fennel and drizzle over the sauce. Crumble 2 pancetta slices over each dish and garnish with fennel leaves.

A wine that works

Both the orange and the pea bring sweetness to this dish, while the fennel, anise and cinnamon add spice, so the wine needs to be able to stand out in its own right. 'Grand Elevage' from Jean-Marie Guffens of Verget is an equal blend of meursault and puligny-montrachet grapes. A bold, juicy Chardonnay with lemon, eucalyptus, minerals and a little oak.

Also try

Georg Breuer 'Sauvage' from the Rheingau, Germany.

A note for the cook

People often cook sausages too quickly. To bring out the full flavour and make sure they're thoroughly cooked, sear the bangers on all sides in a hot pan, reduce the heat and cook gently to your taste.

Remember not to overwork the mash – it gets gloopy if you do. Stop mashing just as soon as you think it's the right consistency.

This traditional, much loved dish is a staple at ely winebar, where we use our own, organic free-range pork to make our bangers. All we add is a little salt, pepper, garlic and ginger. If you're lucky, your local butcher will make his own sausages – the plumper the better. Ask for them to be flavoured to your taste – they'll usually oblige.

bangers and mash

What you need

1kg rooster potatoes, peeled
75g butter
100g shallots, finely sliced
500ml cream
75g garden peas
8 of your favourite sausages
rock salt, black pepper

Serves 4

What to do

First, chop the potatoes into quarter pieces and cook in plenty of boiling, salted water until soft. Melt the butter in a separate pot and sweat the shallots until they are translucent. Add the cream to the pot and bring to the boil. Add the peas and simmer for 1 minute. Drain the potatoes and place a dry, clean cloth over them for 5 minutes to dry them out a little.

Put the sausages on to grill or fry, according to preference (see below), keeping an eye on them while you complete the next step.

Mash the potatoes until they are completely lump-free. Add half the shallot mixture and mix. Then add the rest of the shallot mixture and stir vigorously. Season to taste.

Place a generous spoon of the potato mix with a couple of sausages on each plate and serve with an onion gravy or a grainy mustard. Delicious with a tomato and onion relish (see page 224).

A wine that works

It's got to be Domaine Alary 'la Brunotte' from the village of Cairanne in the Rhône valley. The lovely peppery bite, which comes from the grenache, balances the richness of the organic pork, while being full-bodied enough not to be overpowered by the buttery mash.

Also try

Finca Viladellops from Penedés in northern Spain.

The quality of the main ingredients are the key to this dish. Make sure that your beef is well hung and the prawns are fresh.

surf 'n' turf

What to do

Ask your butcher to trim and cut the fillet into 4 equal portions. Finely chop the shallots and half the capers. Mix the shallots, chopped capers and some freshly ground black pepper into the butter. Either divide this among 4 small, individual ramekins for serving, or roll it into one long sausage shape using parchment paper. Place in the fridge.

Quarter the tomatoes and lemon and set aside.

Heat a grill pan until smoking. Meanwhile drizzle the steak with olive oil, and season with salt and pepper. Remove the prawn shells along the back.

Cook the fillets for 2-3 minutes on each side for medium, or 1½ minutes for rare and 4-5 minutes for well-done. Set aside in a warm place to relax. Meanwhile cook the prawns on the same grill pan for 1½ minutes on each side.

Place some lettuce leaves with 2 tomato quarters at one end of each plate with a wedge of lemon. Then add 2 dublin bay prawns and the fillet steak, with 2 sprigs of rosemary as a garnish. Add the butter to the plate, either in the small ramekins, or sliced from the 'sausage', and place the remaining capers on top of the butter.

A wine that works

Fish or meat, red or white? A happy compromise might be the power and finesse of a great white Burgundy. Domaine Leflaive Puligny-Montrachet Les Pucelles offers minerality, extraordinary texture, intense flavour and a very long finish. What a compromise!

Also try

Domaine de Fondrèche Persia, a white Côtes du Ventoux.

What you need

750g fillet steak
2 large shallots
50g capers
rock salt and black pepper
250g butter, soft
2 tomatoes
1 lemon
olive oil for seasoning
8-12 dublin bay prawns (whole)
2 baby gems or 1 cos lettuce
8 sprigs of rosemary

Serves 4

A note for the cook
To make a quick jus to serve with the lamb, place the roasting tray you cooked the lamb in over a medium heat, add a glass each of stock and red wine, simmer to reduce by half and season.

All our organic lamb comes from our neighbours in The Burren, in particular, Patrick and Cheryl McCormack, who live in the 'Craggy Island' house used in the *Father Ted* TV series.

organic spring lamb
with smoked gubbeen dauphinoise and roasted vegetables

What you need

3 tsp ground cumin

rock salt, black pepper

4 x 4-bone racks of lamb, each about 200g (ask your butcher to prepare them for you)

120ml olive oil

25g sea salt

2 cloves garlic, peeled and roughly chopped

2 aubergines, halved lengthways, then quartered

150g cherry vine tomatoes (still on the vine)

For the potatoes

170ml cream

110ml milk

1 egg

rock salt, black pepper

600g potatoes, peeled

1 medium onion

50g smoked gubbeen cheese, grated

Serves 4

What to do

Preheat the oven to 140°C. To prepare the potatoes, whisk the cream, milk and egg together and season. Finely slice the potatoes and onion and layer into an ovenproof dish. Cover with the cream mixture. Sprinkle the smoked gubbeen over the top. Bake for 55 minutes.

Mix the ground cumin with some salt and pepper. Sprinkle over the lamb and set aside.

Heat half the olive oil on a roasting tin. Add the sea salt, garlic and aubergines. Place in the oven 15 minutes before the potatoes have finished cooking. Remove with the potatoes. Set both potatoes and aubergines aside, covering the potatoes with tin foil to keep warm.

Turn the oven up to 200°C and allow it to reach the correct temperature.

Heat the remaining oil in a roasting tray in the oven for 5-7 minutes. Seal the lamb in the tray by placing each end of the rack firmly on the hot surface for 30 seconds. This helps seal in the juices. Then roast in the oven for 25-30 minutes (this will cook the meat to 'medium').

Add the cherry vine tomatoes to the aubergines and return the tray to the oven 8-10 minutes before the lamb has finished cooking. Remove the vegetables, cover with foil and allow the lamb to rest at room temperature for 10 minutes.

Arrange a rack on each plate or cut into chops and serve with the vegetables.

A wine that works

Traditionally, lamb has been paired with Pinot Noir – Burgundy, to be exact. But try the truly rewarding 'l'Ame Soeur' – a Syrah from Stéphane Ogier in the northern Rhône. A baby Côte-Rôtie that's fragrant, full-bodied and smoky with spice, herbs and black fruit. Supple and elegant.

Also try

Cornish Point Pinot Noir from central Otago in New Zealand.

This dish is a complete meal in one. 'Risotto allo zafferano', or saffron risotto, is traditionally served with 'ossobucco', from the Lombardy region in northern Italy, and together they make a great combination. Ask your butcher to slice the meat.

ossobucco with risotto milanese

What you need

For the ossobucco

2 tbsp olive oil

2 carrots, diced

2 celery sticks, diced

1 onion, diced

1 clove garlic, chopped

2 sprigs thyme, chopped

2 sprigs rosemary, chopped

4 x 300g slices of veal shank

rock salt, black pepper

2 tbsp plain white flour

350ml red wine

500ml vegetable or chicken stock

1 x 800g tin chopped tomatoes

1 tbsp tomato purée

zest of ½ orange and ½ lemon

For the risotto

1.75 litres vegetable or chicken stock (see page 224)

10 threads of saffron

4 tbsp olive oil

1 small onion, finely chopped

350g risotto rice (preferably carnaroli)

85g butter

6 tbsp grated parmesan cheese, plus extra for serving

rock salt, black pepper

Serves 4

What to do

First, make the ossobucco. In a large, wide pan – a roasting tray or large frying pan is ideal – heat the oil over a medium heat. Add the carrots, celery, onion, garlic, thyme and rosemary. Stir and cook until the onion and garlic are translucent. Season the meat slices with salt and pepper, and dust with flour. Pop the meat in the pan with the vegetables. Stir and cook the meat and vegetables over a medium heat until the meat begins to brown, then add the wine. Cook until the liquid has reduced by half, then add half the stock, and reduce again by half. Add the chopped tomatoes and gently stir. Cover and cook for 30 minutes. Stir every now and again.

When the 30 minutes are up, add the tomato purée and the remaining stock. Reduce the heat to simmering point and allow the ossobucco to cook, covered, for another hour. The ossobucco is ready when the meat is almost falling off the bone.

While the meat is cooking, prepare the risotto according to the recipe on page 225, adding half the saffron to the stock to start with. Once half the stock has been used up, add the rest of the saffron to the risotto. When the risotto is ready, remove the pan from the heat and add the butter, parmesan cheese, salt and pepper to taste. Stir vigorously for about 30 seconds to give a creamy, glossy finish to the risotto.

Remove the meat from the heat, adding the zests of orange and lemon. Season well and serve with the risotto milanese. If you want to add texture to the dish, serve with chargrilled asparagus tips.

A wine that works

Tenuta Fontodi, Chianti Classico, is pure sangiovese. It's organically grown and has ripe, earthy dark fruit while still being elegant, and without the lean, bitter style that some Chiantis play on. The wine has the weight and acidity to match this full dish.

Also try

Sequoia Grove, Cabernet Sauvignon from Rutherford in Napa Valley, California.

If anyone was in any doubt about the benefits of organic farming from the point of view of taste, pork is the meat to try. Organic pork, of all organic meats, really shows the extra flavours and textures that organic farming can bring. If you can't get hold of suckling pig, you can use ordinary pork loin instead.

roast suckling pig
with black pudding and glazed baby carrots

What to do

Preheat the oven to 200°C. Divide the pre-rolled pork into 4 pieces. Add a large knob of butter to a large frying pan. Place over a medium heat until the butter sizzles. Add the pork to the pan and fry until the skin is crisp. Transfer to a roasting dish in the oven for 20-25 minutes, basting regularly.

While the pork is cooking, blanch the baby carrots and beans in a large pot of boiling salted water until barely cooked through but still tender. Remove from the pot and place in ice-cold water until cool. Drain and set aside.

Peel and chop the large carrots, place in a pot of lightly salted boiling water and cook until tender. Purée while hot, slowly adding the cream. Add a knob of butter and 1 tsp sugar.

Gently reheat the baby carrots and beans by tossing in a hot pan with a knob of butter. Lightly fry the black puddings in a little oil.

Arrange a portion of pork, black pudding, beans and carrots on each serving plate and finish with a spoon of carrot purée.

A wine that works

Abadia Retuerta Special Selection – a lovely, full-bodied savoury red from the town of Sardón de Duero, just outside the Ribera del Duero D.O. in Spain. Made from tempranillo (tinto fino) it has spice, leather and tobacco, and is bold enough to stand up to the rich flavours of this dish.

Also try

Alta Vista Malbec Mendoza, Argentina.

What you need

butter

1 x 1-1.5kg loin of organic suckling pig

bunch of baby carrots, peeled, leaving the little green tip, plus 4 large regular carrots, peeled

150g extra fine beans, tailed

rock salt

2 x 4in Clonakilty black puddings, skinned and halved

vegetable oil

50ml cream

1 tsp sugar

Serves 4

A note for the cook

Ask your butcher to bone and roll the suckling pig for you, leaving enough skin from the belly to cover the meat when rolled.

For a more formal presentation, place a stack of green beans on one side of the plate, with the pork sitting on top, and lay some baby carrots over the black pudding next to this. On the other side, spoon some carrot purée on the plate, then drag it out with the spoon to form a 'teardrop' shape.

Fresh, fruity and good for you – this delicious frozen treat offers guilt-free indulgence.

frozen yogurt berry cup

What you need

200g mixed nuts (pecans, walnuts, almonds)

500g mixed berries (strawberries, raspberries, blueberries, blackberries), fresh or frozen, plus a few fresh berries to serve

500g set organic plain yogurt, chilled

2 tbsp good honey

mint leaves, to serve

Serves 4-6

What to do

Toast the nuts by placing in a frying pan over a medium heat and tossing until golden brown – take care not to burn.

Put three-quarters of the fruit in a food processor and blend for 30 seconds. Add the yogurt and honey and blend for 1 minute until smooth. Taste for sweetness and add more honey if necessary. Layer the yogurt with the remaining berries in tall glasses, bowls or cups and freeze for a minimum of 2 hours.

To serve, top with the toasted nuts and some mint leaves.

A wine that works

Lustau East India is a blend of old, dry Oloroso and old sweet pedro ximénez, aged in American oak. There is a lovely richness, and it's sweet and nutty just like the dessert.

Also try

A glass of Bollinger Special Cuvée Champagne.

vanilla panna cotta
with a fresh berry sauce

What you need

1 vanilla pod
200ml double cream
200ml whipping cream
110g caster sugar
2 gelatine leaves
250g mixed seasonal berries
juice of ½ lemon
mint sprigs, to serve
icing sugar, to serve

Serves 6

What to do

Line 6 ramekins, each about 7cm in diameter and 5cm deep, with cling film. Begin by splitting the vanilla pod and removing the seeds with the back of a knife. Pour the two creams into a small saucepan and bring to the boil, adding the split vanilla pod and seeds and 50g of the caster sugar.

Soak the gelatine leaves in cold water. Remove the boiled cream mixture from the heat and remove the vanilla pod. Gently squeeze the gelatine and add to the cream, whisking thoroughly until dissolved. Pass through a fine strainer and pour into ramekins, making sure the vanilla seeds are evenly distributed. Cover the ramekins with more cling film to prevent a skin from forming, and place in the fridge until set (1-2 hours).

Reserving 6 whole berries for the garnish, place the berries, lemon juice and remaining caster sugar in a large saucepan and bring to the boil, stirring frequently. Carefully turn the panna cottas out of the ramekins, placing each one in the centre of a small pasta bowl. Use a spoon to spread the berry compote around each panna cotta. Garnish with the mint and whole berries and dust with the icing sugar.

A wine that works

Taittinger 'Nocturne' Champagne has, as the name suggests, been blended with after-dinner in mind. It has a fuller, richer style than other, drier champagnes and offers an intense smoothness. The overall style brings a softness to the mouth, a gentle acidity and a somewhat creamier texture. It's a great way to enjoy champagne when the crisper, more lively styles are too much at the end of a meal.

Also try

Château Tirecul la Gravière Monbazillac.

espresso crème brûlée

What you need

250ml cream

4 egg yolks

90g caster sugar

1 espresso cup of very strong
filter coffee, cold, about 100ml

3 tbsp Bailey's Irish Cream

caster sugar and icing sugar

fresh berries and crème fraîche,
to serve

Serves 6

What to do

Preheat the oven to 110°C. Heat the cream to almost boiling point, then remove from the heat.

Whisk the egg yolks and sugar until creamy in a heatproof bowl. Slowly pour the heated cream over the egg yolk mixture, whisking constantly to prevent the eggs from cooking. When all the cream is incorporated, stir for 2-3 minutes to ensure everything is well mixed. Then add the coffee and Baileys, tasting and adding more coffee if you wish.

Place 6 ramekins or espresso cups, each about 7cm in diameter and 5cm deep, on a deep roasting tray. Divide the mixture among the ramekins. Pour water into the tray up to the half-way point of each ramekin. This way of cooking – known as a bain-marie – helps to cook the brûlées in a moist environment, preventing them from drying out at the top.

Cook for 45-60 minutes. Leave to cool in the water of the bain-marie, then refrigerate until needed. Just before serving sprinkle with a mix of caster sugar and icing sugar, and caramelise the top with a blow-torch.

Serve with fresh berries and crème fraîche.

A note for the cook

Always add the hot cream to the egg mix and never the other way round. If you want to caramelise the top of each dessert you really need a blow torch. A domestic grill risks turning the brûlées into scrambled eggs!

A wine that works

Domaine du Mas Blanc Dr Parce – an aged Banyuls showing smooth, soft, intense black fruit; toasty on the nose. This is pure grenache – ultra-ripe. All in all, a French port.

Also try

Fernando de Castilla 'Antique' Pedro Ximénez from Jerez in Spain.

'Food is not about impressing people. It's about making them feel comfortable.'

Ina Garten

Of all of the seasons, summer spoils us. Week after week, from early May to September, fresh and locally grown ingredients appear at their peak in our fields, markets and shops, offering us the kind of variety no other season can compete with.

summer

Bundles of runner beans and broad beans, punnets of strawberries, raspberries, tomatoes, courgettes, peas, rocket and more, all vie for our attention. It's a time for simple, easy cooking – a roast organic chicken with a fresh salad, for example – and for eating outside whenever possible. When lunch is a whole baked sea bream, fragrant with fennel, or salmon with lemon wedges, new potatoes and garden peas, washed down with a chilled white wine or rosé, you know that summer has truly arrived.

There are many versions of this Spanish classic. This one takes its cue from one of the authentic Andalucian versions. Refreshing on a hot summer's day, gazpacho makes a perfect starter to a barbecue.

andalucian gazpacho

What to do

Remove the crusts from the bread. Cut 3 slices into small cubes and reserve. Soak the remaining slices in water for 10 minutes. Squeeze out the excess water and set aside.

Cut a cross in the base of each tomato then blanch, in batches, in a pan of boiling water for 10 seconds. Strain and place in a bowl of iced water. Peel when cool. Halve the tomatoes. Spoon the seeds into a bowl and put the tomato flesh into a separate bowl. Strain the juices from the seeds back over the bowl of tomato flesh, discarding the seeds.

Roughly chop 1 cucumber, half of the red pepper and 1 shallot. Add to the tomatoes. Blend the soaked bread and garlic in a processor until a paste forms. Add the tomatoes and roughly chopped vegetables and process until smooth. Gradually add 100ml oil, then the vinegar and cumin. Season to taste. Refrigerate the soup until chilled, 2-3 hours.

Finely chop the celery stalks and leaves, the remaining cucumber, pepper and shallot. Heat a small pan over a medium heat, add the almonds, tossing until they are golden brown – take care not to burn. Remove from the pan and wipe the pan clean. Heat the remaining oil over a medium heat and add the bread cubes, tossing until they are golden brown.

Serve the chilled gazpacho in bowls, drizzled with extra virgin olive oil. Place the vegetable accompaniments, croutons and almonds in separate bowls to pass around the table.

A wine that works

Fino sherry – such as Lustau – served chilled. Fino is the lightest in style and alcohol of all sherries. Always bone-dry, with hints of sea salt and grilled almond nuttiness. Treat your sherries like white wine – serve them chilled and use within two to three days of opening.

Also try

Domaine Roulot Bourgogne Aligoté.

What you need

6 slices day-old, rustic-style bread (1 medium-sized loaf)

1kg ripe plum tomatoes

2 cucumbers, peeled, halved and seeded

1 red pepper

2 shallots

1 clove garlic

140ml extra virgin olive oil

1 tbsp sherry vinegar

1 large pinch ground cumin

rock salt, black pepper

2 celery stalks with leaves

125g blanched almonds, halved

Serves 6

A note for the cook

This dish is best prepared the day before you want to eat.

If you have time, soak the squid in milk for a couple of hours before marinating, to break down its natural acidity. This will tenderise it. Pat dry on paper towels.

Squid is so quick and simple to cook; this zingy recipe is fast, fresh food at its tastiest. Ideally, marinate the squid overnight for best results.

pan-fried squid
with chilli and coriander

What you need

400g fresh squid (ask your fishmonger to clean it for you)

200ml olive oil

180g fresh coriander

3 red chillis

1 clove garlic, crushed

zest and juice of 1 lime

watercress or rocket, to dress plate

rock salt, black pepper

lemon wedges, to serve

bean sprouts, to garnish

rocket essence (see page 224, optional)

Serves 4

What to do

Slit the squid tube to open it out into one flat piece and score on the inside with a knife.

Warm the oil to room temperature (37º C) in a pan. Chop the coriander and 1 of the chillis and add these to the oil with the crushed garlic and the lime zest and juice. The tepid temperature of the oil will draw out the flavours of the herbs and chilli.

Transfer the oil to a plastic container, allow to cool slightly, then add the squid. Cover the container and place in the refrigerator overnight so the squid has a chance to take on the flavours.

Heat a pan on the hob until smoking, or prepare the barbecue. Remove the squid from the oil and give it a gentle squeeze to get rid of some of the oil. Place in the dry pan or on the barbecue grill and briefly colour on both sides. This should take no more than 3 minutes. When cooked, place on the plate with the salad leaves. Slice the remaining chillis. Scatter over the squid with the bean sprouts, and dress the plate with the rocket essence, if using. Season with salt and pepper and serve with a wedge of lemon.

A wine that works

Asian dishes require wines with moderate alcohol levels, soft tannins or crisp acidity and even a little residual sugar. A Mosel Riesling such as the Riesling Classic by Max Ferd. Richter has delicate floral aromas, a delicate flavour and a nice balance between sweetness and acidity.

Also try

Stéphane Montz Vin de Pays Collines Rhôdaniennes Viognier combines lower acidity and higher alchohol.

This all-time favourite starter uses everyday ingredients and is simple to make.

caesar salad

What to do

Make the dressing. Put the egg yolks in a food processor and blend slowly, pouring in the oil, then the vinegar and lime juice. Add all the remaining dressing ingredients and blitz until smooth. Refrigerate until needed.

Preheat the oven to 180°C. Mix the bread cubes with the clarified butter and place on a baking tray. Bake until golden brown. Set aside to cool. This can be done in advance.

Grill the bacon for 3 minutes or until crisp.

To assemble the salad, toss the leaves in a bowl with the dressing. Divide between 6 plates, topping each with croutons, crispy bacon and the cheese shavings.

A note for the cook

Remember to add your dressing to the salad as you are about to serve. And bear in mind, too, that less is more!

A wine that works

The unmistakeable bite of the garlic and anchovies calls for a bright white, such as the Dona Rosa Albariño from Rías Baixas in Spain. It's a fleshy wine with lively peach character and a refreshing lift. Perfect with this dish (and a little sunshine).

Also try

A Chardonnay such as a Bourgogne Blanc from Jean-Philippe Fichet.

What you need

For the dressing

2 organic egg yolks

200ml vegetable oil

1 tsp white wine vinegar

1 tsp lime juice

2 cloves garlic

5 anchovies in oil

½ tbsp capers

½ tbsp thyme leaves

½ tbsp flat-leaf parsley

½ tbsp worcestershire sauce

½ tsp tabasco

1 tbsp dijon mustard

50g parmesan cheese, finely grated

Serves 6

For the salad

4 slices bread, crusts removed and cut into cubes

100g butter, clarified (see page 223)

12 slices bacon

4 small heads cos lettuce, leaves washed and patted dry

200g grano padano cheese, cut into shavings

rock salt, black pepper

The warmed chorizo in this summer salad gives an oily, spicy flavour, while the beans balance the dish with a fresh bite. Prepare a little ahead to give time for chilling. The truffle oil brings out the earthiness of the potatoes beautifully, but extra virgin olive oil would be fine as a substitute.

bean salad with chorizo

What you need

200g extra fine green beans

rock salt, black pepper

9 new season baby potatoes

truffle oil, or best quality extra virgin olive oil

8 slices of chorizo (not dried – ask for chorizo for cooking)

frisée lettuce or baby rocket, to garnish

Serves 4

What to do

Place the beans in a pot of boiling salted water, put on the lid and blanch for 30 seconds. Place in iced water to stop the cooking process, then remove, drain and allow to come to room temperature.

Cook the potatoes in plenty of boiling salted water, drain and refrigerate until cool. Slice the potatoes, then allow them to come to room temperature. Drizzle lightly with a tiny amount of truffle oil and season. Set aside until you need to dress the plate.

Grill the chorizo on one side only, until it starts to give out oil. Reserve any oil that escapes during cooking to add colour and flavour to the dish later. Keep the chorizo warm so that there will be hot and cold ingredients in the final dish.

Layer the beans, potatoes and chorizo, either in a big serving bowl, or on individual plates. Drizzle with a little more truffle oil and the leftover chorizo cooking oil. Season and garnish with a small amount of French frisée lettuce or some baby rocket.

A wine that works

What's required here is a wine that works with both the beans and the chorizo. A Tokay Pinot Gris from Alsace, such as Domaine Weinbach Cuvée Laurence, shows layers of smoky peaches and honeysuckle. It's an opulent style of wine with grip, power, elegance and finesse all in one glass.

Also try

A Gewürztraminer from Domaine Sipp Mack, also from Alsace.

A light, refreshing salad that's quick and easy to make – and healthy, too!

cucumber and crab salad
with a mango smoothie

What to do

Drain the defrosted crab and dry on a clean, dry cloth.

Flake the crab into a bowl, removing any bits of shell you may find. Mix three-quarters of the crème fraîche with the crab and diced shallot and season with salt and pepper. Set aside in the fridge.

Using a peeler, run it from the top to the tail of the unpeeled cucumber to create long strips, working through, rather than round it, and discarding the outer strips on each side. Make sure you do not use the seeded centre of the cucumber. You will need 3-5 strips per person.

Peel and chop the mango. Put in a blender with the lime zest, juice, sugar, and the rest of the crème fraîche. Blitz to make a smoothie.

Place a spoonful of crab at one end of each cucumber strip, and roll up. There should be a small hollow above the crab for the smoothie.

Dress the centre of each plate with a handful of leaves. Then stand the rolls upright, arranging them around the leaves. Pour some of the smoothie into each roll, dotting more of the smoothie round the plate between the rolls to decorate.

A wine that works

St Hallett Eden Valley Riesling has limes on both the nose and the palate with plentiful tropical fruit flavours, such as passion fruit, giving a nice long finish. It is a very smart example of what Australia can do with the riesling grape.

Also try

Fillaboa Albariño from Rías Baixas in Spain.

What you need

250g good quality frozen crab meat, defrosted

1 small tub of crème fraîche (about 200g)

1 shallot, finely diced

rock salt, black pepper

1-2 cucumbers

1 mango

zest and juice of lime

25g caster sugar

selection of summer leaves

Serves 4

A note for the cook
You can make these rolls up to 3 hours in advance, cover with clingfilm and chill in the fridge. The amount of cucumber you need may depend on your skill in preparing the strips!

An interesting way to serve smoked salmon – and children love it! Perfect with the treacle brown bread. It's best made the day before you want to eat so the flavours have a chance to mingle and develop.

smoked salmon pâté
with treacle brown bread

What to do
Blend the cream cheese, butter and lemon zest.

Transfer to a bowl and fold in the smoked salmon and dill. Season to taste with the pepper and lemon juice. Spoon into individual ramekins, cover with cling film and leave in the fridge overnight or for at least 2 hours. Serve with brown bread on the side.

A note for the cook
If you are serving this for a dinner party, you could unmould the pâtés on to individual plates and drape some strips of smoked salmon around. Garnish with sprigs of fresh dill.

A wine that works
Vouvray, Chenin Blanc, from the Loire Valley. 'Les Argiles' from Domaine François Chidaine is a medium-bodied wine with a touch of residual sugar, a hint of honey, silky texture, crisp acidity and a dry finish.

Also try
Dog Point 'Section 94' Sauvignon Blanc, Marlborough, New Zealand.

What you need
500g cream cheese

250g butter, melted

zest and juice of 1 lemon

300g organic smoked salmon, chopped

25g chopped dill

black pepper

treacle brown bread, to serve (see page 225)

Serves 8

A note for the cook
This chicken makes a lovely Sunday lunch served with a mixed salad, fresh baguette and olive tapenade – even better if it's warm enough to eat outdoors.

The salt seals rather than flavours in this recipe, preserving the meat juices and producing a fabulously moist chicken. This is very much one for keen cooks, or those wanting to push the boat out, as rock salt is not cheap to buy in such quantities. However, you will be rewarded with a magnificent and unusual dish that more than delivers on flavour.

sea salt baked whole chicken

What you need

3kg rock salt

200ml water

1 small bulb fresh ginger, finely chopped with a little olive oil

6 large cloves garlic, finely chopped

2 spring onions, chopped

20ml sherry

1 whole star anise

1 medium organic whole chicken

15ml dark soy sauce

50ml peanut oil

For the dip

100ml dark soy sauce

50ml sesame oil

zest and juice of 1 lime

2 tbsp honey

Serves 4

What to do

Preheat the oven to 200°C. Mix the salt and water together in a large bowl, or bowls. Mix the ginger, garlic and spring onions together in a small bowl and add the sherry and whole star anise. Stuff the chicken cavity with this mix and seal with a skewer. Rub the outside of the chicken with dark soy sauce and allow to stand until the sauce is absorbed. Place a layer of at least 6cm of the salt mixture in a baking tray. Coat the chicken with peanut oil and place in the middle of the tray. Use the remaining salt mixture to cover the chicken, pressing firmly down on the skin. Place in the preheated oven for 30 minutes per 450g.

Meanwhile, mix the dip ingredients together and blend well.

When the chicken is cooked, remove from the oven and release from the salt packing by tapping with the back of a spoon. Allow to stand for 15 minutes to cool. Serve with the soy sauce dip.

A wine that works

Organic chicken can be fantastic, with a firmer texture and a flavour closer to guinea fowl than its over-produced brothers and sisters. The Pacific Rim ingredients and fine chicken need a serious wine with its own hint of the tropical. Grosset 'Piccadilly' Chardonnay, from the Clare Valley in South Australia, offers up generous flavours of nectarines and grapefruit, balanced by quality oak and a long, intense, slow finish.

Also try

Max Ferd. Richter 'Brauneberger' Riesling Spätlese Trocken from the Mosel in Germany.

A speciality of Tuscany, veal chop is best cooked to medium so that the meat is sweet and tender. Rib-eye or filet mignon also work well in this recipe.

grilled veal chops and radicchio
with lemon caper sauce

What to do

To make the dressing, whisk the olive oil with the vinegar, capers, parsley, lemon zest and garlic in a small bowl until well blended. Season with salt and pepper. This can be done 2 hours ahead and left to stand at room temperature.

Preheat the oven to 180°C. Parboil the potatoes, drain them and leave to cool, then place in the fridge to chill. Peel the potatoes, slice them, then toss in 2 tbsp olive oil and a pinch of rock salt. Roast the potatoes for 15 minutes until golden brown.

Meanwhile, place a baking tray in the oven to preheat. Heat a large, heavy frying pan. Brush the veal chops with 1 tbsp olive oil and sprinkle with salt and pepper. Place them in the pan and colour on each side. Transfer to the preheated baking tray and cook in the oven for 10 minutes. Three minutes before the end of cooking, toss the tomatoes with 1 tbsp olive oil, sprinkle with sugar and place on a roasting tray in the oven.

Toss the radicchio leaves lightly with some of the dressing. Heat a frying pan and add the leaves. Reduce the heat and cook for 3-4 minutes until wilted and golden brown, pressing lightly to flatten.

Divide the radicchio and veal chops evenly between 2 serving plates. Spoon the remaining dressing over, and serve with the roasted baby potatoes and the tomatoes.

A wine that works

'Guidalberto' from Tenuta San Guido, who also make the famed 'Sassicaia', in Bolgheri, Tuscany. 'Guidalberto' shares the same soil and climate as Sassicaia but is intentionally different in style. A blend of merlot, cabernet sauvignon and sangiovese, it has dark cherry and cedar characters from the merlot, a lovely ripe, rounded tannin structure, toasted oak and earthy character from the cabernet and perfume and strawberry fruit from the sangiovese. All of these come together to give a long, intense finish.

Also try

Canoe Ridge Merlot from Château Sainte Michelle in Washington State, USA.

What you need

10 baby potatoes

4 tbsp olive oil

rock salt, black pepper

2 veal chops

bunch of cherry tomatoes on the vine

caster sugar

6 radicchio leaves

For the dressing

3 tbsp extra virgin olive oil

1½ tbsp white balsamic vinegar, or a good quality chardonnay or white wine vinegar

1½ tbsp capers

handful flat-leaf parsley, chopped

zest of 1 lemon

1 small garlic clove, finely chopped

Serves 2

boning fish

Before you begin

When boning a whole fish the following points should be looked for to ensure freshness.

Eyes: bright, full and not sunken, no slime or cloudiness

Gills: bright red in colour with no bacterial slime

Flesh: firm and resilient so that when pressed the impression goes quickly. The fish must not be limp

Scales: these should lie flat and be moist and plentiful

Skin: this should be covered with a fresh sea slime or be smooth and moist with a good sheen and no abrasions

Smell: this must be pleasant with no smell of ammonia or sourness

Gutting

Fish should be gutted as soon as it leaves the water. The gut contains enzymes that break down the flesh rapidly, leading to spoilage. This can be done after the fish has been descaled and rinsed.

Slit the belly of the fish to expose the gut. Pull out the gut and remove as much of the blood line along the inner spine as possible. Use scissors to remove the gills at each side of the fish. Rinse the cavity under cold running water.

Scaling and trimming

Work in a sink under running water. Hold the fish gently by the head to keep it steady. Working from the tail to head with a strong blade scrape the fish, being careful never to angle the sharp end of the knife into the flesh. Always drag it facing away.

Filleting a round fish

Place the fish, head pointing away, on a cutting board. Using a sharp boning knife, make a crosswise cut just below the gill to separate the flesh from the head. Run the knife along the back from head to tail along the central bone. Lift the flesh as you go to make sure you are getting most of the meat. Lift the fillet and make a crosswise cut to separate the flesh from the tail. Proceed the same way for the other fillet. Trim away belly flap and remove visible pin bones with a pair of tweezers.

Filleting a flat fish

Cut the head by following the base of the head to avoid cutting the meat. Place the fish, head towards you, on a cutting board. Locate the central bone that divides the upper and lower fillets and make an incision with a knife. The tip of the blade should rest against the central bone. Slide the blade carefully between backbone and flesh, lifting the fillet away from the bone. Remove the other fillets in the same manner.

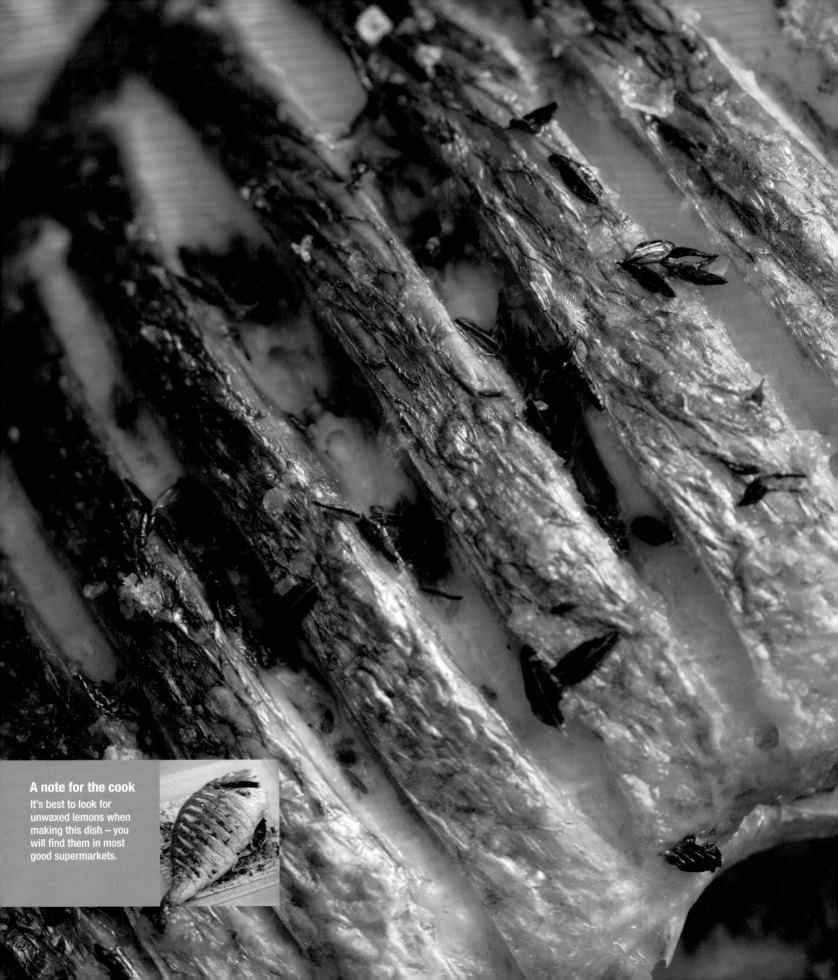

A note for the cook
It's best to look for unwaxed lemons when making this dish — you will find them in most good supermarkets.

Sea bream is a white-fleshed fish with a delicate flavour. This recipe results in a lovely crispy exterior and subtle flesh, which is beautifully offset by the fennel.

whole baked sea bream
with fennel and roast lemon

What you need

4 x 400-600g sea bream
(gutted, scaled, fins removed –
ask your fishmonger to do this
for you, or see pages 92-93)

1 fennel bulb

2 lemons, unwaxed

rock salt, black pepper

bunch of thyme, leaves picked

Serves 4

What to do

Preheat the oven to 190°C. Score the fish and pat the skin dry with a clean tea towel – this will help the skin to crisp.

Shred the fennel with a knife or mandoline, if you prefer. Quarter one of the lemons. Stuff the fennel into the cavity of each fish along with a wedge of lemon, and season with salt and pepper.

Place the fish on a tray lined with baking parchment. Season the skin of the fish, making sure that salt and pepper gets into the incisions made by scoring. This will introduce flavour into the flesh of the fish. Sprinkle the fish with the thyme leaves.

Bake for 8-12 minutes to ensure the fish is cooked right through – fish on the bone is denser than a fillet and needs extra cooking time.

Halve the remaining lemon and squeeze lemon juice over the top of each fish. Serve with new potatoes with mint and butter and extra fine green beans

A wine that works

Sipp Mack, a Pinot Blanc from Hunawihr in Alsace. This wine is relatively full-bodied with stone fruit flavours and balanced acidity. It has enough depth of flavour to cope with the fennel and lemon, but not too much, so that the fish is allowed to show through.

Also try

An alternative would be an Italian Pinot Grigio, such as Cesconi.

Homemade pasta is easier to make than you might think.

lasagne sheets

What you need

350g good Italian '00' flour, plus extra for dusting

2 eggs and 3 egg yolks (all large)

pinch of fine table salt

1 tsp olive oil

1 tbsp tepid water (or more if needed)

Serves 6

What to do

Put the flour, eggs and salt into a food processor and blitz until the mixture resembles coarse crumbs. Add the olive oil and blitz again briefly until the dough starts to come together. Add the water, being careful not to add too much – you need to make sure the dough does not become too sticky. Blitz again, then tip into a bowl and knead together for about 2 minutes. Turn on to lightly floured surface, wrap with cling film and leave aside to rest for half an hour in fridge.

Then, cut the dough into two pieces and work with one at a time. Roll out the dough thinly on a lightly floured surface and feed through the pasta machine several times until it is about 1mm thick. Store the sheets under a damp cloth while you are working

When ready to use the pasta, cook the sheets in boiling, salted water for about 2 minutes. Drain and use immediately, or put into iced water for 5-10 minutes.

A note for the cook

If you don't have a pasta machine, roll the pasta out into square sheets with a rolling pin on a floured surface. This recipe makes about 400g.

The lovely, fragrant scent of basil is one of the delights of summertime.
This delicious, vegetarian lasagne makes the most of that favourite herb.

pesto lasagne

What you need

400g lasagne sheets
(see page 97)

1 quantity pesto
(see page 45), doubling the
quantity of basil to 400g

250g tub ricotta, drained

3 large, ripe tomatoes

50g parmesan cheese, grated

50g pine nuts, toasted

1 bunch of basil, shredded

rocket leaves, to serve

Serves 6

What to do

Make the lasagne sheets. Preheat the oven to 180°C.

Put the pesto in a large mixing bowl and mix in the ricotta. Slice the tomatoes.

Arrange the lasagne sheets in an ovenproof dish, and spread with the pesto mix. Follow with a layer of tomatoes. Keep layering the pasta, pesto and tomatoes, finishing with a layer of pesto mix. Bake for 10-12 minutes, until cooked through. Meanwhile, preheat the grill.

When the lasagne is ready, sprinkle with the parmesan and grill for a few minutes until golden. Cut into wedges, sprinkle with toasted pine nuts and basil leaves and serve with rocket salad.

A note for the cook

The pesto mix can be prepared in advance, but the lasagne sheets should be cooked just before you are about to assemble the lasagne.

A wine that works

Pinot Grigio can be a little neutral but Alois Lageder in the Alto Adige of Northern Italy offers more than most. Alongside bracing crispness and acidity, with flavours of lime and a hint of ginger spice and mineral, this wine still gives plenty of ripe fruit and is well able to handle the pesto in this dish.

Also try

'Wild Boy' Chardonnay by Au Bon Climat in Santa Barbara County, USA.

A note for the cook

You can vary the vegetables depending on what is available in the shops and markets.

If you prefer, you can cook the vegetables on a barbecue or hot griddle.

If you have gas, roast the peppers directly in the flame until blackened, place in a bowl, cover with cling film and peel off the skin when cool.

This lovely, colourful side dish takes minutes to put together. Delicious with roasted or barbecued meats.

roasted vegetable platter
with buffalo mozzarella and parma ham

What you need

2 large aubergines

2 red peppers

2 yellow peppers

3 medium courgettes

1 bunch spring onions

1 bunch asparagus

3 medium red onions

1 bulb of garlic, sliced in half horizontally

olive oil

rock salt

sprig of thyme

sprig of rosemary

bunch each of parsley and chives (optional)

2 buffalo mozzarellas, to serve

6-8 slices Parma ham, to serve

Serves 6

What to do

Preheat the oven to 220-240°C and place a large roasting tray in the oven.

Cut the vegetables into large wedges of approximately the same size and put them in a bowl. Drizzle over enough olive oil to coat, sprinkle with rock salt and use your hands to mix. Add the thyme and rosemary.

Throw the vegetables into the preheated roasting tray and colour them for 1 minute on the hob. This gets the heat into them and stops them going soggy.

Transfer the tray to the oven and cook for 6-8 minutes. Chop the parsley and chives and scatter over the vegetables. Arrange the vegetables on a large serving dish.

Quarter the mozzarella and arrange over the roasted vegetables. Drape with slices of parma ham.

Serve immediately. If you like, you can serve the vegetables with fresh, warm, crusty bread, drizzled with extra virgin olive oil.

A wine that works

This dish is simplicity itself, evoking images of whiling away a balmy evening with a wine such as full-bodied, minerally Pouilly-Fuissé 'Terroir de Fuissé' by Olivier Merlin. It is rich, yet elegant, with lively aromas of apple, pear, some citrus fruit and a touch of oak. It's a wine that will open up and develop while you pick away at the roasted vegetables.

Also try

Ata Rangi 'Craighall' Chardonnay, from Martinborough in New Zealand.

preparing a lobster

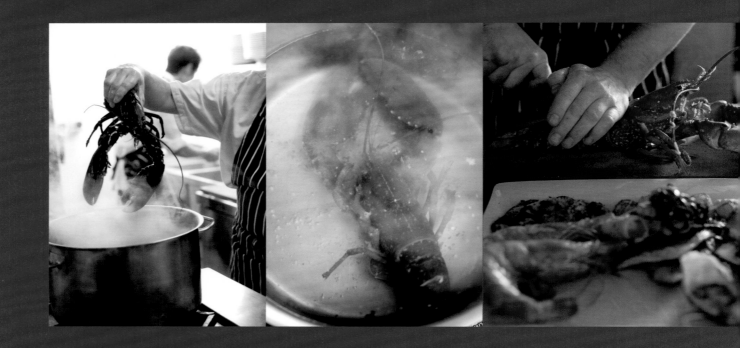

Bring a large pot of lightly salted water to the boil. Make sure that the water is boiling vigorously when you cook the lobster, or it will let out ink from the sac on the back of its head and taint the meat. Place the live lobster in the pot. Cover and simmer for 15-25 minutes for a salad, or 7-8 minutes if you are going to recook the lobster in a sauce, depending on size. Remove the lobster and leave to cool. Then, cut the lobster in half, lengthwise, with a long knife. Remove the 2 gills (near the head), the dark vein that runs down the tail and the small stomach sac in the head. Take out the tail meat, then crack open the claws with the back of a knife and remove the meat in one piece. For a delicious salad, cut into small chunks, mix with salad leaves and a lemon and herb dressing, and new potatoes.

This was a very popular dish in the early days of ely and was inspired by the Head Chef at the time, Franco. It's makes a great starter for a dinner party. Ask your fishmonger to prepare and clean the squid. Adapt the ingredients to your tastes.

seafood cold charger

What to do

Make sure all the mussels are open and discard any that are closed.

Cook the lobsters in boiling, salted water for 20-25 minutes. Once they are out of the water, the residual heat will continue to cook them. Poach the prawns for 1½ -2 minutes in boiling salted water. Remove and set aside. Like the lobster, they will continue to cook a little.

Add the squid to the water and cook for 30-50 seconds. Add the scallops and open mussels and cook for a few seconds. Remove from the water. Place the mussels, lobsters, prawns, squid and scallops on a large platter and leave to cool for a few seconds. Refrigerate and allow to cool completely.

Heat 50g clarified butter in a pan. Remove the scallops from the fridge and add to the pan. Cook briefly on each side for 40-50 seconds, or a maximum of 90 seconds to cook them through thoroughly. Remove from the pan and set aside. Wipe the pan and add the remaining butter. Add the salmon fillets and cook on both sides for 2-3 minutes in total.

Remove the mussels from the fridge. Heat the white wine in a large pan and add the mussels. Cook for 1½ minutes. If any mussels don't open, discard them. Remove the remaining mussels from the pan and leave to cool.

Remove the chilled seafood from the fridge and shell the lobster (see page 102) and prawns. The prawn shells will just peel away. You can leave them with the shell on if you prefer. Shuck the oysters (see page 120) at the last minute to ensure freshness.

Now arrange the shellfish around a large platter and garnish with lemon wedges.

Mix the finely chopped shallots with the red wine vinegar in a small pot or ramekin and serve alongside. Pour over some extra virgin olive oil. Tear or chop the herbs and scatter over.

A wine that works

Domaine Félines Jourdan Picpoul de Pinet, with its ripe pear and honey aromas and fresh fruit. Surprisingly full and rewarding for a medium-bodied wine.

Also try

Bernard Defaix Chablis Premier Cru from the Côtes de Léchet.

What you need

1kg mussels

2 large Irish lobsters

10 jumbo tiger prawns, or dublin bay prawns

500g squid (ask your fishmonger to clean it for you)

10-12 fresh scallops

100g butter, clarified (see page 223)

4 x 150g fillets of salmon

50ml white wine

8-10 oysters

1-2 lemons, quartered

2 shallots, finely chopped

250ml red wine vinegar

extra virgin olive oil

bunch each of basil, parsley and dill

Serves 8-10

The sweet, firm lobster flesh in this stunning, but straight forward dish is perfectly complemented by the creamy coconut milk.

coconut lobster
and dublin bay prawns

What you need

3 tbsp olive oil

2 tsp mustard seeds

2 fresh green chillies, chopped

2 cloves garlic, chopped

1 tsp chopped fresh ginger

4 lime leaves (available from large supermarkets)

4 shallots, chopped

2 tsp turmeric

1 tsp ground coriander

1 tsp ground cumin

400ml coconut milk

rock salt, black pepper

3 x medium live lobsters, about 250-300g each

24 dublin bay prawns, shelled

plain basmati or jasmine rice, to serve

Serves 6

What to do

Pour the olive oil into a frying pan and scatter the mustard seeds into the pan. Add the green chillies, garlic and ginger and cook for 1 minute. Add the lime leaves and chopped shallots and cook for 1 minute. Next, add the ground spices. Stir continuously, then add 4 tbsp water. Add the coconut milk and simmer for 5-10 minutes. Taste and season if required.

Prepare the lobsters according to the method on page 102, working in batches if necessary. Allow the lobsters to cool and place in the refrigerator to chill. Reserve the shells once you have extracted the meat.

If necessary, gently warm the sauce. Add the prawns and lightly poach them for 2-3 minutes, then add the lobster meat and simmer for a further minute. Return the lobster meat to the shell. Serve the lobsters and prawns with plain steamed rice.

A note for the cook

If lobster is unavailable, monkfish makes a nice alternative.

A wine that works

A rounded Sauvignon Blanc works very well with the coconut. The 'Le Chêne' Sancerre by Lucien Crochet has great elements of citrus fruit, hints of spice, especially ginger, and a little Madagascar peppercorn, all of which complement not just the coconut, but the shellfish and spices of this dish.

Also try

For a real treat, a Pouilly-Fumé by Didier Dageneau.

A great way to use meringue, especially broken left-overs.
This really is one of the simplest desserts you can imagine.

ely mess

What you need

4 egg whites

200g caster sugar

100ml cream

50g blueberries

50g raspberries

100g strawberries

icing sugar, for dusting

fresh mint leaves,
to garnish (optional)

Serves 4-6

What to do

Preheat the oven to 140ºC. Whip the egg whites in a large bowl until stiff. Be careful not to overbeat. Add half of the sugar slowly, a spoonful at a time, whipping continuously. Fold in the remaining sugar. Line a baking sheet with greaseproof paper and spoon the meringue mix on to the sheet, spreading it out evenly.

Cook in the oven for 1 hour, then turn off the heat and leave the meringue in the turned-off oven until it's completely cold. When it is ready, the greaseproof paper should peel off the meringue easily.

Whip the cream and break the meringue into bite-sized pieces. Fold the fruit and meringue through the cream, reserving a few berries to garnish.

Serve in a glass dish or bowl and garnish with the reserved berries, dusted with icing sugar and fresh mint leaves, if liked.

A note for the cook

It's a good idea to prepare the meringue the night before, as you can leave it to cool in the turned-off oven overnight. If you don't have fresh fruit use frozen mixed berries, but drain them first. If cherries are available, use a couple to top each serving.

A wine that works

Brown Brothers Orange Muscat and Flora, from Milawa, Victoria, Australia, is a delicate dessert wine, with a fruit-salad sweetness and light spring-flower and orange-blossom aromas. There's a touch of acidity to balance the sun-ripened fruit.

Also try

Château Court-les-Mûts, from Saussignac in Bordeaux.

A recipe that will impress, while being really quite simple to pull off.

melon and champagne jelly
with iced papaya soup

What you need

1 medium canteloupe melon
300ml champagne
150ml water
75g caster sugar
8 leaves of gelatine
1 large ripe papaya
splash of Malibu or gin
ice cubes
1 small bunch of mint, shredded
amaretti biscuits, to serve
vanilla ice cream, to serve

Serves 6

What to do

You will need 6 dariole moulds, each measuring about 7cm across the widest part and 5cm in depth. Peel the melon and remove the seeds. You can cut the flesh into cubes or, using a parisienne scoop, make melon balls. Place the melon pieces in the fridge at this point until you need them.

Place the champagne, water and sugar into a pot and heat gently, being careful not to boil. Meanwhile, soak the gelatine in cold water. When soft, remove from the cold water, squeeze the leaves gently and add to the mix. Stir until you are sure they are well dissolved.

Place 3-4 of the melon balls or cubes into 1 dariole mould per serving. Pour the champagne mix into the ramekins filling them right to the top. Place in the fridge and allow to set for 2-4 hours.

Just before serving, peel and deseed the papaya and place the flesh in a food processor with a splash of Malibu. Add 5-6 cubes of ice, then blend until smooth. Divide among espresso cups or champagne glasses.

To remove the jellies, dip the moulds into hot water for a few seconds to loosen, then invert carefully on to a plate. Top each jelly with an amaretti biscuit and garnish the papaya soup with shredded mint.

A note for the cook

It's worth sourcing leaf gelatine here. It can be difficult to get exact results with powdered gelatine. The soup must be served ice cold for best results. At ely, we serve this with a scoop of ice cream on a tuile and dust the plate with icing sugar. If melon is unavailable, you could use red berries.

A wine that works

Charpentier Champagne is a lovely Champagne with flavours of green apples and classic yeasty tones. It has enough body to complement the ingredients of this dish and won't break the bank.

Also try

Sagramoso Blanc de Noirs Brut, Napa Valley.

Sometimes the simplest dishes create the fondest memories.
A great Sunday brunch favourite.

eggy bread
with strawberry jam and clotted cream

What to do

Whisk 3 egg yolks and 1 whole egg together with the milk. Soak the bread in this mixture for a few seconds, then fry in butter until golden brown, allowing 10g butter per 2 slices bread. Ensure you wipe the pan clean each time to avoid burning the butter.

To make the jam, wash the strawberries and remove the stalks. Cut into quarters. Place the sugar in a pot with 3-4 tsp water. Heat gently until the sugar dissolves, then add the strawberries. Simmer for 10-15 minutes. Mash lightly with a fork and leave to cool.

Serve the fried bread with the cream and jam on the side, and a pot of your favourite coffee.

What you need

4 organic eggs
(yolks only of 3, and 1 whole)

250ml milk

8 slices bread (a doughy white bread works well here)

40g unsalted butter

200g strawberries

150g caster sugar

1 tub clotted cream, to serve

Serves 4

'**Food is our common ground, a universal experience.**'

Sheilah Graham

As the days slowly shorten and the sun plays harder to get, our appetites begin to change, too. Where just weeks before, it seemed natural to toss a salad together on a whim, now our thoughts turn to a bowl of soup, or a comforting casserole.

autumn

It's a good time for homegrown fruits and berries too, as autumn apples and pears put mouthwatering tarts and fruits poached in spiced, aromatic wine on the menu. Late-ripening tomatoes are at their juiciest and perfect for rich sauces, while the fishermen bring us the best of the sea – crabs, mussels, oysters, lobster, squid, scallops and prawns. Wine-wise, it's no longer all about whites and rosés, as reaching for those robust reds and fuller whites comes naturally again.

A simple soup with a sophisticated twist. You could leave out the oysters for an everyday lunch.

sweet potato soup
with poached oysters

What to do

Peel and roughly chop the sweet potatoes, garlic and shallots. Heat 1-2 tbsp olive oil in a pot. Add the vegetables and sauté with the bouquet garni for 10 minutes, without colouring, until al dente.

Add the white wine. Reduce by half and then add the vegetable stock. Bring to the boil then turn down the heat and simmer for 10 minutes.

Meanwhile, shuck the oysters (see page 120).

Take out the bouquet garni and remove the soup from the heat. Blitz the soup in a blender and add the cream. Season to taste.

Place 2 oysters in each soup bowl. Pour over the hot soup. The heat of the soup will slightly poach the oysters. Serve immediately, drizzled with the rocket essence, if liked. The quantities here are quite generous, so if you have any leftover soup, it will keep nicely in the fridge for up to 3 days.

A wine that works

A glass of Fino sherry is a very civilised accompaniment to most soups. Try the Campo de Guía by Gutierrez Colosia; it has a slightly fruitier style than most Finos.

Also try

Lustau Papirusa Manzanilla, which is a very dry, lighter Fino.

What you need

4 medium/large sweet potatoes

2 cloves garlic

2 medium shallots

olive oil

1 bouquet garni (see page 223)

300ml white wine

1 litre vegetable stock
(see page 224)

8 medium oysters

250ml cream

rock salt, black pepper

rocket essence (optional,
see page 224), for serving

Serves 4

shucking an oyster

Discard any oyster shells that are open, or that don't close immediately once tapped. To 'shuck' the oysters, you'll ideally need a sharp 'shucking knife'. For extra protection, drape a towel over your open palm. Hold the oyster firmly, knife in the other hand. Have a bowl ready underneath to catch any liquid. Slip the blade between the top and bottom shell next to the hinge on the back. Run the knife from this point around the oyster until you get to the other side. Be firm, but take care not to stab yourself. Using a twisting motion, prise the top and bottom shells apart. Cut the oyster free from its shell, sliding your knife firmly under the knob attaching it to the shell on its underside. Rinse the shells. Return the oysters to their half shells for serving and place on a large plate. You could sit them on a bed of crushed ice to hold them in place. Strain the reserved juices and pour back over the oysters. Serve with fresh herbs and red wine vinegar mixed with finely chopped shallots, or lemon wedges.

If you're a fan of oysters, you'll love this rich and beautifully presented dish. It's essential that you use oysters and scallops that are sparklingly fresh.

carpaccio of scallops
and warm oyster risotto

What to do

Preheat the oven to 180°C. Chill the scallops and slice as thinly as possible (if you put them in the freezer for 10 minutes they will be easier to slice). Roast the peppers whole in the oven in a little olive oil and salt for approx 20 minutes or until cooked through. When they are cooked, remove from the oven and cover – trapping the steam will make it easier to take the skins off. After a few minutes, remove the stalk, squeeze to remove the seeds, then peel. Finely dice the flesh and place in a bowl with half the shallots and all the chives. Drizzle with the honey.

Arrange the pepper mix in a circle on each serving plate and layer the scallops on top. You can use a tian ring here. Allow 2 scallops per person. Prepare the rocket essence.

Prepare the risotto according to the recipe on page 225, using the remaining shallots, the olive oil, the arborio rice and stock. Shuck the oysters (see page 120).

Place a small tian ring or round pastry cutter on a plate beside the scallops and red pepper. Fill with risotto and press down firmly with a spoon. Place an oyster on top. Remove the tian ring carefully. Repeat with each serving plate. Season as required – do not use too much salt as this will 'cook' the scallops. Garnish by drizzling the plate with the rocket essence. Dress with some fennel leaves and sprinkle with cracked black pepper.

A note for the cook

It's very important to use a really sharp knife for slicing the delicate scallops. Choose one that's as flat and sharp as possible and make sure the scallops are well chilled and firm.

A wine that works

The natural richness of the scallops and the creaminess of the risotto will bring out the intense minerality, gun-flint and chalk aromas of Didier Dagueneau's Pouilly-Fumé Bouisson Renard. With flavours of passion fruit, cassis, hints of salt and chalk and a trace of smoke, this is one of the world's best Sauvignon Blancs from the world's best Sauvignon Blanc producer.

Also try

Domaine Huet 'Le Haut-Lieu' Vouvray Sec from the Loire.

What you need

8 large scallops, roe on or off, as preferred

2 red peppers

olive oil

rock salt and black pepper

2-3 shallots, diced

15g fresh chives, finely chopped

1 tsp honey

rocket essence, to serve (see page 224)

75g-100g arborio rice

150ml vegetable stock (see page 224)

4 large oysters

bunch fresh fennel leaves, to serve

cracked black pepper, to serve

Serves 4

A refreshing alternative to the popular dish of mussels with white wine and cream sauce.

mussels with fennel and pernod

What to do

Prepare the mussels (see note for the cook, below). Sauté the fennel and shallot in a small amount of oil over a medium heat. When they have softened slightly, add the mussels and leave for 1 minute, then add the pernod. Flambé the pernod, then allow the alcohol to reduce. Add the cream and reduce again until the mussels are just coated.

Serve in a large bowl garnished with lemon slices, fennel leaves, sprigs of flat-leaf parsley and crispy leeks, if liked.

A note for the cook

Scrub the mussels first in clean water to remove the barnacles and pull off any beards. It's much easier to do this if you take 2 mussels and use the pointed end of one to clean the other. Check if an open mussel is safe to eat by tapping it gently on a counter top. If it closes easily, it's ok to eat. If it remains open, discard.

A wine that works

The strong flavours of fennel and pernod could seem to be a problem when it comes to choosing a wine. However, a white wine such as Côtes du Rhône Villages 'La Font d'Estevenas' from Domaine Alary in Cairanne, makes a great match. There are hints of aniseed, and it's fairly fat with minerals, nuts and honey with a clean, fresh finish.

Also try

Grosset Semillon/Sauvignon from Clare Valley, South Australia.

What you need

1 fennel bulb with leaves, diced and leaves reserved for garnish

1 shallot, finely diced

1 tbsp extra virgin olive oil

800g-1kg fresh mussels

100ml pernod

150ml cream

½ lemon, sliced, to garnish

flat-leaf parsley, to garnish

crispy leeks, to garnish (optional, see page 130)

Serves 4

This brilliantly simple starter looks impressive and is incredibly healthy
– none of the ingredients are cooked, so all the goodness remains.

salmon tartare
with watercress and cucumber ribbons

What you need

1 cucumber

200g fresh, organic, Irish farmed salmon

small bunch dill

2 small shallots

50g crème fraîche

juice of ¼ lemon

rock salt, black pepper

50g watercress

mixed leaves and brown bread, to serve

Serves 4

What to do

Take a peeler and run it from the top to the tail of the whole, unpeeled cucumber to create 4 long strips – these will be used to wrap the salmon. You should end up with long, translucent strips with dark green borders on either side. The borders will help the strips hold their shape.

Dice the salmon, dill and shallots. Reserve 4 tsp crème fraîche. Place the salmon, dill and shallots in a bowl with the remaining crème fraîche and lemon juice, mixing well to ensure all ingredients are coated. Season to taste.

Divide the salmon mix into 4 and place each portion in the centre of a plate in a cylindrical shape. Wrap each one with a cucumber strip. Place 1 tsp crème fraîche on top of each portion. Pick and wash the watercress and place a few leaves on top of each bundle of salmon. Sprinkle with rock salt.

Serve with mixed leaves and traditional brown bread, if liked.

A note for the cook

You want to make sure the taste of the fresh dill comes through; half of one of the packets you can buy at the supermarket should be about right.

A wine that works

Domaine Roulot's Bourgogne Aligoté has 'haunting purity and directness' with a clean, attractive nose, a delicate sensation of apples and lime and a lively finish.

Also try

Georg Breuer 'Terra Montosa' Riesling Trocken, from Rheingau in Germany.

These have been on the menu since day one at ely. They make a great dish for lunch, or an informal dinner party.

ely fishcakes

What to do

Lay the bread slices on a plate to dry them out, or place in the oven at a low temperature for a few minutes. Remove the crusts, if liked, and whiz the bread in a processor to make breadcrumbs.

Boil the potatoes in plenty of salted water until cooked. At the same time, bake the salmon in the oven for about 8-10 minutes. Poach the cod for 3-4 minutes in the milk with a pinch of salt and pepper. Sauté the onion in half the butter. Drain the potatoes and place back over a very low heat, covered with a dry, clean cloth, for a few minutes. This will help to dry them out a little.

Mash the potato with the remaining butter, then add the onion. Strain the cod through a sieve, discarding the milk. Flake the cod and salmon and mix with the potato and the crab meat. Season with salt and pepper. Add the chives and dill. Allow the mix to cool.

Preheat the oven to 180°C. Divide the mix into 4 or 6 portions, shape into individual cakes and coat with the breadcrumbs.

Heat a little olive oil in a small frying pan. Seal the fishcakes by cooking for a few seconds on each side in the olive oil. Then place in a baking dish in the oven for 10-15 minutes.

To make the sauce, mix the capers, dill, shallot and crème fraîche together and season with salt and pepper. Serve the fishcakes on a bed of lettuce drizzled with the caper dressing.

A wine that works

Pouilly-Fumé 'Chatelain Prestige' from Domaine Chatelain is a rounder style of Sauvignon Blanc than its neighbourly Sancerre. It gets a smoky or flinty flavour from the limestone and flint soil and has naturally high acidity, plus herbal undertones. Excellent with the fish flavours and potato.

Also try

Pieropan Soave from Veneto in Italy.

What you need

2 slices of white bread
200g potatoes, peeled and chopped
200g salmon, filleted, skinned and fine-boned
200g cod, filleted, skinned and fine-boned
125ml milk
rock salt and black pepper
1 large onion, finely diced
100g butter
100g crab meat, fresh or frozen
25g chives, finely chopped
25g dill, finely chopped
olive oil
lettuce, to serve

For the sauce

50g capers, chopped
50g dill, chopped
1 shallot, finely diced
150-200g crème fraîche

Serves 4-6

A note for the cook

Before you coat the fishcakes with the breadcrumbs, place them in the freezer for 30 minutes or up to 1 hour. This will help them keep their shape when you fry them.

You can save time by preparing the sauce the day before you cook the fishcakes. Simply cover and keep in the fridge overnight.

If you don't have monkfish this works well with any firm-textured fish.

monkfish with chive risotto
and crispy leeks

What to do

Place the monkfish on a plate lined with a paper towel and refrigerate until it's time to cook.

Julienne the leeks (cut them into very thin, finger-length strips), place in a bowl and coat with flour. Pour the oil in a pan – you will need about 2cm depth – and, when hot, add the leeks. Deep-fry until golden brown, then remove with a slotted spoon and place on a paper towel. Season with salt and leave to dry. Preheat the oven to 180°C.

Heat the clarified butter in a frying pan. Place the monkfish on the pan and colour until golden brown on both sides. Remove from the pan and season. Place on a wire rack in a roasting tray and cook for 5 minutes.

While the monkfish is cooking, prepare the risotto following the method on page 225. Stir in the chives at the end. Prepare the rocket essence, if using.

Drizzle the serving plates with rocket essence. Place a portion of risotto on each of the serving plates, with a nest of crispy leeks on top. Put the monkfish alongside the risotto.

A note for the cook

At ely we serve this dish with just a small amount of risotto. If you'd like to offer more then simply increase the quantities as desired.

We love the colour and texture that pea shoots give to a finished dish. Look for them in punnets at good supermarkets, where they are starting to become more available.

A wine that works

Jean Thévenet of Domaine de Roally, from Mâcon in Burgundy, has been referred to as the 'Maestro of Mâcon', and makes wonderful Chardonnay. It has a fuller style due to the late harvesting, leading to honey and citrus flavours. There is no oak, just pure fruit flavours and a lengthy finish.

Also try

Torres 'Milmanda' Chardonnay from Conca de Barberà in Spain.

What you need

4 pieces of monkfish, each about 180g

1 large leek (white only)

10g flour, for frying leeks

about 500ml vegetable oil

rock salt, black pepper

50g butter, clarified (see page 223)

For the risotto

about 350ml vegetable stock (see page 224)

2 tbsp olive oil

100g shallot

200g risotto rice (preferably Carnaroli)

85g butter

rock salt, black pepper

75g chives, finely chopped

rocket essence (see page 224, optional)

pea shoots, to garnish (optional)

Serves 4

A sophisticated twist on a much-loved classic. The bubbles in the beer are the secret ingredient here for crispy batter.

beer batter fish and chips

What you need

For the batter

500ml beer, cold

300g plain white flour or tempura flour, plus extra for coating

1 level tsp salt

1 egg white

For the fish and chips

1 litre vegetable oil

4 large potatoes (roosters), peeled and cut to chip size

4 cod fillets, each about 200g

rock salt

plain flour, for coating fish

1-2 lemons, quartered, to serving

For the tartare sauce

50g capers

50g gherkins

good sprig of chopped parsley

150g good mayonnaise

juice of ½ lemon

Serves 4

What to do

You will need 2 deep chip pans and baskets, or a counter-top deep-fat fryer for this recipe. Begin by mixing the batter ingredients together in a bowl. Set aside in the fridge to chill for 1 hour.

To make the tartare sauce, dice the capers and gherkins and chop the parsley. Mix with the mayonnaise in a bowl and add the lemon juice to finish.

Heat the oil in the pan or deep-fat fryer to 140°C and parcook the potato chips until slightly soft. Lift the basket from the oil and toss the chips on to a tray lined with paper towels to dry off excess oil.

Season the fish with salt. Pour the flour into a large mixing bowl and dip the seasoned fish fillets in the bowl so they are evenly coated. Next, dip the fillets in the beer batter.

Heat the oil to 195°C. Put the fillets one at a time into the chip basket in the pan (or the deep-fat fryer) and cook until they are golden and crisp – about 4-5 minutes, depending on the size of the fish. Remove and place each fillet on a paper towel to dry off excess oil.

When the fish is cooked, drop the chips in the fryer for about 2 minutes to finish the cooking.

Serve the fish and chips sprinkled with salt and accompanied by lemon wedges and tartare sauce.

A note for the cook

Don't leave the batter to stand for longer than an hour or the beer will separate.

A wine that works

Petaluma's Hanlin Hill Clare Valley Riesling from the Adelaide Hills in Australia. It's light and crisp with lovely lime flavours, a touch of apple and a long, bright finish. It will bring out the delicate taste of the fish and help balance the mayonnaise.

Also try

Try something a little different, such as a dry sherry (Fino).

Halibut is native to Irish waters and comes into season in the autumn. It's a flat, white, slightly oily fish. If you don't want to make the beetroot gratin to serve with this, roasted beetroot also makes a great accompaniment.

pan-fried halibut
with jerusalem artichoke purée, beetroot gratin and parsnip crisps

What to do

Prepare the beetroot gratin if you are serving it with the fish.

To make the parsnip crisps, peel the parsnip, then use the peeler to cut the flesh into long, thin strips. Deep-fry the strips in sunflower oil, or bake, salted, for 1-2 hours at 60-80°C.

Peel the artichokes and boil in salted water for 20 minutes. When soft, strain and place in a food processor while still hot – this will help to melt the butter and heat the cream. Add the clarified butter and cream. Purée until smooth – this may take 3-4 minutes. Taste and season.

Now for the fish. Halibut is a fish that cooks very quickly. Heat the olive oil in a frying pan and place the fish bone-side down. Fry to golden brown. Turn over, reduce the heat and leave for 2-3 minutes. Season to taste. Meanwhile, gently reheat the purée and gratin for serving.

To serve, place a piece of fish on each plate with a stack of the beetroot gratin, or other accompaniment, and spoon some purée on the side. Garnish with parsnip crisps.

A note for the cook

Season the fish after it is cooked. If you season it before cooking, this will dry it out.

A wine that works

A good alternative to Pouilly-Fuissé is a Saint Véran, such as the one made by Domaine Olivier Merlin, from the village of Saint Véran in Mâcon. This Chardonnay has subtle oak flavours with ripe fruit, pears and citrus fruit and an underlying minerality.

Also try

Domaine Bel Air, Pouilly-Fumé, Loire.

What you need

beetroot gratin
(see page 225, optional)

1 parsnip

sunflower oil, for deep-frying
(optional)

rock salt and black pepper

500g jerusalem artichokes

50g butter, clarified
(see page 223)

250ml cream

1 tsp virgin olive oil

4 x 180g pieces of
fresh halibut

Serves 4

A great alternative to the Sunday roast. The more time given to its cooking, the greater the flavours and texture.

slow-cooked lamb shanks
in red wine and juniper berries, with parsnip mash

What to do

Preheat the oven to 160°C.

Season the lamb with salt and pepper. Heat the olive oil in a frying pan and brown the lamb shanks. In a heavy ovenproof dish with high sides, fry the onions, carrots, garlic and celery until brown and caramelised. Add the lamb shanks. Pour the bottle of wine over the lamb. Add the juniper berries, herbs and a little salt and pepper. Cover and place in the oven. Cook for 2 ½-3 hours.

Towards the end of the cooking time, prepare the mash. Peel the parsnips and quarter them lengthways. Remove the core of the parsnip (the hard spine that runs through the centre of the parsnip). Peel the potatoes and cut to a similar size to your parsnip quarters.

Place the potatoes and parsnips in a large pot with the thyme sprigs, cover with water and bring to the boil. Cook until tender and discard the thyme. Drain and mash with the butter. Warm the milk and add to the mash to create a creamy consistency. Season to taste.

When the meat is soft and just falling off the bone, gently lift the shanks out and leave to one side. Strain the liquid, reserving the vegetables, and skim off the fat. Reduce the strained and skimmed gravy to about 300ml by gently simmering in the cooking dish. Taste and adjust the seasoning.

To serve, put the mash in individual serving bowls and place a lamb shank on top, spooning over some of the gravy or jus. Place the reserved vegetables in a bowl and serve on the side.

A note for the cook

If you prefer, you can serve the lamb shanks with a selection of steamed vegetables, depending on what's around. Toss them in butter and chopped herbs.

A wine that works

If you have been decadent enough to use a nice bottle of wine with this recipe, then that's what you could drink. Either way, a northern Rhône would do very well for both tasks, especially the 'No Wine's Land' from Domaine du Coulet. This is a medium-bodied Syrah that gets its name from the fact that the vineyard lies (unclaimed) between the appellations of Cornas and Saint Joseph. There's dark fruit on the nose and palate, blackcurrants, black olives and a touch of vanilla. The wine has freshness to it due to the high minerality of the soil.

Also try

Its big brother, the 'Brise Cailloux' from Cornas.

What you need

6 lamb shanks, each about 400g

rock salt and black pepper

3 tbsp olive oil

2 onions, peeled and roughly chopped

2 carrots, peeled and roughly chopped

1 whole head garlic, halved

1 celery stick, quartered

1 bottle full-bodied red wine

12 lightly crushed juniper berries

sprig each of thyme and rosemary

bay leaves

For the parsnip mash

4-5 medium parsnips

2 large baking potatoes

2 sprigs of thyme

knob of butter

milk, to cover (about 150ml)

Serves 6

There are a lot of ingredients in this recipe, but it's really worth the effort.
A Moroccan equivalent to the Irish Stew.

lamb tagine

What you need

800g–1kg lean lamb shoulder, diced

plain flour, to coat lamb

extra virgin olive oil

1 large Spanish onion

1 each red and yellow peppers, diced

2 large or 3 medium carrots, diced

4 cloves garlic, crushed

4 bay leaves

1 sprig thyme

1 sprig rosemary

1 small, red chilli, dried or fresh

2 cinnamon sticks

2 star anise

10g fresh ginger, peeled and grated, or ½ tsp ground

20g dried ground cumin

100ml honey

800g tinned chopped tomatoes or passata, or enough to submerge all ingredients

1 aubergine

1 courgette

Serves 6

What to do

Lightly coat the lamb in flour and brown in a little oil on a hot pan. You will need to do this in batches. Set aside and remove any excess fat.

In one large frying pan (or two, if necessary), fry the onion, peppers, carrots and garlic in some olive oil until they are soft. Add the lamb, bay leaves and fresh herbs.

Now add the chilli, cinnamon sticks, star anise, ginger and cumin. Stir well to coat the lamb and vegetables. Drizzle the honey over the lamb, then pour in the tomatoes or passata. Stir well. Reduce the heat to a simmer and cook for 1-2 hours, stirring occasionally. Take off the heat and leave to cool.

Slowly reheat the tagine when you are ready to serve. Chop the aubergine and courgette into large chunks, fry in some olive oil and add to the tagine. Doing this last prevents the aubergine and courgette from being discoloured by the sauce. Serve with couscous (see note for the cook).

A note for the cook

This delicious lamb tagine tastes even better the day after cooking, when the flavours have had a chance to blend and settle.

It's best served with couscous. Rub oil into the couscous (before cooking) to prevent it sticking together. Mix equal quantities of hot stock and couscous, cover with cling film and leave for 5 minutes. Remove the cling film and run a fork through the couscous to separate. Season, add some fresh mint, and serve.

If you like, you can top each dish with a handful of cress and some parsnip crisps (see page 134).

A wine that works

En Sol Majeur Corbières, from Domaine du Grand Arc, gives dark plummy fruits on the nose, with full-bodied black cherries and strawberries and soft velvety tannins which stand up to the spices. The fruit flavours work beautifully with the sweet honey in the tagine.

Also try

Casa Lapostolle 'Cuvée Alexandre' Merlot from the Colchagua valley in Chile.

The subtle sweetness of the maple syrup is the perfect partner to the bacon in this simple recipe – a stylish twist on an Irish tradition.

baked loin of bacon
with a green peppercorn and maple crust

What to do

Place the bacon in a large saucepan, cover with water and simmer gently for approximately 1½-2 hours, until the skin peels away easily. Mix the green peppercorn mustard and maple syrup together in a small bowl. Place the bacon on a roasting tray. Drizzle over a little extra syrup before covering with the mustard mixture. Bake in the oven at 180°C for 30-40 minutes – until the mustard is a light, golden brown.

Meanwhile, cook the potatoes in boiling, salted water. Remove from the heat when they are soft, drain and mash. Heat the butter and cream in a small saucepan and add to the potatoes, mixing well. Season with salt and pepper.

Heat a little butter in a frying pan and add some freshly ground pepper. Add the cabbage and sauté for a few minutes, being careful not to overcook it.

Carve the bacon and serve with the cabbage and potatoes.

A wine that works

A white Châteauneuf-du-Pape from Lucien and Marie-José Michel of le Vieux Donjon. It's a fruity, dry wine with ripe pears and provençal herbs, weighty and rich. The wine is made from clairette, roussanne and grenache blanc and is organically farmed.

Also try

Domaine Weinbach 'Clos des Capucins', a Pinot Blanc from Alsace.

What you need

1kg loin of bacon

3 tbsp green peppercorn mustard

100g maple syrup, plus extra for drizzling

1kg rooster potatoes, peeled and chopped

75g butter

500ml cream

rock salt, black pepper

butter, for frying

1 medium savoy cabbage, finely sliced

Serves 4

Offal is a much maligned ingredient. Combined in a rich sauce with wild mushrooms and covered in flaky pastry, it's one of life's great gifts. There is nothing better on a cold day.

kidney and mushroom pie

What you need

olive oil

1 large carrot, finely diced

3 baby potatoes, pre-cooked, chilled and diced into cubes

300g wild mushrooms, washed

2 sticks celery, finely diced

2 banana shallots, or 4 ordinary shallots, finely diced

1 sprig thyme

1 small bunch tarragon

50g butter, clarified (see page 223)

16 lambs' kidneys (try to keep the kidney blood to help thicken the sauce)

150ml red wine

200ml roast bone stock, see page 224, or good-quality bought beef or lamb stock

rock salt, black pepper

1 egg, beaten

2 sheets ready rolled puff pastry

Serves 6

What to do

Heat the oil in a large frying pan. Add the carrot, potatoes, mushrooms, celery, shallots, thyme and tarragon and sauté until al dente. Remove and sieve to get rid of any excess oil (so as to avoid splitting the sauce). Wipe the pan clean and put back on heat. Add the clarified butter and sauté the kidneys for 3 minutes. Add the wine and any blood and leave to bubble for a couple of minutes to reduce slightly. Add the sautéed vegetables. Cook for 2 minutes over a medium heat.

Next, add the stock. Simmer to reduce for 5-6 minutes. Season to taste. Divide the mixture among 4 large ramekins, ovenproof bowls or other suitable heatproof containers. At ely, we use our soup bowls.

Preheat the oven to 200°C.

Egg-wash one side of each sheet of rolled pastry, cut in half and drape one piece over each dish, egg-side down. Trim the sides, but make sure the edges of the pastry stick to the dish as this will give the pie a domed effect. If you like, you can decorate the top with leaves cut from any excess pastry. Now egg-wash the outside to give a golden colour to the cooked pastry.

Cook for 8-10 minutes. Remember, this is just to cook the pastry. Serve with fries and a mixed green salad.

A note for the cook

Ask your butcher to skin the kidneys, split them, and remove the fat centre. If you have time, marinade the kidneys before cooking. Place in a pyrex dish and add 1 glass of red wine, a shot of sherry or sherry vinegar, 1 carrot, 1 sprig of rosemary, 1 halved head of garlic, some peppercorns and a bay leaf. Cover and place in the fridge for 1-2 hours.

A wine that works

This is a lovely, rustic dish that is rich and a little glutinous. The wine needs good acidity to complement the texture. Domaine de l'Arlot Côtes de Nuits Villages 'Clos du Chapeau' has plummy fruit with earthy, gamey characteristics and farmyard aromas with medium body and a dry finish.

Also try

Cigliuti Dolcetto d'Alba, from Piedmont in Italy.

A luscious chocolate dessert, which is best made a little in advance.

chocolate and hazelnut torte

What to do

Preheat the oven to 160°C. Butter a 12in tart ring, with removable base, or a standard Swiss Roll tray.

Begin with the base. Blitz the hazelnuts in a food processor, or wrap them up in a clean tea towel and bash them with a rolling pin.

Beat the butter, sugar and egg yolks in a bowl until pale. Gradually fold in the flour and mascarpone. Add the poppy seeds and crushed hazelnuts, then the orange juice, stirring gently to incorporate. Whip the egg whites until stiff and fold into the mixture. Pour into the tart ring or tray and bake for 15 minutes. Remove from the oven and leave to cool slightly.

Reduce the oven to 150°C.

Now for the topping. Melt the chocolate in a heatproof bowl over a pot of boiling water. Boil the water and 165g sugar in a pot until the temperature reaches 110°C (the soft-boil stage). Stir the sugar and water mix into the melted chocolate, then add the butter. Beat the eggs with 3 tbsp sugar until pale. Fold the chocolate mixture into the eggs.

Pour the topping over the baked base and return to the oven for 12 minutes. The torte will rise in the oven, but will go down again as it cools. Leave to cool to room temperature, then place in the fridge for at least 4 and up to 12 hours until set.

To serve, cut the torte into slices and serve with crème fraîche and a fruit compôte (preferably bitter red fruits)

A wine that works

Lustau Oloroso is a truly rich, yet equally dry wine with an intense nose of roasted nuts, a touch of acetone and some creamy traces. It has a dry palate with spices and dates and a wonderfully complex and long finish. A lovely go-between for the chocolate and hazelnut.

Also try

Domaine Mas Blanc Banyuls, France.

What you need
For the base

165g soft unsalted butter, plus extra for greasing

125g roasted hazelnuts

125g caster sugar

4 large eggs, separated

30g plain flour

125g mascarpone

2 tbsp poppy seeds

juice of 1 orange

pinch of salt

For the topping

375g dark chocolate (minimum 70% cocoa)

125ml water

165g caster sugar, plus 3 tbsp

150g salted butter

5 large eggs

crème fraîche and fruit compote, to serve (optional)

Serves 8-12

Although no cooking is required and it can be prepared in minutes, this is a very special dessert. The name means 'pick-me-up', and although there are many variations to be found, at ely we prefer this simple recipe.

tiramisu

What you need

4 large eggs, separated

120g caster sugar

1 tsp vanilla sugar or few drops of vanilla essence

100ml single cream

500g mascarpone cheese

4 espresso cups of cold, strong espresso coffee, about 400ml

4 tbsp coffee liqueur (kahlua), or amaretto

approx 20 savoiardi biscuits (lady fingers)

cocoa powder, for dusting

Serves 6

What to do

Beat the egg yolks with the caster sugar and vanilla sugar in a bowl until thick and mousse-like. Beat the egg whites until the mixture forms peaks. In another bowl, beat the single cream into the mascarpone to loosen it, then carefully fold in the egg yolk mixture and finally fold in the egg whites. Spread half the mixture over the base of a large, shallow pyrex serving dish, measuring approximately 30 x 15cm.

Mix the espresso coffee and liqueur together in a shallow dish and quickly dip in the savoiardi biscuits, one by one, placing them immediately after dipping on top of the layer of mascarpone mix. When all the biscuits are layered over the mascarpone mix, spread the remainder of the mix on top to cover them completely. Chill in the fridge overnight or for at least 6 hours.

Before serving, dust the tiramisu generously with cocoa powder.

A note for the cook

Instead of making a large tiramisu, you can make individual portions in glasses, cups or other small containers. It's best to prepare this dessert a day in advance.

A wine that works

Has to be a glass of Vin Santo 'Tegrino' from Cantine Leonardo in Italy. A balance of sweetness, acidity and concentration, with a delicate, creamy, honey-roasted flavour.

Also try

Taittinger Nocturne Champagne.

The juiciest pears are plentiful at this time of year and take centre stage in this delicious dessert.

poached pears

What to do

Peel the pears and turn them in a bowl in the lemon juice to prevent from going brown.

Put the red wine, cassis, sugar, cinnamon, star anise and orange juice in a large pot – big enough to hold the pears in one layer – and bring to a simmer.

Add the pears and weigh them down with a small plate placed on top to ensure they are fully submerged in the liquid. Simmer gently for 20–25 minutes. Do not boil.

Remove the pot from the heat and allow the pears to cool in the syrupy cooking liquid. Remove the pears from the liquid with a slotted spoon, reserving the liquid.

Serve warm or chilled with ice cream, or natural yogurt, and amaretti biscuits. Drizzle the pears with the syrup before serving.

A note for the cook

The delicious cooking liquid from the pears can be used to make a lovely syrup; reduce it gently in a pot until syrupy and serve drizzled over ice cream. Alternatively, leave the liquid to cool then cover and refrigerate. For an autumnal spiced drink, place a small measure of the liquid – according to taste – in the bottom of a glass and top up with sparkling wine.

A wine that works

A Loire Chenin Blanc, such as Quart de Chaume, from Domaine des Baumard.

Also try

Its big brother, the `Trie Spéciale' Savennières, from Baumard.

What you need

4 conference pears
juice of 1 lemon
1 litre red wine
250ml crème de cassis
200g caster sugar
2 cinnamon sticks
2 star anise
juice of 1 orange
ice cream or natural yoghurt, and amaretti biscuits, to serve

Serves 4

'Seeing is deceiving.
It's eating that's
believing.'

James Thurber

Warming comfort food comes into its own in the cold, dark winter months. As we feel like slowing down ourselves, we want food that will boost our energy, but that's quick and easy to prepare on a cold winter's night.

winter

It's the season for rich stews that taste even better the next day – and the day after that again. Nourishing soups made with chunky root vegetables like turnips, swedes, parsnips, celeriac and carrots are at the heart of everyday cooking. A lunch of roast loin of venison, red cabbage and herb roast potatoes – accompanied by a heady red wine – seems like the perfect way to laze away a Sunday.

A great starter for a winter lunch.

smoked bacon and parsnip bisque

What to do

Fry off the bacon in a pot, leaving any fat or sediment that comes out – this will flavour the vegetables. Remove the bacon to a plate lined with paper towels. To the same pot, add the olive oil, vegetables and thyme. Cook the vegetables until they colour and soften slightly.

Add the vegetable stock and bring to the boil. When the stock comes to the boil, lower the heat and simmer for 15 minutes. Add 200ml cream and the bacon to the soup, reserving a small amount of bacon for the garnish. Stir well, blitz in a blender and pass through a sieve. Season to taste. Spoon into serving bowls and add a swirl of cream to each bowl. Scatter over the reserved bacon and sprinkle with black pepper.

Serve with traditional bread, and butter. This is delicious served with parsnip crisps, see page 134.

A wine that works

Casa Lapostolle 'Cuvée Alexandre' Chardonnay from Casablanca Valley in Chile has masses of sun-ripened fruit and nicely integrated oak, all held in check by its French ancestry. The oak in the wine highlights the smokiness of the bacon.

Also try

Château Thieuley 'Cuvée Francis Courselle' from Bordeaux.

What you need

150g smoked bacon, roughly chopped

50ml olive oil

½ large onion, diced

3 sticks celery, coarsely chopped

1 medium carrot, coarsely chopped

2 cloves garlic, chopped

3 medium parsnips, peeled and coarsely chopped

sprig fresh thyme

450ml vegetable stock (see page 224)

250ml cream

rock salt, black pepper

Serves 4-6

The tanginess of the pickled cabbage cuts through the smooth richness of the liver to great effect in this straightforward recipe. This is quite a filling, satisfying winter dish; if you prefer, you can use a slightly smaller weight of calves' liver.

calves' liver with pickled cabbage

What you need

1 small Dutch cabbage, shredded

150ml sherry vinegar

50ml white wine

50g butter

4 shallots

caster sugar, to dust

olive or sunflower oil, to coat pan

600-800g calves' liver (around 200g per serving)

about 350ml red wine jus (see page 224)

4 x approx 8cm pre-cooked mini tartlets made from shortcrust pastry

rock salt, black pepper

Serves 4

What to do

Place the cabbage, vinegar and wine in a large pan, bring to a gentle simmer and cook until tender – about 20-25 minutes.

Preheat the oven to 180°C. Melt the butter in a roasting tray on the hob, throw in the shallots and dust with caster sugar. Roast in the oven for 10-15 minutes. Meanwhile, coat a frying pan with oil and fry the calves' liver until medium – about 10-15 minutes. Remove and leave to rest.

To serve, heat the red wine jus in a pan and warm the tartlets in the oven for 3-4 minutes. Place 1 pastry case in the centre of each plate and fill with the cabbage. Slice the liver, season, and arrange neatly on top of the cabbage, then place the shallots on top and drizzle with the jus.

A note for the cook

Season the liver after cooking rather than before. Seasoning before cooking causes unpleasant spots to appear on the liver flesh.

You can buy shortcrust pastry tartlets from most good supermarkets.

If you don't want to make the red wine jus, simply throw a wine glass each of beef stock and red wine into the pan you cooked the liver in, simmer to reduce by half and season.

A wine that works

'Les Clots' by Luc Lapeyre in Minervois, is a blend of grenache, syrah and carignan, giving a concentration of dark fruit, a peppering of spice, a long, rich finish – and the back-bone to work with the pickled cabbage.

Also try

Luciano Sandrone Dolcetto d'Alba.

A note for the cook

It's worth seeking out Szechuan peppercorns from a good-quality deli — they have a particular pungency which works beautifully in this recipe.

To serve this dish 'Alba Style' — a version that's very popular with the truffle-hunters of the Alba region of Italy — dress the beef with asparagus, celery, parmesan shavings, white truffle shavings, olive oil and lemon juice.

This is extremely simple to prepare, but do make sure you buy a good piece of fillet and use a very sharp knife.

beef carpaccio

What you need

400g beef fillet
1 tbsp Szechuan peppercorns
½ tsp black peppercorns
2 tbsp honey
50g brown sugar
25ml port wine
25ml brandy
rock salt and black pepper
150g French green beans
4 tbsp extra virgin olive oil
juice of 1 lemon
1 bunch rocket
85g parmesan cheese, thinly sliced

Serves 4

What to do

Place the meat in a sealed container in the fridge for 2-4 hours. Meanwhile, place the Szechuan peppercorns and black peppercorns in a food processor and blitz, or grind up in a pestle and mortar.

Remove the meat from the fridge and rub the pepper mix into the flesh, coating thoroughly. Place the honey, sugar, port and brandy in a bowl and mix well. Pour this mix over the spiced meat. Cover and refrigerate overnight.

Remove from the fridge the next day, wrap tightly in clingfilm and freeze for 1 hour (this will make it easy to slice the meat very thinly). Cut the meat into slices about 1-2mm thick.

Blanch the green beans in boiling, salted water for 30-40 seconds. Refresh in iced water and set aside.

Arrange the meat in a circle round the edge of 4 large serving plates. Do not overlap the slices. Season with salt and pepper, then brush with olive oil and lemon juice. Place the rocket in the centre of each plate, then arrange the green beans and parmesan shavings over this. Serve with *grissini* (Italian bread sticks) or crusty bread.

A wine that works

A light Pinot Noir would seem an ideal choice, but you should also consider a white wine such as 'Clos de Saint Yves' from the charming and talented Florent Baumard. It's a Chenin Blanc from Savennières in the Loire, with intense fruit, quince, camomile and honey, plus grip and minerality. It works well with the rich texture of the meat and the peppery accompaniments.

Also try

Domaine l'Hortus 'Grande Cuvée' Coteaux du Languedoc, which can have Pinot Noir characteristics due to its high altitude.

An excellent starter to impress your guests.

foie gras with fig tart
and crispy shallots

What you need

4 x 50g slices of foie gras

200g frozen puff pastry

flour, for dusting, and coating shallots

4 fresh figs

1 tbsp caster sugar

2 tsp sherry vinegar

2 shallots

about 500ml sunflower oil, for deep-frying

rock salt

mustard cress

Serves 4

What to do

Keep the foie gras in the fridge until needed. Leave the pastry to defrost at room temperature for 1 hour. Line a baking sheet with greaseproof paper. Preheat the oven to 180°C. Roll the pastry gently on a very lightly floured surface and cut into 4 x 8-10 cm squares. Place on the baking sheet, score each square with a sharp knife and bake for 7-10 minutes. When ready, remove and set aside. Top and tail the figs. Slice into discs and arrange on the top of the pre-cooked pastry in flower shapes. Mix the sugar and sherry vinegar and sprinkle over the figs – this will draw the flavour out.

Heat a frying pan on the cooker until smoking. Remove the foie gras slices from the fridge and place on the frying pan – foie gras does not need oil for frying as it is 90% fat. Fry until golden brown on one side (approx. 10 seconds), then turn over and repeat. Remove the foie gras and place on top of the fig tarts. Heat in the oven for 2-3 minutes.

Finely slice the shallots into rings. Coat them with flour and deep-fry in 3-4cm sunflower oil until golden brown. Remove the tarts from the oven. Season the foie gras with rock salt and arrange the shallots neatly on top. Garnish with mustard cress.

A note for the cook

You can buy pre-sliced foie gras from the freezer section of good supermarkets. If you are slicing it yourself, chill the foie gras first and use a very sharp knife.

A wine that works

A classic accompaniment to foie gras is Sauternes, one of the sweet wines of Bordeaux. While many Sauternes are expensive (often justifiably so, due to the rigours of harvesting the botrytis-affected grapes) an easy way of enjoying these styles of wine is to buy them in the half bottle. A good example of Sauternes is Château Laville (available in half bottles), made by Jean-Christophe Barbe. It may take six passes through the vineyard to get the grapes he wants and the resulting wine has a lovely intensity of sweet fruit but shows a fresh acidity that carries the richness of the food. Tip: try your Sauternes with an oriental dish that has a little ginger.

Also try

Domaine Weinbach Tokay Pinot Gris 'Cuvée Laurence' from Alsace.

Seafood, in general, contains an abundance of minerals such iron, zinc and iodine. Bouillabaisse is a great way to serve up plenty of shellfish and seafood in a wonderful dish that's perfect for a celebration with a group of friends.

bouillabaisse

What to do

To make the rouille, preheat the grill to high. Cut the red pepper in half, remove the seeds and place, skin-side up, under the hot grill until the skin blackens and blisters. Place in a bowl, cover and leave to cool before peeling away the skin. Roughly chop the red pepper flesh. Soak the bread in water, then squeeze dry. Put the red pepper, bread, chilli, garlic and egg yolk in a processor and mix together. Gradually add the oil and continue to mix until the rouille is smooth with the texture of thick mayonnaise. Cover and refrigerate until required.

To prepare the soup, heat the oil in a large pot and cook the fennel and onion for 5 minutes, until golden. Meanwhile, if you're using fresh tomatoes, score a cross in the base of each, cover with boiling water for 30 seconds, then plunge into cold water. Drain and peel. Halve, remove the seeds and chop, discarding the cores.

Add the tomatoes to the pan and cook for 3 minutes. Stir in the stock, the saffron, bouquet garni and orange zest. Bring to the boil for about 10 minutes. Remove the bouquet garni and zest and push the soup through a sieve. Return to the pan, season well and bring back to the boil. Reduce to a simmer and add the fish and shellfish. Cook for 5 minutes or until the fish is tender and the shellfish have opened. Discard any that do not open. Serve with the rouille and crusty bread.

A note for the cook

If you prefer, you can buy good quality, ready-made fish stock. However, it's well worth the small effort to make your own.

A wine that works

This is a meaty, rich, tomato-based fish casserole that calls for a red wine. Domaine Clavel 'les Garrigues' is a blend of grenache, syrah and mourvèdre and has echoes of Châteauneuf-du-Pape. There's rich, ripe, dark berry fruit, with a touch of herbs and spice and vanilla from the oak.

Also try

Fairview 'Pegleg' Carignan from Perdeberg in South Africa.

What you need

For the rouille

1 small red pepper
1 slice white bread, crust removed
1 small red chilli
2 garlic cloves
1 organic egg yolk
80ml olive oil

For the soup

2 tbsp olive oil
1 fennel bulb, thinly sliced
1 onion, chopped
750g ripe tomatoes
(or tinned, chopped)
1.25 litres fish stock (see page 223)
pinch of saffron threads
bouquet garni (see page 223)
zest of 1 orange
rock salt, black pepper
12 large uncooked prawns, peeled
800g monkfish fillet, cut into bite-size pieces (you can also use salmon, sea bass, snapper, red mullet or john dory)
18 mussels, cleaned
12 king scallops
18 clams, cleaned

Serves 8

Pasta alla carbonara is a speciality of the Lazio region of Italy, and the traditional recipe calls for *guanciale* (air-dried pig's cheek). However, pancetta is usually substituted today.

real carbonara

What to do

Drop the spaghetti into a large pot of salted, boiling water. Stir occasionally until al dente. Drain, reserving a little of the cooking water for the eggs.

Meanwhile, heat the oil in a frying pan and fry the cubed pancetta until crisp. Beat the eggs yolks in a large bowl, season with black pepper and add the grated cheese, then a little of the pasta cooking water. Quickly stir the freshly drained pasta into the egg mixture.

Serve immediately in bowls with fresh parmesan shavings and a green salad.

A wine that works

An Italian Pinot Noir with a lovely aromatic nose and depth of flavour, Franz Haas Pinot Nero has that touch of acidity to cut through the eggs and pasta.

Also try

Domaine des Nugues Beaujolais.

What you need

600g spaghetti

2 tbsp olive oil

400g pancetta, cubed

6 medium-sized organic egg yolks

black pepper

4 tbsp freshly grated parmigiano or pecorino, plus extra shavings, to serve

Serves 6

This one-pot wonder is still a favourite at ely winebar.

irish stew

What to do

Heat the olive oil in a frying pan, add the lamb and seal on all sides. You will need to do this in batches.

Place all the ingredients in a large pot on the hob. Add enough water just to cover and season lightly – remember you can add more later. Bring to the boil, cover and simmer over a low heat for 1½-2 hours until the meat is very tender. It should cut easily – even with a spoon. Taste and season again if required.

Serve in deep bowls with traditional brown bread.

A wine that works.

This is a simple dish, with a clear juice and a delicate, sweet flavour from the organic lamb. Lombeline Beaune is a delicate Pinot Noir, with light fruit and tannins that quietly compliment the stew, and with its own sweet berry fruit.

Also try

La Rioja Alta 'Viña Alberdi' Rioja.

What you need

1 tbsp olive oil

1kg stewing lamb, diced

500g rooster potatoes, peeled and halved

2 medium onions, diced

4 medium carrots, peeled and sliced

rock salt, black pepper

Serves 4

A note for the cook
If you don't have a
griddle pan a heavy duty
oven-proof pan will do.

'Bleeding' the cabbage
(leaving it to steep in
the vinegar) prior to
cooking helps preserve
its vibrant colour.

Venison is a low-fat meat with lots of flavour, and it's full of protein.
It makes a great seasonal alternative to fillet of beef.

chargrilled venison
with red cabbage, prunes and roasted figs

What you need

2 figs

150ml red wine vinegar

1 tsp icing sugar

50g brown sugar

100ml crème de cassis

150g red cabbage,
finely shredded

50g dried prunes

1 cinnamon stick

olive or sunflower oil,
for cooking venison

2 x 180g pavés of
venison loin

Serves 2

What to do

Split the figs into 4. Place on a baking tray, drizzle with a little of the vinegar and lightly dust
with icing sugar. Cook for 15-20 minutes at 50°C, or as low as your oven will go. Set aside
and keep warm until ready to serve.

Meanwhile, place the brown sugar and crème de cassis in a pot and heat gently. In a bowl,
combine the red cabbage with the remaining vinegar and leave to stand for 5-10 minutes.
Add to the pot together with the prunes and cinnamon stick. Turn up the heat slightly.
Stir well, cover and cook for 20-25 minutes, stirring every 2-3 minutes. When cooked,
strain over another pot, reserving the liquid. Set the cabbage aside and cover with cling film
to keep warm. Reduce the strained liquid over a gentle heat to make the sauce.

Preheat the oven to 180°C. Heat a griddle pan until smoking. Oil the venison very lightly
and sear on each side to get a chargrilled effect. Place on a roasting tray in the oven for
4-5 minutes for medium-rare. If you prefer, leave in the oven for longer. Remove the venison from
the oven and slice neatly.

To serve, divide the cabbage between 2 serving plates, place the venison on top,
coat with the sauce and arrange the figs as desired.

A wine that works

Domaine Le Sang des Cailloux, a Vacqueyras from the southern Rhône is exceptional
value and competes nicely with the best of Châteauneuf-du-Papes. It has a Provençal nose
of herbs and garrigue; black fruits, pepper and roasted herbs on the palate. Rich, rewarding
and lovely with this dish.

Also try

Alvaro Palacios's 'Les Terrasses' from Priorat in Spain.

From the very beginning, the organic burger has been our best-selling dish. We use top-quality organic beef, not too lean or overly minced, so our burgers stay juicy and keep their flavour.

ely organic burger

What to do

In a large bowl, combine the beef, shallot, parsley, egg and breadcrumbs. Mix well and season. Divide the mixture into 4 and shape into burgers. Place the burgers on a lined tray and refrigerate until you are ready to cook them.

Preheat the oven to 200ºC. Heat a pan with a metal handle and seal the burgers on each side until brown. You could also seal them on a hot griddle. Transfer to the oven and cook for 20-25 minutes. If you don't have a pan with a metal handle, preheat a roasting tray in the oven instead.

Before serving, place a slice of brie on top of each burger and garnish with some salad.

A note for the cook

If you prefer smaller portions, simply divide the mix into 8 and reduce the cooking time.

When you're sealing the burgers, make sure the pan is hot to prevent sticking.

Feel free to add some horseradish sauce or your favourite relish to the pre-cooked mix. Other toppings could be caramelised onions with melted cheddar, a fried egg and bacon, foie gras or whole roast tomatoes.

At ely, we serve the burger on a bed of homemade tomato relish and dress the plate with rocket essence (see page 224).

A wine that works

Crozes-Hermitage from Domaine Yann Chave, one of the northern Rhône's up-and-coming producers, is a gorgeously big, smoky Syrah with youthful tannins and dry, dark fruit. Perfect for the simplicity of a great burger.

Also try

Hewitson 'Ned & Henry', a shiraz/mourvèdre blend from the Barossa Valley.

What you need

800g coarsely ground organic beef

1-2 shallots, diced

few sprigs parsley, chopped

1 large free-range egg, beaten

100g fresh white breadcrumbs

rock salt, black pepper

sunflower or olive oil for frying

200g ripe brie (at room temperature), sliced into 4

salad leaves, to serve

Serves 4

boning a chicken

Poultry signs of quality

A really fresh chicken should have plump, moist breasts, a pliable breast bone and firm flesh. Its skin should be white and unbroken and with a faint tint. Avoid poultry that has signs of drying, discolouration, blemishes or bruising. Fresh poultry has a mild scent and is free of strong odours.

Watch out for coarse scales and large spurs on the legs. These, along with long hairs on the skin, are all signs of a bird that's past its best. Buy poultry that feels cold to the touch. Fresh poultry needs to be cold at all times to help prevent bacterial contamination. Make poultry, along with meat and fish, among the last items you put in your basket.

Cleaning

Pick out any pens or down, using a small knife. If there are any hairs or tiny feathers left on the chicken you can use a blowtorch to singe them, taking care not to scorch the skin. Using a decent-sized sharp knife, split the neck skin by gripping firmly and making a lengthwise incision on the underside. Using a meat cleaver, cut off the head as close to the body as possible.

Removing wingtips

Remove the first two wing joints by cutting across them with a heavy knife. These wing tips can be kept for stock.

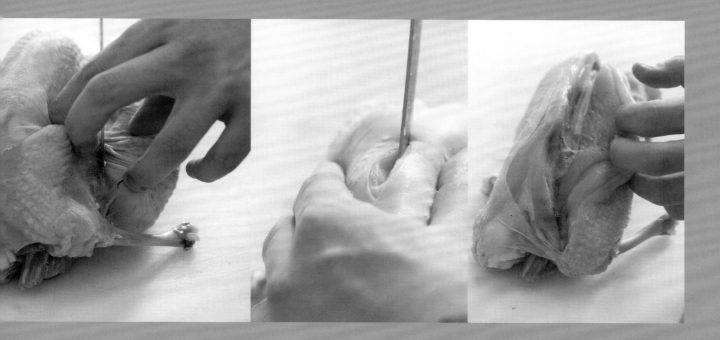

Removing breasts

Lay the chicken down on one breast. Make a cut along the cartilage that runs from neck to tail, between the breasts, working the knife down into the flesh.

Make a cut along one side of the breastbone to free the breast from the ribcage. Pull the meat away from the bones as you make the cut so that you leave as little meat on the ribcage as possible. Make a cut through the joint that attaches the wing to the rib cage. At this stage you can now keep the breast as a supreme, with a wing attached, or the wings and skin can be completely removed.

Removing legs

Lay the chicken on its back on a chopping board. Using a sharp knife make a cut between the leg and the breast. Bend the leg away from the body and press your fingertips into the back of the joint to pop it loose. Continue to cut the leg away from the breast. Make a cut completely around the end of the drumstick to sever the flesh, tendons and skin from the bone.

Quartering a chicken

Using poultry scissors, start at the neck and work your way down along the cartilage between the breasts. Repeat on the other side until you have 2 halves. Using a clean, sharp knife, cut straight down through the bone of each half, applying enough pressure to make sure the knife goes through the bone.

A modern twist on an old French classic. At ely, we serve this with creamy mashed potato.

chicken chasseur
with morel mushrooms

What to do

Start by soaking the morels in boiling water until thoroughly wet and soft to the touch.

In a large pot (big enough to hold the chicken), sauté the carrot, shallots and celery in half the butter until al dente. Add the thyme and bay leaves and then a splash of red wine. Strain the morels, roughly chop and add to the saucepan with the vegetables. Add the stock and reduce to a simmer.

Heat a frying pan and fry the chicken pieces in the remaining 50g of butter until golden brown on both sides – this will add flavour to the dish. Place the chicken pieces in the simmering liquid. Add the cream and reduce by one-quarter. Season to taste. Chop the tarragon leaves and add at the last minute – this ensures that you don't blacken the herb with too much heat and also brings out its full flavour.

Serve in a bowl, on a bed of mashed potato, scattered with the spring onions.

A wine that works

A light merlot-based wine will bring out the flavour of the mushrooms. Château Calon from Montagne, Saint-Emilion, has dark fruit, ripe, rounded tannins and a decent finish.

Also try

Le Volte from Ornellaia in Bolgheri, Tuscany.

What you need

100g dried morels

½ medium carrot, diced

2 banana shallots, or 4 ordinary shallots, diced

1 stick celery, diced

100g butter

2 sprigs thyme

4 bay leaves

150ml red wine

300ml roast bone stock (see page 224), or good quality, ready-made chicken stock

1 organic, corn-fed chicken, quartered (see page 172)

100ml cream

rock salt, black pepper

good bunch tarragon

2 spring onions, finely chopped, to garnish

Serves 4

The ultimate in wholesome comfort food.

fish pie

What you need

1 medium onion, sliced

100-150g butter

50g flour

½ bottle unoaked dry white wine

550ml cream

250g salmon, filleted, skinned, fine-boned and chopped

250g cod, filleted, skinned, fine-boned and chopped

250g crab meat, fresh or frozen

3 large floury potatoes, such as roosters, peeled and chopped

rock salt, black pepper

50g dill, chopped

50g parsley, chopped

1 egg yolk

Serves 4-6

What to do

Start by sweating the onion in half the butter in a pan. When the onion is translucent, slowly add the flour to make a roux. Over a very low heat, stir in the white wine and 500ml of the cream. Add the fish and crab meat and cook for 12-15 minutes.

Meanwhile, preheat the oven to 180°C. Cook the potatoes in plenty of boiling, salted water until soft. Drain and place back over a low heat covered with a dry, clean cloth for a few minutes. This will help to dry them out a little. Mash the potato with the remaining cream and butter, to taste. Season well with the salt and pepper and set aside.

Add the dill and parsley to the pan with the fish and crab meat, and season with salt and pepper. Turn the seafood mix into a large, ovenproof dish and cover with the mash. Brush the top of the potato with the egg yolk.

Bake for 7-10 minutes, or until the potato is golden brown on top.

A note for the cook

This is a great dish to cook for a casual weekend dinner or Sunday lunch. Best of all, most of the work can be done the night before.

Just work through the recipe right up to the point where you assemble the pie, then cover and put in the refrigerator overnight. All you have to do the next day is bake the pie for 15-20 minutes at 180°C.

A wine that works

The creaminess of this dish needs a wine with the ability to cut through the sauce while lifting the mild fish flavours. 'José Pariente' by Bodegas dos Victorias in Rueda, Spain, is made from the verdejo grape. It's almost sauvignon-blanc-like in its freshness, with layers of fruit flavours and a ripe, citrus acidity.

Also try

Broglia 'Tenuta la Meirana' Gavi de Gavi.

A note for the cook

In season, wild pheasant should be readily available. Try to buy Irish if possible. At ely we present the dish on a rectangular plate as follows: slice each breast in half diagonally and stand on the plate in the centre. Place two ovals of mash at opposite ends of the plate. Place the leg and thigh next to the mash, at opposite angles from the breasts. Lightly scatter the vegetables around the plate. Drizzle over the jus.

The earthiness of the celeriac works beautifully with the gamey flavour of the pheasant. A great one for a dinner party. You can vary the vegetable accompaniments according to what's available.

roast pheasant
with celeriac purée and baby vegetables

What you need

125g butter, plus extra for greasing

10 thin slices of small pork belly or streaky bacon

1 wild pheasant (ask your butcher to prepare it by removing legs and taking breasts off the bone)

rock salt, black pepper

1 large potato (rooster), peeled and quartered

250g celeriac, peeled and chopped

4 spears green asparagus

50g garden peas

4 young carrots, peeled

4 young leeks, trimmed

100ml red wine jus (see page 224)

Serves 2

What to do

Preheat the oven to 180°C. Begin by cutting 2 sheets of foil, no more than 8cm in length and width. Rub with butter. Lay the pork belly slices on the sheets so that the slices overlap each other. Place one pheasant breast on each sheet. Season with salt and pepper. Roll the bacon or pork belly slices completely around the pheasant breasts, then roll up in the foil, twisting it at each end.

Place the legs and the thighs in a roasting tray in the oven and cook for 35 minutes. After about 10 minutes, place the pheasant breasts in the oven and cook for 15-20 minutes. When all the meat is cooked, remove from the oven and leave to rest for 5-10 minutes.

While the pheasant is in the oven, cook the potato and celeriac in boiling, salted water until tender. Strain and mash well, adding 75g of the butter. Blanch the asparagus, peas, carrots and leeks in boiling salted water for 30-40 seconds, then refresh in iced water. Set aside until needed. Heat the remaining 50g butter in a pan until it foams. Add the vegetables and sauté for 1½ minutes. Remove from the heat before the butter browns. Place the red wine jus in a pan and keep over a gentle heat.

Split the pheasant leg from the thigh and trim any excess skin off the bone down to the knuckle, keeping the bones as clean as possible. This will help with presentation. Remove the foil from the breast. Serve the pheasant with the mash and the baby vegetables, drizzling the jus over the pheasant.

A wine that works

Vigne dei Fantini, Barolo, by Silvano Bolmida, is not your typically tannic, austere style of Barolo but a modern, fuller wine. Velvety, sweet and ripe with an enticing bouquet of dark cherries and violets, this is a very rewarding wine whose fuller style works well with the dry meat that is roast pheasant, while not overpowering the dish.

Also try

Domaine de Montcalmès from the Coteaux du Languedoc.

A great dessert for when you just want to make use of storecupboard ingredients.
You can leave out the brandy cream if you are serving children.

banana pancakes
with brandy cream

What you need

200g plain flour

2 eggs

100ml milk

1½ tbsp water

100g butter, plus extra
for frying pancakes

4 bananas

3-4 tbsp brandy

100ml cream

Serves 4

What to do

Ideally, make the pancake batter the day before, or at least 1 hour in advance.

Sieve the flour into a bowl. In another bowl, whisk the eggs, milk and water together. Make a well in the centre of the flour, then slowly stir the egg mixture into the flour. Cover and keep in the fridge overnight.

Heat a non-stick pan. Add a small cube of butter and allow to melt. Ladle in enough pancake mixture to make a circle that holds its shape. Turn as it cooks. Place each cooked pancake in a stack on a warmed plate and cover with a humid tea towel. Keep warm.

Meanwhile, peel the bananas and cut in half lengthways. Melt a knob of butter in a frying pan and cook the bananas until slightly golden. Remove the bananas, carefully pour the brandy into the pan to deglaze and add the cream. Slowly reduce by half.

Place 2 pieces of banana on top of each serving. Drizzle with the brandy cream.

A note for the cook

These are American-style pancakes – they use a thick batter which holds its shape. Making the batter in advance allows the gluten content of the flour to relax resulting in lighter, pancakes.

DANGER! Brandy is highly flammable. Be very careful when you're deglazing the pan, especially if using gas. Reduce the flame first.

A wine that works

Lustau 'East India' has a lovely, creamy, caramelised nose; a sweet palate, with hints of dates and a touch of bitter chocolate. This blend of the palomino and pedro ximénez grapes gives a full, complex and long finish. A real treat that works well with the sweetened banana and the heady brandy.

Also try

A ten-year-old Tawny port such as Warre's 'Otima'.

A three-step, foolproof dessert!

rhubarb fool

What to do

Top and tail the rhubarb and chop into 2cm chunks.

Place the rhubarb and sugar in a large pot, and bring to a gentle simmer. Cook until soft (approx 10-15 min). Allow to cool.

Whip the cream, fold the rhubarb into the cream and serve with ginger biscuits, brandy snaps, or other dessert biscuits.

A note for the cook

Keep 1 rhubarb stalk aside for a garnish. Peel and string the stalk and chop neatly into equal lengths. Dust with icing sugar before serving. If you like, you can add colour by topping the fool with red berries.

A wine that works

This doesn't need anything too serious – a little fruit and sparkle. Le Contesse Prosecco from Italy has lovely floral aromas and delicate fruit on the palate with a mellow finish.

Also try

Your favourite Champagne.

What you need

500g rhubarb
100g caster sugar
200ml double cream
dessert biscuits,
to serve

Serves 4-6

These gorgeous brownies are heavenly served with ice-cream, as a dessert. They're also ideal for storing as treats for your coffee break – if you can resist them for that long!

jamaican coffee pecan brownies

What to do

Line a baking tray, measuring approx 38 x 26cm, with greaseproof paper, or lightly grease a glass ovenproof dish. A lasagne dish is ideal. The tray or dish should be 2cm minimum in depth.

Combine the sugar, butter, cocoa, ground coffee and salt in a metal or heatproof bowl. Place the bowl over a saucepan of simmering water and leave until the butter melts, stirring occasionally to help blend the ingredients – the texture will be grainy.

Remove the bowl from the water and allow the mixture to cool to lukewarm. Whisk in the eggs and vanilla. Sieve the flour over and fold in. Take three-quarters of the pecan halves and roll up inside a clean tea towel. Bash lightly with a rolling pin to break up. Stir the pieces into the mix.

Pour the freshly brewed coffee over the mixture with the chocolate and stir until melted and smooth. Pour the mixture into the prepared dish or tray and spread evenly. Allow to cool and thicken for approximately 1 hour. Preheat the oven to 180°C. Bake in the oven for 25 minutes or until a skewer inserted into the brownies comes out clean.

Remove from the oven and cut into squares. Dress the brownies with the reserved pecans and ginger or candied orange peel. Dust with icing sugar. Serve warm with vanilla ice-cream.

A wine that works

Warre's Otima 20-year-old Tawny port has beautiful, soft, nutty aromas that come from having spent a full 20 years in seasoned oak barrels. It's rich, smooth and delicate with balanced acidity and tannins that complement the dark chocolate.

Also try

A top quality Chilean cabernet-style wine such as Clos Apalta from Casa Lapostolle.

What you need

400g caster sugar

375g unsalted butter

75g cocoa powder

3 tbsp finely ground Jamaican blue mountain (or your favourite) coffee beans

½ tsp salt

3 large eggs

1½ tsp vanilla extract

150g plain flour

100g pecan halves

6 tbsp freshly brewed Jamaican coffee

100g dark chocolate, 70% cocoa solids, chopped (Valrhona is ideal)

30 thin strips crystallised ginger, or candied orange peel

icing sugar, for dusting

Makes 15

A melt-in-the-mouth dessert for chocoholics everywhere.

warm dark chocolate fondants

What you need

125g dark chocolate, 70% cocoa solids, chopped

125g unsalted butter, plus a little extra for greasing the moulds

3 medium organic eggs

3 medium organic egg yolks

65g caster sugar

100g plain flour

1 tbsp cocoa powder, plus a little extra for the moulds

To serve

vanilla ice-cream or mango sorbet

thin dessert biscuits (optional)

Serves 6

What to do

Put the chocolate and the butter in a heatproof bowl and stand over a pan of simmering water. Leave to melt, stirring until smooth. In another bowl, whisk the eggs, egg yolks and sugar together. Add the melted chocolate mixture and fold in the flour and cocoa until evenly combined.

Lightly grease 6 x 7.5cm ramekins with butter and dust with cocoa. Stand them on a baking tray and pour in the chocolate mixture until about three-quarters full. Place in the fridge for 1 hour to set.

Preheat the oven to 200°C. Place the ramekins into the oven for 10 minutes. The fondant should be spongy on the top but still soft in the middle – you can check by gently inserting a small knife and the chocolate mixture should run free.

Serve the fondants warm with a scoop of vanilla ice-cream or mango sorbet and a thin dessert biscuit.

A note for the cook

At ely, we like to serve this dessert with a refreshing mango coulis.

A wine that works

Banyuls, a 'vin doux naturel', or 'naturally sweet wine', from the southern limit of Roussillon in France, is one of the few wines that go well with chocolate. Made predominantly from grenache, the heady aromas of macerated red fruits give way to mocha flavours and a dry, powerful finish. The concentration achieved by the grenache, and the heat and time works well with the chocolate, especially dark chocolate.

Also try

A red Zinfandel, from California.

'Tell me what you eat, I'll tell you what you are.'

Brillat-Savarin

'The mighty trio of ely winebar, ely chq and ely hq. Which to choose?
Absolutely the most delicious Dublin dining dilemma.'

our restaurants

ely hq – the place was kickin'. The punters were groovy – bankers, rock bands drinking bolly, hip young women – and were almost as groovy as the staff.

And we ate so well it wasn't true, with chef Tom Doyle firing out some delicious, inspired cooking. Ace food, ace place. But then... so are all three elys, from the little original on ely place to the swish ely chq just north of the river.

Erik and Michelle Robson's achievement seems to us to be amongst the most considerable in Dublin hospitality in recent years, and their secret is to understand polite service, good food and great wines, and to inspire their crews to match them every step of the way. Which one to choose? No dilemma was ever so delicious.

Bridgestone Guide 2008

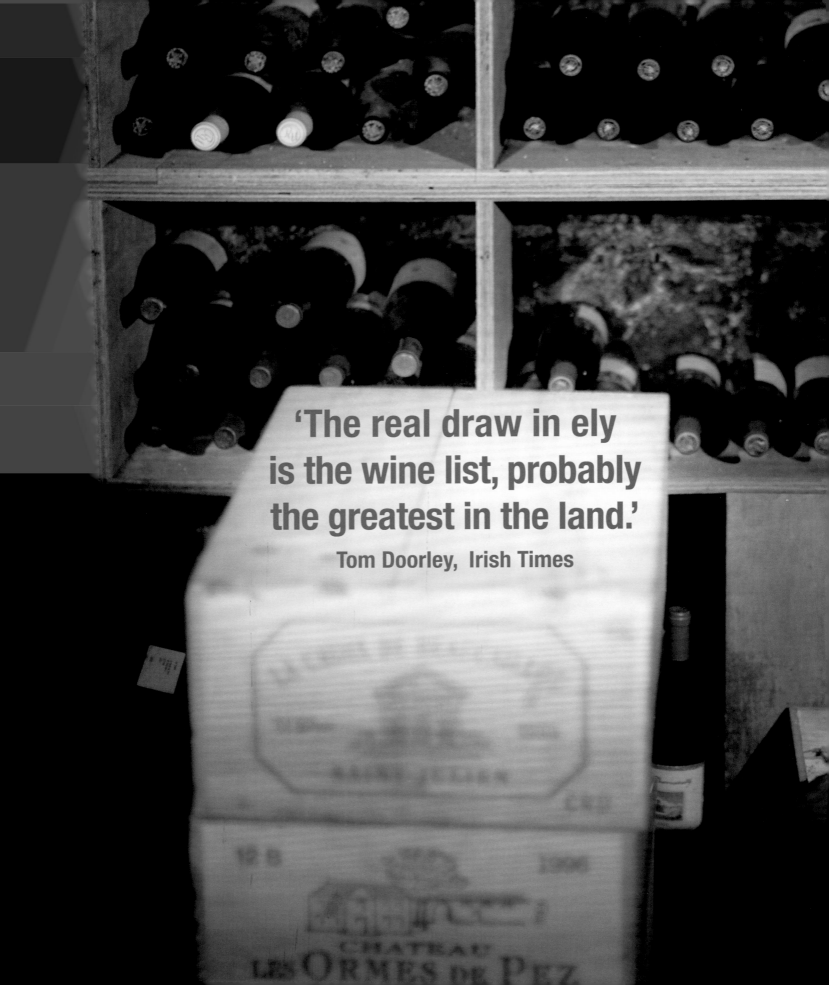

'The real draw in ely
is the wine list, probably
the greatest in the land.'

Tom Doorley, Irish Times

ely winebar

Located in a beautifully refurbished building in the heart of Georgian Dublin, ely winebar is where it all started. Open since December 1999, it has earned a reputation for being the best place in Dublin city to relax over a glass of wine and enjoy a good meal. With one of the most comprehensive wine lists in the country, it offers a comfortable and relaxed environment where our customers can enjoy great wines and good, honest food with the minimum of fuss and pretension.

ely winebar is at ely place, dublin 2

While developing the wine list at ely winebar over the past decade we have discovered some really good wines. An important aspect of choosing our wines has been the ratio of quality and character to value; and that each wine reflects its origin in its style. An example is Domaine Alary 'La Brunotte' from the village of Cairanne in the Rhône Valley.

discovering good wines

A good rule of thumb is that the more money you spend on a bottle of wine, the more interesting and involving it will be. However, you don't have to spend an exorbitant amount to get good quality. Modern winemaking techniques, generations of experience and stringent standards mean that most of today's wines are well made.

In a restaurant, remember that trading up and spending an extra €10 or so should give you a wine of vastly improved quality.

People often play it safe, and order the house wine, or a wine they've had before. But being a little adventurous now and again and ordering outside your comfort zone will bring its own rewards. So, if you always opt for an Australian Shiraz, ask your wine waiter to recommend a Northern Rhône. Similarly, if you are tired of oaky Chardonnays, why not try a Mâcon or a Chablis? These wines will deliver all that's good about Chardonnay, without overpowering your palate with oak.

By engaging with the wine waiter and trying new wines, you'll learn more about the amazing array of grape varieties that are out there, and who is making the wines that you really enjoy.

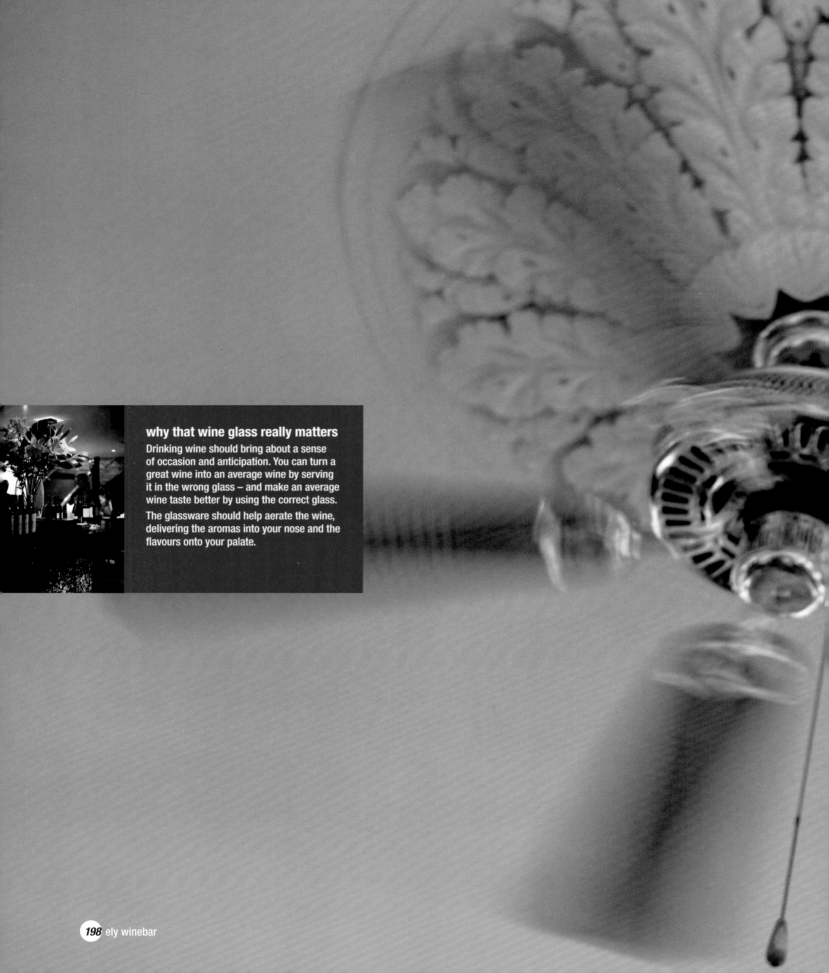

why that wine glass really matters

Drinking wine should bring about a sense of occasion and anticipation. You can turn a great wine into an average wine by serving it in the wrong glass – and make an average wine taste better by using the correct glass.

The glassware should help aerate the wine, delivering the aromas into your nose and the flavours onto your palate.

focus on glasses

The bottom of the glass should be bowl-shaped, with the rim of the glass sloping inwards to capture and concentrate the aromas.

The bowl of the glass should be wider for red wines, which will benefit from a little swirling around.

The more subtle bouquet of a light and delicate white wine will concentrate better in a tall glass with a tapered rim.

A tall, slim flute glass will help champagne keep its sparkle.

Wine tastes better served from the appropriate glassware – Riedel has perfected the art of making the right glass for the right wine. At ely, we use the Schott Zwiesel range which is also dishwasher-friendly.

'The wine list verges on
the encyclopaedic – it's very
long and full of surprises,
the sort of list that makes you go
'ooh' and occasionally 'aah'.'

Paolo Tullio, Irish Independent

Situated on Dublin's waterfront in the bustling Irish Financial Services Centre, the chq, or 'custom house quay' building – an award-winning architectural masterpiece – was the choice for our second venue.

ely chq

At ely chq, our guests can choose from a list of over 500 wines and enjoy wonderful, continental cuisine. Stack A, as it was originally called, was completed in 1821 by one of the most remarkable engineers of his era, John Rennie, as a cast-iron, bonded wine and tobacco warehouse. Now renamed chq, the building has been beautifully restored and enhanced by an international team of architects, glass and lighting consultants.

The chq building has been referred to over the years by locals as the 'Banquet Hall' because it was the venue which hosted one of the greatest social events of the mid-nineteenth century. At the Crimean Banquet, 1856, Queen Victoria – alongside 1,000 dignitaries – honoured 3,000 Irish soldiers who had returned from the Crimean War.

The chq building is certainly the jewel in the crown of Dublin's ever-evolving Docklands. When our guests walk into our stunning vaulted wine cellars there is a real sense of taking a step back in time. We have restored the vaults and created a relaxed lounging area with two private dining rooms for private functions and wine tastings. In contrast, reflecting the contemporary vibe of this bustling waterfront district, the impressive glass atrium bar, upstairs, has its own oyster bar and serves beers, spirits, cocktails and wines, while the heated, waterside patio allows for atmospheric dining al fresco. ely chq spectacularly showcases what we do best at ely: great wines and smooth food in a relaxed, convivial atmosphere.

ely chq is at the ifsc, dublin 1

centuries of good taste

The Crimean banquet, held at custom house quay in 1856, included 250 hams, 230 legs of mutton, 25 sides of beef, 500 meat pies, 100 venison pasties, 100 rice puddings, 1½ tons plum pudding, 200 turkeys, 200 geese, 2,125 gallons of wine and 3,500 pints of port. Although the menu has changed somewhat, perhaps this extraordinary feast was an early taste of a gourmet tradition that would continue some 150 years later!

'If you can organise
your kitchen,
you can organise
your life.'

Anon

ely hq

With a brand new space as a blank canvas for our third location, we were able to create a distinctly contemporary venue at ely hq in hanover quay. The lively atmosphere, bright, stylish interior, heated waterside patio and young, upbeat staff echo the modern and urban surroundings of this developing area.

You can choose from an extensive wine list as well as a selection of cocktails, beers and spirits at ely hq. The food menu, while based on ely's popular signature dishes, has a cosmopolitan feel, with a strong emphasis on seafood.

ely hq is at hanover quay, dublin 2

ruby cosmo

Chill a large Martini glass. In a Boston glass or cocktail shaker, 'muddle' (or mix), seeds and juice from 2 fresh pomegranates and 12.5ml sugar syrup*. Add 37.5ml Gosling's Black Seal rum, 25ml cranberry juice, 12.5ml fresh lemon juice, 5ml raspberry liqueur and 4 mint leaves.

What to do

Shake the ingredients hard and double-strain into the Martini glass.

Thread 1 raspberry on a cocktail or prism stick, follow with 1 sprig of mint and another raspberry. Lay the stick across the glass.

*To make a sugar syrup, gradually stir 2 parts sugar into 1 part boiling water until completely dissolved.

ely mojito

'Muddle' (or pound) ½ lime, 6-8 mint leaves and 2 tsp brown sugar in a whiskey glass. Fill the glass with crushed ice. Add 37.5ml good quality rum (we use Matusalem Plantation) and 12.5ml Matusalem Classico. Fill to the top with champagne. Top glass with crushed ice and garnish with a mint sprig and lime wedge.

People eat with their eyes first and foremost – this is the golden rule. Any chef will tell you that even the most delicious dish can go untouched if it isn't presented properly, simply because the way food looks affects our perception of how it will taste.

dressing the plate

Think about the presentation of your dish long before you buy your ingredients.

Plan everything in threes: texture, colour and shape.

Take a dish like supreme of chicken on a bed of creamed potato as a perfect example. Sounds great on a cold winter's day – how comforting! However, once you've placed the white chicken on top of the white potato on a white plate the whole thing has gone from a mouthwatering prospect to a dining disaster.

By spending a little time planning the presentation of your meal you can transform even the most simple of foods into a recipe with appetite appeal.

Texture The chicken supreme is the meat texture and the creamed potato is the smooth texture. Simply add a third texture – crunch – with a stir-fry of mixed vegetables.

Colour Wrap your chicken in bacon and roast it in the oven.

Chop spring onions and mix through the creamed potatoes.

For the stir-fry use vibrant colours, such as a julienne of green beans, and red and yellow pepper (all finely sliced into equal lengths).

Shape Place a round of spring onion creamed potato at the side of your plate. Fan your julienne of vegetables in front of the potato. Slice the chicken at an angle and place on top of the potatoes and vegetables.

And finally, don't overdo it – keep it simple and clean.

'You don't have to cook fancy or complicated masterpieces – just good food from fresh ingredients.'

Julia Childs

Bathing in coffee grounds fermented with pineapple pulp is a traditional Japanese therapy for reducing wrinkles and improving the skin. While we don't suggest that you try this at home, we do believe that a perfect cup of coffee brings great benefits. We also think that the enjoyment of a meal can depend on the quality of the coffee that comes afterwards.

the ground rules of great coffee

Our trusted coffee supplier, Robert Roberts, has worked with us at ely since the beginning. The company's regular on-site training programmes have created a wonderful awareness and appreciation of quality coffee amongst our staff. The coffee at ely is monitored by Robert Roberts on a monthly basis, so we can be sure we're always serving the best.

Enjoying great coffee at home

Always start with fresh, cold water.

Water should be heated to 92°-96°C. It should never be boiled.

Ensure coffee is fresh. It is a perishable product. Once opened, store in an air-tight container to preserve its freshness.

Be generous with coffee. Allow approx 7g (¼ oz) for every 180ml (6fl oz).

Serve as soon as possible. Never reheat or leave on a hot surface for too long.

No matter which equipment you're using, keeping it clean – to remove the oily residue left by the coffee – is a key factor in the art of making the perfect cup every time.

'Finding good quality cheese in Ireland has become easier in recent years, with more and more independent, speciality food shops springing up around the country.'
Kevin Sheridan

making the most of cheese

At ely, we trust our friends and long-time suppliers, Sheridans Cheesemongers, to guide us when it comes to serving a great cheeseboard to our customers

When you're putting together a cheeseboard, the general idea is to serve a selection of cheeses which will offer you and your guests contrasting flavours and textures. Try to buy where you can taste; your eyes will never tell you as much as your taste buds.

Ideally, mix a nice soft cheese, a blue cheese, a hard cheese, a washed rind cheese (they're the smelly ones with the pinkish rinds), and if possible, a sheep's or goat's milk cheese. But remember, it's better to have one ripe and gorgeous cheese than five mediocre pieces.

After you buy your cheese, be sure to look after it. Cheese is a living, breathing food and needs to be treated with some care to get the best from it. This is particularly true of the softer cheeses. Cheese should always be served at room temperature because serving it cold substantially inhibits the flavour. Ideally, buy your cheese from someone who has cared for it properly, then serve that same evening.

Cheese that you can't use the same day can be stored in an unheated room or garage, though fridges are not as bad for cheese as they are sometimes made out to be. The main problem is their dry atmosphere rather than the cold temperature. If you do store your cheese in the fridge, always remove it several hours before serving.

Make sure your cheese is well wrapped in a breathable covering such as wax paper. This is particularly important for cheeses with mould or culture rinds and fresh goat's cheeses; plastic will suffocate them and often cause 'off' flavours.

There are no set rules for serving your cheeses; some people like to have their cheese before dessert and others prefer it after, or instead of, dessert. I think it is good to serve something with the cheese which will act as a foil against any richness and clean the palate between cheeses. Fruit is really good for this; a fresh pear or apple is ideal. The fruit must be ripe though, so if you don't have any to hand, serve a chutney, fruit jelly or dried fruit.

Cheese is a wonderful food and needs very little preparation. Everything depends on the quality of the cheese you source. So take your time, seek out the best and enjoy!

glossary and notes

oven temperatures

gas mark	°C
½	120
¾	140
1	150
2	160
3	180
4	190
5	200
6	210
7	220
8	240

weights

grams	ounces
25	1
50	2
75	3
110	4
150	5
175	6
200	7
225	8
250	9
275	10
315	11
350	12
365	13
400	14
425	15
450	16/1lb

volumes

millilitres	fluid ounces
25	1
55	2
75	3
120	4
150	5
175	6
200	7
225	8
250	9
275	10
425	15
570	20/1 pint
725	1 ¼ pints
850	1 ½ pints
1 litre	1 ¾ pints

ingredients and cooking terms

salt and pepper

We find the best salt for cooking is rock salt because it is pure and unrefined and does not attract moisture from the atmosphere like refined table salt. We always use freshly ground black pepper. White pepper can be used where you don't want the pepper to be visible in a pale dish.

size of eggs

These are large, unless otherwise stated. Always use the freshest organic eggs in recipes where the egg is not cooked.

cream

We use single cream, unless otherwise stated.

bouquet garni

A bunch of herbs that are either tied together by the stems or placed in a muslin bag and used to flavour soups, stews and broths. You can buy dried bouquet garni in the supermarket, but it's easy enough to make your own. At ely, we tend to use a bay leaf, a sprig of thyme, some flat-leaf parsley and celery leaves, wrapped up in the outer leaf of a leek and tied with kitchen string. You can substitute rosemary for thyme if you like, although thyme works best with fish. For fish, you could put some dried fennel seed in the centre of the herbs before wrapping them in the leek.

clarified butter

Butter that has been heated so that the whey sinks to the bottom, leaving a clear part on top. It can be heated to higher temperatures than normal butter without burning. Place the butter in a small dish in the microwave on a low heat for 3-4 minutes. Do not stir. Skim off any impurities, then decant the oil from the top, leaving behind the whey. This is your clarified butter. This can be done over gentle heat in a pan, but a microwave works best as it can be hard to avoid burning the butter on the hob.

blanch and refresh

This is when we plunge foods – usually vegetables – into boiling water for a few seconds, then remove and place in iced water. This keeps the vibrant colour of the vegetables, without cooking them all the way through.

basic recipes
fish stock for bouillabaisse

What you need

2 tbsp olive oil

1 carrot

2 sticks celery

1 medium onion

white of 1 leek

about 2kg fish bones, typically red mullet

2 bay leaves

4 sprigs parsley

4 sprigs dill

What to do

Heat 2 tbsp olive oil in a large pot. Roughly chop the carrot, celery, onion and leek into large chunks. Add the fish bones and sauté until nicely caramelised and with a good bit of colour. Cover with cold water (about 1.5 litres), add the herbs and simmer for 30 minutes, skimming any impurities from the top. DO NOT BOIL. Tip the contents of the pan into a blender and blend until smooth. Pass through a fine sieve to remove any bone shard. You can freeze the stock for up to 3 months.

Makes 1.25 litres

clear fish stock

The ingredients are the same as for bouillabaisse stock. Just leave out the olive oil and make sure the fish bones are white, with no heads and no blood.

What to do

Clean all the fish bones of blood. Roughly chop all the vegetables as before. Place them, with the fish bones and herbs, in a large pot and cover with cold water (about 1.5-2 litres). Simmer over a medium heat for 30-45 minutes, skimming any impurities from the top. DO NOT BOIL. Strain through a colander. If you like, you can flavour the stock with a glass of dry vermouth, such as Noilly Prat. You can freeze the stock for up to 3 months.

Makes 1.25 litres

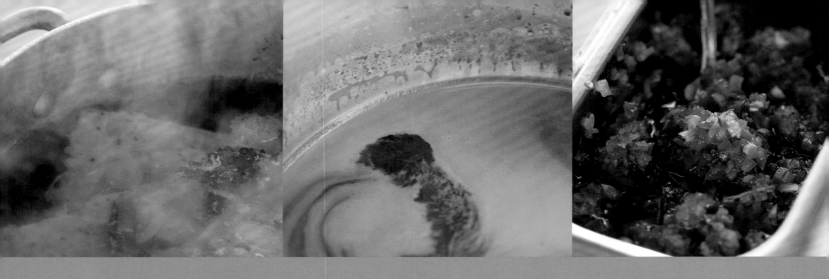

chicken stock

What you need

2 chicken carcasses

3-4 small to medium onions, roughly chopped

2-3 large carrots, roughly chopped

1 tsp peppercorns

3 sprigs thyme

3 bay leaves

3-4 sprigs parsley

½ bottle dry white wine (about 350ml)

What to do

Place all the ingredients into a large pot and cover with approx 2 litres cold water, ensuring that the chicken carcasses are completely submerged. Bring to the boil and simmer for 1 ½-2 hours until reduced to approx 1.5 litres; top up with more water if necessary. Occasionally skim the film off the top of the stock with a clean spoon. When ready, strain the stock and allow to settle. Skim the fat or any impurities off the top. You can freeze this stock for up to 3 months.

Makes about 1.5 litres

vegetable stock

What you need

1 carrot	2 sticks celery
1 medium onion	white of 1 leek
2 bay leaves	1 fennel bulb
pinch of salt	

What to do

Roughly chop all the vegetables into large chunks and put in a large pot. Add enough water to cover (about 1.5 litres) and bring to the boil. Turn off the heat and leave to settle for 10-15 minutes. Strain through a colander and allow to cool. You can freeze the stock for up to 3 months.

Makes about 1.5 litres

red wine jus

This red wine jus gives a lovely glossy finish to meat dishes and has a rich, deep flavour. If you haven't any roast bone stock to hand, you can use good quality bought stock or stock paste.

What you need

1 bottle red wine, or about 750ml

400ml roast bone stock

What to do

Heat up a large pot on the hob. Add the red wine and simmer gently. Heat until reduced to half its volume, with a syrupy texture. Add the stock and simmer until reduced by half. You can freeze the jus for up to 3 months.

Makes about 500ml

roast bone stock

This simple stock gives an incredible intensity of flavour. You can order the veal bones from the butcher.

What you need

2kg veal bones (shin bones with marrow)

1 large onion, halved

2 sticks celery, halved

4 soft tomatoes, halved

bouquet garni (see page 223)

2 cloves garlic, crushed

2-3 tbsp sunflower oil

What to do

Preheat the oven to 200ºC. Place all the ingredients in a roasting tray. Drizzle with the oil, toss to coat and roast for 45 minutes, or up to 1 hour, until dark brown.

Tip the contents of the tray into a large pot. Cover with cold water (about 2 litres) and bring to the boil. Simmer for 30-60 minutes, skimming off impurities regularly. Strain. This will freeze for up to 3 months.

Makes about 1.5 litres

tomato and onion relish

This is great served with the ely burger (see page 170) and bangers and mash (see page 57).

What you need

2 shallots

4 large plum tomatoes

100-150ml white wine vinegar

50g brown sugar

sprig thyme

1 clove garlic

rock salt

bunch of basil

What to do

Finely chop the shallot. Roughly chop the tomatoes, keeping the seeds to add bulk. Put the vinegar, sugar and thyme into a pot. Bring to the boil, reduce the heat and simmer until syrupy. Add the shallot and tomatoes and mix together. Add the garlic. Cook on a medium heat for 10-15 minutes until the liquid has reduced slightly. Taste and add a pinch of salt, if necessary, but no pepper. Tear or roughly chop the basil and add just before serving.

Serves 4-5

rocket essence

We use this lovely, vibrant green essence to dress many of our dishes. It's simple, tastes delicious and really makes an impact.

What you need

100g rocket

150ml extra virgin olive oil

What to do

Blanch the rocket in a pan of boiling water for a few seconds, then immediately refresh in iced water. Add the olive oil and blitz in a blender for 10 minutes. Season to taste.

Serves 4

basic risotto

What you need

1.75 litres vegetable or chicken stock

4 tbsp olive oil

1 small onion, finely chopped

350g risotto rice (preferably carnaroli)

85g butter

6 tbsp grated parmesan cheese, plus extra for serving

rock salt, black pepper

What to do

Bring the stock to a boil in a medium-sized saucepan. Reduce the heat and allow to simmer gently. In a separate pan, heat the olive oil over a medium heat. Add the onion and, stirring all the time with a wooden spoon, cook until it softens and becomes translucent.

Add the rice and cook, stirring, for about 3 minutes, making sure that every grain is coated with oil. Add 1 cup (250ml) of the stock and stir until absorbed. Continue adding the stock, about ½ cup (125ml) at a time, stirring frequently and making sure all the liquid is absorbed before adding more. Continue to stir in the stock, ½ cup (125ml) at a time.

When most of the stock has been added – this should take about 15-20 minutes – test a grain of rice. The risotto is ready when the rice is just tender and creamy, but still 'al dente', with a little bite to it. Remove the pan from the heat and add the butter, parmesan cheese, salt and pepper to taste. Stir vigorously for about 30 seconds to give a creamy, glossy finish to the risotto.

Serves 4

beetroot gratin

What you need

4 large heads beetroot

6 cloves garlic

sunflower oil

800ml cream

1 nutmeg, grated

6-7 large potatoes, peeled

butter, for greasing

rock salt, black pepper

What to do

Boil the beetroot with the skins still on – do not top and tail. Remove when just cooked and allow to cool. Remove the skins with a wet cloth. Peel the garlic cloves and purée them in a small blender with a drop of sunflower oil.

Bring the cream to a simmer with the garlic purée and grated nutmeg, then remove from the heat. Preheat the oven to 160°C.

Slice the beetroots and potatoes as thinly as possible.

Grease a suitable dish. Start layering with potato and then follow with beetroot, seasoning every second layer with salt and pepper and continuing until all potato and beetroot slices are used. Ensure the last layer is potato. Pour the cream over and place a sheet of greaseproof paper on top.

Place in the oven and cook for 30–40 minutes.

Remove and eat straight away or allow to cool, refrigerate and use within 3 days. To reheat, place in the oven at 150ºC for 5-6 minutes. Serve with the halibut (see page 134). This is also perfect with roast game and venison.

A note for the cook

If you wish to create 'stacks' of the gratin for a more formal presentation, prepare and cook 1 day in advance. Place a weight on top of the cooked, layered beetroot and potato and refrigerate overnight. Use a pastry cutter or cup to cut to shape. Place the stacks on a baking tray and cook at a moderate heat for 3-4 minutes.

Serves 4-6

treacle brown bread

What you need

500g wholemeal flour

225g strong white flour

½ tsp salt

½ tsp baking soda

1 dsp brown sugar

135ml vegetable oil

200ml black treacle

250ml O'Hara's or other stout

600ml buttermilk

unsalted butter

large oat flakes, for topping

What to do

Preheat the oven to 180°C. Mix the flours, salt, baking soda and brown sugar in a food processor. Add the oil, black treacle, stout and buttermilk. Mix well.

Grease 2 x 1kg loaf tins with unsalted butter and scatter a light coating of oat flakes into the tin. Pour the bread mix into the tins. Bake for 1 hour, then remove from the oven. Take the loaves out of the tins and return to the oven on a rack for another 10 minutes. Remove and allow to cool before serving. The bread will keep in the freezer for around 1 month.

A note for the cook

To check if the bread is cooked, tap the base of the loaf with your knuckle. If it produces a hollow sound, it's ready.

Makes 2 loaves

grape varieties

barbera

A deep-coloured, wild-fruit flavoured wine with refreshing acidity, ideal for cutting through rich, meaty dishes and Italian cuisine. In its simplest form, gutsy and thirst-quenching, in its more serious guise, aged in barrique (a small, oak barrel), smooth and sophisticated.

cabernet sauvignon

The noble Bordelais grape has travelled far. Every wine-growing region has its own style of cabernet sauvignon, with its blackcurrant and cedar characteristics. Renowned for its longevity, many of the greatest wines in the world, and many of the simpler ones are likely to have this structured, sturdy, elegant grape variety as at least part of the blend. It demands red meats and strong hard cheeses.

cabernet franc

Although best known when blended with merlot on the Right-Bank of Bordeaux, the cabernet franc grape – often described as 'austere' – can reach untold heights in the Loire Valley and some other wine regions. Raspberries and pencil shavings are the give-away aromas which work well with lamb, pork, game and charcuterie.

carmenère

A rare old Bordeaux variety. It yields small quantities of exceptionally deep-coloured, full-bodied spicy wines and has now become synonymous with Chile. Hearty steak and game dishes can take this extrovert variety with ease.

dolcetto

Known as 'The little sweet one', this grape is normally very dry! Deep limpid red, this vivacious grape is full of ripe berries but with a refreshing bitter twist in the tail, it is made to accompany rich country dishes from Piedmont, warm for winter, cool for summer.

gamay

The Beaujolais grape is paler and bluer than most red grapes, with relatively high acidity and a simple, but vivacious aroma of freshly picked red fruits. Shows best drunk cool, and recommended with cold meats, flowery-rind cheeses such as Brie and Camembert and pastas and pizzas as well as many chicken dishes.

grenache/garnacha

A Mediterranean grape which, although quite pale in colour, packs a vinous punch of pepper and warmth. Although it is often blended with other southern varieties such as syrah, carefully made grenache, from old vines, can be a classic in its own right, particularly in Châteauneuf-du-Pape, the Roussillon and Rioja. Great winter wine with game, powerful red meats and rich casseroles.

malbec

Once popular in Bordeaux but now more readily associated with Cahors in South West France and more so with Argentina, where the varietal produces lush wines with gamey concentration and ageing potential. Perfect with barbecued or seared dishes.

merlot

This blue-black fleshy grape, which imparts softness and roundness to red wines, is Bordeaux's most planted vine by far. Nowadays it also enjoys popularity almost everywhere and, on its own, makes good dark-fruited wines in northern Italy, South Africa, California, Chile, Argentina and lately, New Zealand. Goes well with roasts, steaks and hard cheeses.

montepulciano

A vigorous vine planted over much of central Italy, but most widely in the Abruzzi where it is responsible for the often excellent Montepulciano d'Abruzzo, and in the Marches, where it is the principal ingredient in such reds as Rosso Cònero and Rosso Piceno. Try it with Italian dishes or, indeed, because of lowish acidity, it can complement some spicy Asian cuisine.

mourvèdre/macabeo/maccabeu

Mourvèdre is becoming more and more fashionable in Mediterranean climes. Dense, sturdy and yet with a cool elegance, it is almost always reminiscent of good, smooth, dark chocolate. Game, roast beef and big tomato-based sauces, along with roasted vegetables.

nebbiolo

The king of Italian grape varieties, the deeply layered 'tar and roses' bouquet and complexity on the palate cry out for powerful meaty dishes, especially beef and veal to draw out the flavours. Preferably open a few hours before use, or at least decant if possible. It is the ultimate foil for both white and black truffles.

pinot noir

Pinot noir is arguably the greatest of fine wine grapes and makes the fabulous red wines of Burgundy with scent, flavour, texture and body unmatched anywhere. A particularly old variety, the vine is difficult, only moderately prolific and often less than happy in some of the newer parts of the winemaking world. However, New Zealand, the South of France and some New World regions are getting to grips with it and producing some very different, fruity but worthwhile wines. Roasts, game and washed-rind cheeses shine with this grape.

pinot meunier

Pinot meunier is treasured in Champagne as a fruity dependable constituent in the making of their fine wines. In the three-variety champagne blend, meunier contributes youthful fruitiness to complement pinot noir's weight and chardonnay's finesse.

pinotage

South Africa claims this variety as its own. A cross between pinot noir and cinsault it is capable of making fruity, easy-drinking wines alongside some serious and very stylish wines. Great for outdoor dining and winter stews and roasts.

sangiovese/brunello/prugnolo

Sangiovese, and its synonyms, are Italy's most planted variety. It is the principal variety for the fine red wines of Tuscany, such as Chianti, Vino Nobile and Brunello. Wines made from this grape have noticeable tannins and acidity but a character that varies from somewhat earthy to plummy according to quality and ripeness. Great with lamb, pork, bacon and hard cheeses such as pecorino or parmesan. And of course, pastas and pizzas.

syrah/shiraz

Syrah is the great grape of the northern Rhône; the deep, dark, dense qualities of the wine are characteristically strange and satisfying. Scented with black pepper, capsicums and sometimes violets, the grapes flourish in warmer climes such as California, Australia and South Africa, where it is known as shiraz.

tempranillo

Tempranillo is Spain's answer to cabernet sauvignon, the vine variety that puts the spine into a high proportion of Spain's most respected red wines. Its grapes are thick-skinned and capable of making deep-coloured, long-lasting wines that are not, unusually for Spain, notably high in alcohol. Lamb, chunky vegetable dishes and manchego cheese are perfect partners.

zinfandel

Originating most likely in the Adriatic, this exotic minerally, black-skinned grape, grown predominantly in California, can make dark, brooding wines for barbecued steak or, bizarrely, sweetish, lighthearted quaffing rosés called 'blush'.

albariño/albarinho

Native to the north-west of Spain and Portugal (Rías Baixas and Vinho Verde) this satiny, round variety gives a very refreshing match to the wonderful seafood of the area.

chardonnay

The winemaker's 'artist's palette', chardonnay can take on many styles, depending on its provenance and the winemaker's intentions. From cool, classic Chablis, through creamy, fruity unoaked Mediterranean offerings to huge, oaky, tropical, fruit-filled New World giants, it can be all things to all men, and, according to Bridget Jones, women! Match the style to the dish, oysters and seafood for the austere Chablis, Pacific Rim dishes for the whopping Australian styles.

chenin blanc

Probably the world's most versatile grape variety, it is usually found in light and fruity New World wines, particularly from South Africa where it is known as steen. It also produces some of the finest, longest-living sparkling, dry, medium and sweet white wines in the Loire Valley and Limoux. Perfect with river fish, goat's cheeses, chicken and fish dishes with creamy sauces and fruit, honey and nut desserts.

gewürztraminer

From a pink-skinned grape variety, it is an exotic, distinctively aromatic and somewhat spicy full-bodied white wine, usually from Alsace or Germany, but increasingly elsewhere, including Spain. Excellent with foie gras, ham and pork dishes and Asian cuisine.

grüner veltliner

The classic white of Austria, this is a hidden gem. The wine is capable of beating top chardonnays in blind tastings, yet is little known here. Somewhat spicy and unusual in style, it is full-bodied and very savoury, and suits a wide variety of quite strongly flavoured dishes.

marsanne and roussanne

The twin grapes of the northern and southern Rhône and the Languedoc, this pair make a sturdy, very full-bodied, bone-dry and spicy wine that will withstand most dishes, especially those with strong flavours such as truffles.

muscat/moscato

The 'grapiest' of all varieties, muscat comes in every style from bone-dry, through low-alcohol and lightly frizzante, to full Spumante, and even sweet and sticky. It is the base of many good Vin Doux Naturels such as Muscat de Beaumes de Venise or Muscat de Rivesaltes.

muscadet

The muscadet grape (or Melon de Bourgogne) is almost solely grown for producing the dry, crisp white wines from the Nantes region of the Loire. The perfect foil for shellfish such as crab, lobster or prawns.

pinot bianco/pinot blanc

Although its base is Burgundian, it is more common in Alsace where plantings have increased. It is also to be found in Italy where it yields simple but popular fresh, fruity wines. A good wine to match many varied dishes.

pinot gris/pinot grigio

This grape tends to give flavourful, almost oily wines, rather high in alcohol and slightly low in acidity. More spicy in France than Italy or Argentina. It is full-bodied enough to accompany red meats if red wine is not used.

prosecco

Cultivated all over North Eastern Veneto, especially Valdobbiadene, it renders a sparkling wine with delicate aromas of apples. Widely used as an aperitif or simply to quaff and watch the world go by.

riesling

A great white wine grape associated most obviously, but not exclusively, with Germany and Alsace. It varies in style from the light alcohol wines of the Mosel in Germany through full-bodied classic wines of Alsace to the stony, lemon and lime ripeness of Australian Riesling and wildly aromatic New Zealand styles. The grape can show hints of green apples, lemon or white peach when young, with the typical kerosene bouquet developing with age. Ideal match to ham and pork dishes, strong cheeses, onion tarts and quiches.

sauvignon blanc

An exceptionally fine white grape, distinctively aromatic, it is responsible for some of the world's most popular white wines. Sancerre, Pouilly Fumé and Menetou-Salon, for example, in France and a host of Sauvignons and Fumé Blancs from elsewhere. New Zealand Sauvignon is now considered a classic style. The perfect thirst quencher, it works with so many dishes.

sémillon

Blended with its traditional partner, sauvignon blanc, this golden-berried vine variety is the key ingredient in both the great dry and the sweet white wines of Bordeaux. Sémillon usually predominates and inspires rich, golden, honeyed viscous wines. It can also be used on its own or blended with chardonnay, mainly in hotter countries. Well-matched with rich fish dishes like monkfish or turbot, or poultry with cream sauces.

viognier

A very low-yielding variety with a particular perfume of apricots, peaches and blossom. A relatively drought-resistant variety, it is now thriving in the south of France and is also grown in the New World. Blended with chardonnay at times, it is an intriguing mix. Drink as an apéritif, or with some lightly spiced dishes.

our suppliers

wine

Approach Trade
Mill River Business Park, Carrik-on-Suir,
Co. Tipperary

Burgundy Direct
8 Monaloe Way, Blackrock, Co. Dublin

Berry Bros & Rudd
4 Harry St, Dublin 2

Comans Wholesale Ltd.
Belgard Rd, Tallaght, Dublin 24

Febvre & Co Ltd
Burton Hall Rd, Sandyford Ind Est,
Sandyford, Dublin 18

On the Grapevine
21 St Patricks Rd, Dalkey, Co. Dublin

Gilbeys
Nangor Hse, Nangor Rd, Dublin 12

Le Caveau Ltd
Market Yard, Kilkenny, Co. Kilkenny

Liberty Wines Ireland Ltd
Bankhouse Centre, 331 South Circular Rd,
Dublin 8

Mitchell & Son Wine Merchants
Chq Building IFSC, Dublin 1 and
54 Glasthule Rd, Sandycove, Co. Dublin

Nomad Wine Importers
41 Fitzwilliam Point, Fitzwilliam Point,
Fitzwillam Quay, Dublin 4

Searsons Wine Merchants
Monkstown Cresent, Blackrock, Co. Dublin

Select Wines From Italy Ltd.
Waverly House, Church Rd,
Greystones, Co. Wicklow

Tankersley Wine Brokers Ltd
Tankersley Cottage, Preban,
Tinahely, Co. Wicklow

Tyrrell & Co
Rathernan, Kilmeague, Naas, Co. Kildare

Wicklow Wine Co
Main St., Wicklow, Co. Wicklow

Wine Select
5 Bramley Heath, Castleknock, Dublin 15

Woodford Bourne
79 Broomhill Rd, Tallaght, Dublin 24

Wines Direct Ltd
Irishtown, Mullingar, Co. Westmeath

food

Glencarn Organic Produce
Glencarn, Carron, Co. Clare
— All meats

Mulloy (Thomas) Ltd
3 West Pier, Howth, Co. Dublin
— Fish

Robert Roberts
79 Broomhill Rd, Tallaght, Dublin 24
— Coffee

Sheridans Cheesemongers Ltd
Virgina Road station, Carnaross, Co. Meath
— Cheeses

St Martin Shellfish
Tarmon East, Kilkee, Co. Clare
— Oysters

Skelligs Chocolate Company
The Glen, Ballinskelligs, Co. Kerry
— Handmade chocolates for ely place only

Dromoland Estate
Dromoland Co. Clare
— Game

Finnebrogue Estate
Downpatrick Northern Ireland
— Venison

index

'Drinking good wine
with good food in good
company is one of life's
most civilised pleasures.'

Michael Broadbent